Dance Classics

Dance Classics

A Viewer's Guide to the Best-Loved Ballets and Modern Dances

Nancy Reynolds
and
Susan Reimer-Torn

Photographs by Martha Swope

a cappella books

Reynolds, Nancy,
    Dance classics: major works from the ballet and modern dance repertory /
Nancy Reynolds and Susan Reimer-Torn; photographs by Martha Swope.
        p.   cm.
    Originally published in different form as: In Performance: Harmony Books,
1980.
    Includes index.
    ISBN 1-55652-109-X: $29.95. — ISBN 1-55652-106-5 (pbk.): $14.95
    1. Ballet—Stories, plots, etc. 2. Ballet—History. 3. Modern dance—History.
I. Reimer-Torn, Susan. II. Reynolds, Nancy, In performance. III. Title.
GV1790.A1R43 1991
792.8'4—dc20   90-27665
                                                                     CIP

a cappella books
an imprint of
Chicago Review Press

Editorial offices:
PO Box 380
Pennington, NJ 08534

Business/Sales offices:
814 N. Franklin St.
Chicago, IL 60610

Cover photograph: Martha Swope
Hand coloring: Steve Gross

Cover design: Fran Lee
Editorial direction and interior design: Richard Carlin

All photographs © Martha Swope, with the following exceptions: *Trinity*, *Façade*,
The Still Point, and *Cakewalk*, photos by Herbert Migdoll, courtesy The Joffrey
Ballet; *Summerspace*, photo by Richard Rutledge, courtesy the Cunningham
Dance Foundation; *Rooms*, photo by M. B. Hunnewell.

This book was originally published in different form as *In Performance* by
Harmony Books in 1980.

CONTENTS

ACKNOWLEDGMENTS

For assistance, advice, and cooperation in the preparation of this book, the authors would like to thank the Dance Collection, New York Public Library; Doris Hering, formerly of the National Association of Regional Ballet; Seymour Barofsky; Robert Cornfield; Judy Kinberg, Dance in America; David Vaughan; and particularly Martha Swope. We would like to thank Manuela Soares for her editorial help.

PREFACE

Dance Classics has been designed as a guide to today's most popular dance works as well as a broad introduction to the dance as a lively art. It can also be read as a continuous narrative that touches on more than 150 years of Western theatrical dance, covering its major historical phases, outstanding choreographers, its rules and conventions, styles, evolutions, and revolutions. Each phase is illustrated by the works that have proved their lasting value as repertory pieces. Because this is not only a reference book for specific works, but also an overall look at the development of dance, we have chosen to group the works either by historical period, by type, or by choreographer, rather than purely alphabetically. It is true, of course, that repertory today is kaleidoscopic—that is, works with no common denominator of style, period, or concept are presented side by side. In some ways, therefore, the history of the dances is irrelevant, for it hardly matters whether they are five or 150 years old; something in them commands the stage today that has nothing to do with the age that produced them. Nonetheless, as we began to write the book, certain ballets naturally fell within the scope of the same discussion, and rather than repeat similar observations about each one, it seemed sensible to group them by period and style. Moreover, such an organization enriches the experience of viewing dance. *Giselle,* for example, is most fully appreciated if the viewer has some acquaintance with the Romantic style; while the conventions of *Swan Lake* are illuminated by a general understanding of the working principles of its choreographers, Marius Petipa and Lev Ivanov.

The only section of the book in which choreographers are presented alphabetically is Modern Ballets. The works analyzed there do not follow a continuous line of development (as they do, generally speaking, in the Modern and Contemporary Dance section), and the material does not group itself conveniently by subject matter or theme. In modern ballet (from approximately 1929 on), we have important choreographers working contemporaneously. For example, the two giants, Sir Frederick Ashton and George Balanchine, created masterpieces for more than 50 years apiece; therefore, it is impossible to place them chronologically, for they no more ''belong'' in the 1920s than in the 1950s or 1970s.

For the novice spectator, one of the greatest difficulties in appreciating dance derives from the absence of many set formulas. Unlike, say, classical music, with its sonata allegro form, its symphony, its string quartet, its equal temperament—all of which to some degree condition the audience's expectation—in choreography there are a few formal dictates (some, developed in the Classical era, are discussed in Part One). But if the form of a dance has few structural conventions to support it, the technique employed in the execution of the steps in a ballet is based on a highly codified set of rules. Classical ballet technique is one of the most regulated, refined, and demanding in the world. If one knows something about its development and ideals, one already understands much about Western dance, for ballet technique, rather than a vehicle for expressing individual emotion, serves a predetermined formal aesthetic.

This technique has evolved over 400 years. The aristocratic members of the 16th-and 17th-century European courts used the dance as a means of distinguishing themselves from the common people. Ballet began with the refinement of ordinary folk dances into a precise, highly stylized form. Dancing masters taught the nobility the codified steps and exacting rules of deportment. These social dances, which were used for performances on special occasions, underwent further definition and polish during the baroque reign of Louis XIV in France. The baroque was an age of restraint and control in social etiquette. Emotions were concealed in the interest of outer form, and in the arts, too, a decorative surface was stressed. Furthermore, all the arts were strictly defined by rules, with canons of dos and don'ts issued by royal academies. It is during this period (late 17th century) that ballet, based on earlier court dances, came of age. Thus the ballet's concern for formal perfection, its precisely defined vocabulary of acceptable steps, and the importance of their correct execution become clear. Moreover, its noble background assured that deportment, deference in manner, politeness, exterior control, refinement—in short, the attributes of good breeding—colored the execution of every step. It is this fusion of stylized, courtly elegance, together with ballet's precise canon of steps and poses, that give us the important idea of the *danse d'école*—the classical style and technique together. *Danse d'école* is the unalterable standard to which all works using the classical technique make reference, to a greater or lesser degree.

The execution of classical technique rests on several assumptions. The most basic of these is undoubtedly the turnout—ballet dancers strive in their training to achieve an outward rotation of the legs from the hips. After many years of effort, the turnout becomes virtually incorporated in the dancer's every movement, and the audience comes to accept—and even to expect—it. If a classical ballet dancer is not "turned out," this is either a defect in his or her ability or, very occasionally, a deliberate effect on the part of the choreographer. Along with this developed turnout go straight, taut knees (unless a bend is required, usually in preparation for a jump) and pointed feet with high instep (the higher the better.) Naturally, slim ankles enhance the presentation of the foot. Ideally, ballet dancers have long tapering legs, smallish heads, and long necks.

The basic direction for ballet dancing is "up"; it is said that the dancer "hates the floor." The classical dancer moves with a raised, uplifted torso (unless the choreographer specifically request something else); the center is controlled while the arms and legs execute decorative movements. The ability to leap high into the air, preferably without apparent effort, landing noiselessly, is one of the most important elements in a dancer's vocabulary. In the execution of movements, arms and hands are rounded, with the head and shoulders shaded at specific angles (*épaulement*). In general, it may be said that the exacting training of the classical dancer endows him or her with speed, fleetness, flexibility, and strength, creating its own canon of beauty.

We have been speaking here of the textbook ideal of the classical ballet—the base from which dancers begin. It goes without saying that an ideal is never attained; more importantly, in the 20th century many of these "ideals" are no longer ideals at all. Rules, as the saying goes, are made to be broken, and in our day, not only in the areas of modern dance and experimental dance but in the ballet itself, "rules" have been bent, broken, and in many cases thrown out altogether.

The first cracks in the system appeared around the turn of this century, when Loie Fuller, Isadora Duncan, and Ruth St. Denis (with Ted Shawn) began to perform dances that did not depend on the muscular agility derived from a finely honed ballet technique. The three women danced in bare feet or soft shoes—not in pointe shoes—and wore free-flowing robes rather than the corseted fancy costumes common in the ballet. The soft fabrics and the dancers' loose hair made patterns of their own, which became a part of the visual effects of the dances.

With the development of what we now call modern dance, beginning in the late 1920s, as pioneered by Martha Graham and Doris Humphrey, the conventions taken for granted in the ballet world for centuries were completely overthrown. For the moderns, dance could be heavy; even the dancer could be heavy. Effort could, sometimes *should*, be shown, for emotional effect. The dancer did not have to have perfectly pointed feet, when such a refined, careful finish might detract from the dynamism of a movement. Turnout was not stressed, and often denied. The basis behind the rejection of the balletic ideal was that these new dancers wanted to express everyday human emotions as experienced by "real" people, not the royal or exotic fairy-tale characters that were the province of traditional Classical ballet. This entire aesthetic revolution is more completely described in the Modern and Contemporary Dance section.

There is also "postmodern" dance. This rather vague term is a catchall phrase for a variety of creative movement experimentation, also called "avant-garde dance," that has been going on at least since the 1960s. Some of these new dances are performed in loft spaces (rather than on proscenium stages), in sneakers or socks, in works clothes or track suits. Many of the choreographers use "natural" gesture and a variety of sonic accompaniment that is not necessarily music. Often, but certainly not always, these choreographers do not demand as finely schooled a dance technique as those working in ballet or those closely allied with the modern dance as defined by Graham. Avant-garde works will not be described in this book, for as yet they command a very small audience and cannot be called "classics.'' However, Twyla Tharp and Paul Taylor, to name two important choreographers of today, emerged from this background, and both have won great favor with a larger public.

In the 20th century, the ballet, as will be seen throughout the book, has been by no means untouched by the upheavals in thought and feeling in the modern age. In fact, considering its highly formal nature, it has shown a remarkable adaptability. At the same time, the "old-fashioned" traditional ballets have not become obsolete. The amazing fact is that, without losing its essential identity, the ballet can encompass both works of the past, produced by what we might consider an outmoded aesthetic, and the most progressive works of the present.

Today dance in performance has become "big business," supported by both government and private industry. The audience has increased enormously, and with quality television now presenting dance works, the new audience is almost limitless. The marketing of these programs on videotape and videodisc has further extended the possibilities for dance appreciation. The number of dance companies has also proliferated. Some of the companies have rather elaborate structures—complete administrative staffs, apprentice systems, attachment to a dance academy, a resident costumer or even a costume shop, and fundraising personnel, not to mention technical crews, musicians, and perhaps a notator, photographer, and a press department. At the other end of the scale is the modest company of a few members, often unpaid for their rehearsal time, who must teach or take other jobs to earn a living (since their performance wages will not be sufficient), and who tour in station wagons, perform in gyms, sew their own costumes, use tape rather than live accompaniment, and adopt other cost-cutting procedures.

Traditionally, modern dance troupes have tended to be much smaller than ballet companies—sometimes consisting of fewer than six people. They have usually formed around a single choreographer, who generally also dances the leading roles, with, perhaps, a leading dancer of the opposite sex. (This has begun to change as some major modern dance choreographers have decided to retire from performing but continue to lead their troupes.) The other dancers are commonly supporting players.

Ballet troupes, in addition to being larger, have at least some works in the repertory with opulent costumes and sets. Very rarely are they formed around the artistic vision of a single choreographer (the New York City Ballet, guided for some 40 years by George Balanchine, is the major exception), although all have "artistic directors" who may be the chief choreographers as well. They are seldom the sole choreographers, however (as in a modern dance troupe), and very frequently they no longer perform. In contrast to modern dance troupes, in which there is generally no hierarchy in billing, in most ballet companies, dancers are ranked by prominence: at the top are the ballerinas and the *premiers danseurs* (a man may sometimes be called the *premier danseur noble* if he has a particularly pure classical style). These terms for the male are no longer commonly used; in fact, leading dancers of both sexes are more often referred to as "principal dancers" in a company, although "ballerina" is still in current usage. A notch below these stars come the soloists, or featured dancers, and, supporting the whole, the *corps de ballet* (literally, "body of the ballet"), a group of dancers who frequently perform steps in unison or provide patterns against which (or within which) the stellar dancers perform. In our democratic times, it is not uncommon for a dancer to be a part of the *corps de ballet* one night and assume a leading role the next.

Most companies of any size employ one or more rehearsal masters (they can be of either sex), who rehearse the ballets previously choreographed or help new dancers assume their parts. These incredibly valuable individuals often know virtually every role in the repertory, including all the parts of the *corps de ballet* (in which each dancer can do something slightly different, although all are basically dancing together). In addition to their own memories, rehearsal masters can sometimes rely on notation (a special dance script) or film and videotape. But many dances are not notated, and films or videos sometimes do not show all the choreography (the feet of the dancers in the back may be hidden, for example). In our computer age, the astounding fact remains that dances are still often handed down from generation to generation by the dancers themselves, without benefit of written or visual record. Under these circumstances, it is amazing that even a tiny amount of choreography of other periods has been preserved. It is also understandable, if unfortunate, that so much more dance has been irretrievably lost.

In the course of teaching, steps and nuances become changed as memories falter; thus the "authenticity" of some of the old dances is difficult, indeed impossible, to establish. In fact, the traditional ballets we see are most certainly not performed exactly as the original choreographer conceived them. It is perhaps a point of interest to the casual observer that, for this and other reasons (many having to do with interpretation), the same ballet or dance will look very different from production to production. In our day there is no such thing, for example, as the "original" or "authentic" *Swan Lake*—or, for that matter, the "definitive" *Swan Lake.*

We hope that these notes about the dance and the examination of major works that follows will increase the reader's enjoyment of this rich and beautiful art, so various in its forms, so full of vitality in its presentation, and at present enjoying an unprecedented preeminence.

N.R.

S. R.-T.

A NOTE ON
ACCESS TO VIDEOS

The videotape/VCR explosion (augmented by a revitalized laser-disc industry) has greatly increased public access to the classics of the dance. While nothing replaces live performance, visual records make it possible to become acquainted with a work when no performances are available, to compare its different versions or interpretations, or to study it in depth. In our discussions of dance works and choreographers that follow, we indicate where they are represented on video.

Since new video releases are issued weekly, it is not possible to include a comprehensive and timely list of specific offerings. Rather, we have compiled a list of distributors specializing in titles in the performing arts; the reader should contact them for current releases. Where possible in the text, information about existing videos has been keyed to individual works or choreographers, using the following abbreviations.

VIDEO DISTRIBUTORS

CDF
Cunningham Dance Foundation, Inc.
463 West Street
New York, NY 10014
(212) 255-3130

CVC
Connoisseur Video Collection
8436 W. 3rd St., Suite 600
Los Angeles, CA 90048
(213) 653-8873

DHV
Dance Horizons Video
Princeton Book Company
P.O. Box 57
Pennington, NJ 08534
(609) 737-8177
(800) 326-7149

GVV
Glenn Video Vistas, Ltd.
6924 Canby Avenue, Suite 103
Reseda, CA 91335
(818) 981-5506

HBO
HBO/Cannon Video
1370 Avenue of the Americas
New York, NY 10019
(212) 977-8990
(800) 323-4767

HOME
Home Vision
5547 North Ravenswood Avenue
Chicago, IL 60640-1199
(312) 878-2600
(800) 826-3456

IEI
Image Entertainment, Inc.
9333 Oso Avenue
Chatsworth, CA 91311
(818) 407-9100
(800) 421-4585

KUL
Kultur International Films Ltd., Inc.
121 Highway 36
West Long Branch, NJ 07764
(201) 229-2343
(800) 458-5887

ORION
Orion Home Video
9 W. 57th Street
New York, NY 10019
(212) 980-1117

PAR
Paramount Home Video
5555 Melrose Avenue
Los Angeles, CA 90038-3197
(213) 956-5000

PI-A
Pioneer Artists, Inc., and Pioneer Signature
c/o LDC America
2265 E. 220th Street
Long Beach, CA 90745
(213) 835-6177

PROS
Proscenium Entertainment
P.O. Box 909
Highstown, NJ 08520
(609) 448-9129
(800) 222-6260

RCA
RCA Selectavision Videodiscs
1133 Avenue of the Americas
New York, NY 10036
(212) 930-4714

SPECT
Spectator Video
1145 North McCaddon Place
Los Angeles, CA 90038
[no phone listed]

VAI
Video Artists International, Inc.
P.O. Box 153
Ansonia Station
New York, NY 10023
(212) 799-7798
(800) 338-2566

VIEW
V.I.E.W. Video
34 E. 23rd St.
New York, NY 10010
(212) 674-5550

The *Videolog* (San Diego: Trade Service Corporation), which is updated on a weekly basis, should also be consulted. It may be found in video stores. It should be noted that a certain amount of sleuthing will be involved: shorter works—for example, *The Dying Swan*—are marketed under such generalized titles as "An Evening with the Bolshoi." Less obviously, Tharp's *Push Comes to Shove* forms a part of "Baryshnikov Dances Sinatra"; Tudor's *Lilac Garden* will be found under "ABT in San Francisco."

While the traditional classics are quite well represented on video (largely in performances by European companies), the works of many of the major contemporary choreographers, although extensively shown on television, are generally not yet available to the public for rental or purchase. Over the past 15 years, the largest producers of high-quality dance programming have been "Dance in America" and "Live from Lincoln Center" (together with Lincoln Center "specials"), both under the auspices of public television. These telecasts have included performances of many of the dances discussed in this book—the principal masterworks of Balanchine, Robbins, Taylor, and Tudor, as well as individual works by Arpino, Ashton, Graham, Jooss, Loring, de Mille, and the Diaghilev choreographers.

Negotiations to make these extensive video ''libraries'' available to the public are ongoing, and by the end of 1990, a few titles had been released. The reader is encouraged to contact the producers for the latest information.

Dance Classics

TRADITIONAL
BALLETS

ROMANTICISM

Ballerinas have not always danced on toe. Toe dancing was an innovation that came about gradually. The first dancer believed to have balanced momentarily on her pointes appeared about 1820. By the turn of the 19th century, ballet technique was evolving toward an aesthetic of lightness. The heavy costumes and heels worn in the previous century were discarded, and without heeled shoes, a *plié*, the bend at the knee, could be deeper. Since a *plié* is essential for the execution of jumps, higher jumps became possible. The new shoe also shifted weight to the arch and ball of the foot (half toe); and dancers suspended on wires were lifted briefly onto pointe before being hoisted off by stage machines into the air. A soft slipper with a barely rein-forced toe was coming into use; it was the ancestor of the blocked toe shoe of today.

In the 1830s, the internal changes in ballet technique were swept up in the wave of a larger movement, the Romantic revo-lution in the arts. The Romantics rejected rules governing artis-tic creation, stressing instead individual form and subjective feeling. There was a great concern with passion rather than intellect, and a back-to-nature movement; the industrialization of France and England left the artist feeling trapped by a crowded civilization, starved for gentler landscapes, airier spaces, and pret-tier sights. The Romantics expressed a longing to escape, be it to a self-created world of dreams or to idyllic locales, still unspoiled and unhurried.

Thematically, ballet, which was never before taken very seri-ously by other artists, was a most appropriate vehicle for express-ing the concerns of the Romantics. Ballet scenarios increasingly called for untrammeled, peasant settings, where the folksy dances and colorful costumes added to the faraway feeling. Even

3

more significantly, the ballerina was now able to rise softly to her toes to become the personification of the artist's fantasy. A frail, ghostly specter shimmering in gossamer and moonlight, she was a dream woman only tentatively connected to this world. When a ballerina rose all the way to the tips of her toes, it set her apart from ordinary mortals and also gave the impression, without the benefit of stage machinery (such as the wire harness), that she was barely skimming the ground as she traveled across it.

Other technical inventions of the period made the projection of the Romantic ideals possible on stage to greater effect than before: in particular, the introduction of gas lighting provided a way to achieve eerie, supernatural effects, partial darkness, and blackouts. Previously, candles had illuminated the stage, and, of course, they could not be adjusted at all. Everyone was happy if the candles just stayed lit and didn't set fire to anything; several theaters over the years were burned to the ground because of candles.

For the first time, famous literary figures became involved with ballet. The foremost among them was the poet Théophile Gautier (1811–1872), a very influential critic, whose dance writing is still read today. Among the favored literary pursuits of the time was composing love poems to ballerinas; the ballerina was glorified to the almost complete exclusion of the man (most of the writers were male, after all). The role of the hero became smaller and smaller; his lot was reduced to that of a porter—he existed mainly to carry the ballerina around. (Only in Denmark did the male retain his stature.) Eventually, the situation reached the point where the hero's role was taken by a woman in man's clothing! But by this time, the heyday of Romanticism was over.

The Romantic sensibility left a significant mark on the art and literature of the mid-19th century, in America as well as in Europe. The Romantic ballet, flourishing between 1830 and the late 1840s, is one of the most important developments in the history of Western theatrical dancing. It rivals the great age of Classicism, which reached its apex in Russia in the 1880s and 1890s. Furthermore, the Romantic era is the earliest period to have furnished us with ballets that have been handed down to our day through a tradition of live performance. (Works choreographed before that time must be reconstructed from written and visual documents.) This means that the unbroken history of live performance of dance in the West is a mere 160 years old.

LA SYLPHIDE

Choreography by Filippo Taglioni, 1832; music by Jean Schneitzhoeffer; scenery for first production by Pierre Ciceri; costumes for first production by Eugène Lami. Danish version choreographed by August Bournonville, 1836; music by Herman Løvenskjold.

Inaugurating the Romantic ballet era in France, *La Sylphide* premiered at the Paris Opéra in March 1832 and encompassed many of the elements of the Romantic sensibility. The ballet is set in a rustic Scottish village, where wholesome young people dance folksy reels in celebration of the betrothal of James and Effie. However, young James is suddenly distracted by a winged Sylphide, a fantasy creature who flutters into his peaceful life and seduces him away to her enchanted forest. When James finds he cannot catch the elusive Sylphide, Madge, a witch, suggests he try a magic scarf. However, when he wraps the scarf around the elfin creature, her wings fall off and she expires. As his fantasy dies in his arms, James watches Effie go off in a wedding procession on the arm of his best friend.

La Sylphide provided both the faraway locale and the mystical unreality so popular in Romantic art and was a great success. Significantly, *La Sylphide* also echoed the pessimism of the Romantics, who despaired of ever finding real happiness. James, by attempting to realize a dream, lost everything. The Romantics of the 1830s and 1840s knew that once they abandoned the real world for the ideal, there could be no satisfaction and no return. The Sylphide, like the other bloodless and fanciful creatures who invaded the ballet of the period, was seductive but dangerous, alluring but elusive.

The foremost Romantic ballerina of her day, Marie Taglioni (1804–1884), was the first Sylphide, in a role created for her by her ballet master father, Filippo Taglioni (1777–1871). It is Marie Taglioni who created the image so often associated with the ballerina—a weightless, graceful creature, fragile, chaste, lyrical, and wistful. Her portrayal of the Sylphide epitomized the Romantic style in ballet—curved arms and fingers, a delicately poised head, gentle *épaulement* (lilting bend) of the shoulders. The leg extensions were low and decorous, the balances fleeting on the soft toe shoe, the leaps floating and noiseless. The Sylphide costume, with its décolleté, fitted bodice, bell-shaped skirt made of layers of filmy tulle (through which the new gas lights could shine for special otherworldly effects), and tiny gossamer wings became the uniform of dancers in the many *ballet blancs* ("white ballets") that followed. In 1909, these were the inspiration for Michel Fokine's nostalgic recreation of the vogue in his *Les Sylphides*.

Although the original production of *La Sylphide* took place at the Paris Opéra and is considered a hallmark of French Romanticism, it is the Danish version, choreographed four years later by August Bournonville (1805–1879), that is most often seen today.

La Sylphide begins with young James asleep in a high-back chair in the living room of his home. Kneeling at his feet, watching him, her head coquettishly tilted against one finger, is a winged Sylphide. She dances about him, darting and leaping with light, playful steps. When she kisses him gently, he awakes to behold a living dream. He reaches toward the teasing Sylphide but she simply vanishes up the chimney. Gurn, James's best friend and rival for Effie, his fiancée, appears, and shortly Effie, the young bride-to-be, descends the staircase. James greets his bride, but although he tries to hide it, he is visibly distracted by this glimpse of a world beyond the hearth. Effie's bridesmaids, cheerful, healthy-looking village girls dressed in bright plaids, enter and offer her gifts. James, perturbed, stares moodily into the fire until Madge, the village fortune-teller, steps forward and interrupts his reverie. Her gray hair hangs long and stringy around her white, haggard face; she bends crookedly over her walking stick. James, who resents the interference of this ugly hag, throws her out, but not before she has read the girls' palms and warned Effie that she will not find wedded bliss with James. The others go up the staircase, leaving James alone with his troubled thoughts. What exactly was it that he saw? Why is he unable to forget her?

Just then, the Sylphide reappears in the window, her hands demurely clasped before her. She explains that she has always loved James from afar and now that he is about to marry Effie, she has no reason to live. James, unable to resist, kneels before the sorrowing creature and admits that, despite his real attachment to Effie, he does love the Sylphide. Quickly regaining her

Natalia Makarova and Ivan Nagy in *La Sylphide,* American Ballet Theatre.

flirtatious, high spirits, the Sylphide lightly claps her hands and leaps in a spritely manner from side to side. She run-run-leaps into a charming pose, her tilted head framed by a curved arm. She balances on a bent leg, the other extended behind her in a low *arabesque.* Unaware that Gurn is watching, James kisses the Sylphide. When they hear people approach, she tucks herself into James's high-back chair and he covers her with a plaid shawl. Gurn, returning with Effie and their friends, points accusingly at the chair and whisks away the shawl. To his chagrin, the chimerical creature has mysteriously vanished.

It is time now for the prewedding celebration to begin and all disturbing thoughts to disappear. The guests, dressed in bright kilts, striped socks, fringed sashes, and carrying ribboned tambourines, begin a spirited reel. Effie reminds her distracted groom that they are to dance together. Arms crossed, they face each other, joining in the sideways lunge-step-step of the group dance until its circular pattern winds them away from one another. The Sylphide reappears to James, her fleeting steps in soft slippers contrasting with the clacking heels of the others. The supernatural creature, seen by James alone, weaves and darts in and out of the dancing group as James struggles to keep in step with the others, within sight of the Sylphide. The dance over, James and Effie are on the verge of exchanging vows when the Sylphide, hovering and quivering on her toes, beckons beseechingly to James. Remembering that she will supposedly die without him, James can no longer withstand her call. Just as he is about to put the ring on Effie's finger, he breaks away and rushes out the door in pursuit of the Sylphide. Everyone is stunned and shocked. Gurn, who knows what has happened, comically imitates the flight of the Sylphide by way of explanation. Effie, distraught, tears off her bridal veil and sinks to the floor sobbing.

The ballet's second scene opens in the depths of a dark, brooding forest. A group of humpbacked, hideous witches dance grotesquely around a smoldering cauldron, which Madge the fortune-teller is busy stirring. Amidst smoke and steam and flame, Madge dips her walking stick into the pot and pulls out a long scarf that she has fashioned for her own, soon-to-be-revealed, dark purposes. As the smoke clears and the sun rises, we see a wooded glade columned with tall green trees. James enters and his Sylphide follows. When he tries to take her face in his hands, she darts away. A whole flock of identical, white-clad, winged sylphides appears to dance around the would-be lovers, darting, leaping, and turning from side to side. But each time the enchanted James reaches out toward his Sylphide, she eludes his grasp and vanishes. The young man is baffled by this behavior and seeks the advice of Madge, whom he encounters in the forest. She assures James that he has only to wrap the magic scarf she has fashioned around the Sylphide for her wings to fall off and for him to possess her. James, innocent of her evil intent, kneels before the old witch in gratitude. He races back to the Sylphide, who continues to dance with childlike delight. James presents her with the scarf and wraps it around her arms. Sure enough, the gossamer wings fall off, but to James's horror, the Sylphide stumbles and falls to the ground. Robbed of the possibility of flight, neither her spirit nor her body can live. The other sylphides appear to carry off their fallen sister. She is borne aloft on a floating, flowered bier that crosses the stage suspended on wires. James kneels and weeps in true despair. As if timed to aggravate his sense of loss, bagpipes announce the wedding procession of Gurn and Effie. James watches the contentment and peace he might have had passing by in the distance. Mocking and malevolent, Madge, cackling spitefully, raises her stick triumphantly over the defeated and grieving hero.

Different ballerinas have stressed varying aspects of the Sylphide's character. She can be played as simply mischievous and impish, or her sexual and demonic nature can be stressed. She must contrast strongly with the sweet simplicity of the very human Effie. In the French version, there is a *pas de trois* in the first act, where the Sylphide joins unseen in a duet for James and Effie, imitating the girl's movements in her own more rarefied, ethereal style. The dance clearly reflects James's dilemma, caught between his two loves. The role of James is a challenge for the male dancer. He is a confused, idealistic young man who suddenly realizes he has failed to grasp reality. Madge the witch is also a pivotal figure in the drama, personifying the demonic forces that the Romantics considered sadly inseparable from the dream. Often played by a man *en travestie* (in women's clothing), usually an older dancer, Madge must be sufficiently frightening to scare the people in the back of the theater while avoiding the exaggerated histrionics that would make her seem absurd.

August Bournonville, the most important choreographer in Danish history, was influenced by French Romanticism while studying in Paris. Returning to Copenhagen, he incorporated many of the French themes into the Danish ballet, albeit somewhat toned down to better suit the optimistic Danish view of life. Bournonville developed his own technique based on French academia, but emphasized small, quick steps, twinkling beats, many light jumps, and rapid changes of direction. Arms were open and curved graciously, the chest was expanded and broad, the head slightly inclined—a harmonious, effortless, and cheerful look are the characteristics of Bournonville's style. Unlike the French, who in the thrall of ballerina worship virtually ignored the male, Bournonville, very significantly, greatly developed male virtuosity. In 1836, two years after he saw Filippo Taglioni's *La Sylphide* in Paris, Bournonville choreographed his own version, following the original story but using different music. Retaining the style and prominence of the ballerina, Bournonville also emphasized male variations, giving both James and Gurn solos in the first act and inserting another solo for James in the second act. The male variations are characterized by rapid footwork, leaps to the front with the back leg bent in *attitude* (at a right angle) and the arms open and forward, and brilliant beats with fully articulated feet and curved arms held low and close to the body.

While the original French *La Sylphide* remained in the repertory only until 1860, with attempts at reconstruction in 1946 and 1972, the Danish version has been performed by the Danes ever since its premiere in 1836. It was generally unknown to the rest of the world, however, until it was staged for American Ballet Theatre and the National Ballet of Canada in 1964. Erik Bruhn (1928–1986), a noted Danish dancer who often performed the role of James, restaged it for ABT in 1971. The Danish *La Sylphide* is now widely performed.

Video: HOME, KUL, PI-A.

GISELLE

Choreography by Jules Perrot and Jean Coralli, 1841; music by Adolphe Adam; scenery for first production by Pierre Ciceri; costumes for first production by Paul Lormier.

Giselle is the most important ballet of the Romantic era. All of the Romantic ideals and concerns are touched on in this ballet. On its own terms, too, *Giselle* has always been an affecting tragedy, and the leading part, which demands a highly gifted actress as well as a superior dancer, has always been a touchstone role for ballerinas. The role of Giselle, in fact, has been nicknamed the ''Hamlet'' of ballet, both because it has tremendous emotional depth and variety and because, like *Hamlet* in the theater, the ballet itself has become a timeless standard.

Giselle is in two acts, one a contrast to the other. The first act represents ''real life,'' set in the rustic, traditional Rhineland; the second act is set in a kingdom that none has ever visited— an otherworldly place populated by female spirits who come out only at night. In a sense the two acts represent the dual currents of the Romantic age—the earthly and the supernatural.

A young woman is betrayed by her fiancé, loses her reason, and dies; but later, her love still strong, she saves the man who let her down. As the ballet opens, we see two modest cottages on either side of the stage. The scene is a Rhineland village at vintage time. A young man, Hilarion the gamekeeper, enters. Obviously in love, he is about to knock at the door of the house of Giselle, a young peasant maiden, when he hears a noise and hides.

Two other men enter. One of them, Prince Albrecht, wears a cape and sword. He asks his servant Wilfrid to hide these things so he can resume his disguise as the peasant Loys. Wilfrid puts the incriminating objects in the other cottage.

Albrecht approaches Giselle's cottage and knocks, then ducks behind some trees. Giselle rushes out, happy and expectant, but sees no one. She dances her love joyfully all the same, skipping in a circle, leaping from one foot to the other, then leaping forward in an *attitude* position, finishing in an *attitude* on pointe. She looks for Albrecht, but when he appears, she shyly looks away, eludes him and tries to get back into the house. He pursues her; she is still skittish, but finally joins arms with him as both do little sliding steps sideways. She sits shyly on a bench, but when he gets too close, she runs away. Finally she looks him straight in the eye, and he swears his love. She plucks a flower and starts to play "he loves me, he loves me not," but, looking ahead, she imagines that she will end with "he loves me not." Albrecht discreetly discards one of the petals, then shows Giselle that she is mistaken and that "he loves me" will be the final word. Joyously the two link arms and do the little leaping steps from foot to foot and the leap in *attitude* that Giselle did in her solo. Then they do higher leaps in a circle, one after the other. There is very little supported partnering in this ballet and in the other Romantic ballets that have come down to us; the art of partnering was not developed until the age of the Classical ballet in Russia. For the most part, Giselle and Albrecht either dance apart or with arms linked.

As they are dancing joyously together, Albrecht is confronted by Hilarion, who demands Giselle's attention. Giselle rebuffs him, and Albrecht orders him away. Village peasants enter and dance. Giselle performs a simple solo—step, skip, and hitchkick to the front and a few steps on pointe with a little tiny fluttering motion of the nonsupporting foot *(petits battements)*. Albrecht then joins her and they do the same steps together. Suddenly Giselle hesitates and gasps for breath. She has a weak heart and is not supposed to exert herself. (Such constitutional weakness was much favored by the Romantics, who liked their heroes and heroines to be in the grip of a fate they could not control.) Albrecht is concerned; she makes excuses and brushes him away. He does a few slow leaps and beats of his own, then the two together repeat the earlier steps—step, skip, hitchkick—but this time in subdued fashion.

Giselle's mother, Berthe, comes out of the cottage, scolding Giselle for dancing too much; tenderly she wipes her daughter's forehead. Then fearfully she reminds Giselle that maidens who die before their wedding day will be transformed into Wilis—spirits of young women condemned to dance forever. Hilarion, meanwhile, has found Albrecht's sword in the other cottage. Just as he is about to reveal it, a horn sounds, announcing the arrival of a royal hunting party. Included in the group is Bathilde, Albrecht's fiancée. (During the ensuing scene,

Carla Fracci and Erik Bruhn in *Giselle* (Act II), American Ballet Theatre.

nobody seems to notice that Albrecht is not present.) Berthe offers what modest hospitality she can to the visitors, who sit at a rustic table and accept a drink. Giselle, although awed, creeps forward to admire Bathilde's satin hem. Bathilde catches her caressing it and, charmed by this sweet innocent girl, asks her to dance. As Giselle describes her fiancé, she dances the same step, skip, and hitchkick that she and Albrecht performed together. Bathilde says that she too is engaged to be married and gives Giselle her necklace. Giselle is, of course, flustered by this attention from a royal personage. The hunting party leaves. Hilarion emerges from his hiding place as Giselle dances another solo. Albrecht returns, and Hilarion bows before him mockingly. No one knows what he is up to, but he quickly explains. With a dramatic flourish, he brandishes the royal sword, exposing Albrecht as an imposter. The crowd is in disarray. Hilarion blows the hunting horn to summon back the royal party. When the group returns, Bathilde immediately recognizes Albrecht as *her* fiancé, and asks what he is doing here. In a rush of agitated music, Giselle breaks in and demands to know the truth. As Albrecht's duplicity slowly dawns on her, she races over to her mother, collapsing.

Now the famous "mad scene" begins. Giselle rises, her hair streaming behind her. The music of her former happiness is now played more slowly, plaintively. The flower motif is heard. Giselle stumbles about, miming her earlier meeting with Albrecht with feeble gestures and an unseeing facial expression. In the most touching moment, she wanly removes petals from an invisible flower, shaking her head slowly. She staggers. The music picks up in intensity as she grabs the sword, swinging it in a circle. The crowd steps back, horrified, but Hilarion easily wrests the sword from her. She is beaten. Albrecht can only stand helplessly by. Again the courtship music is heard, and Giselle does a weak version of the steps she once danced with joy. To crashing chords, she rushes first to her mother, then to Albrecht, collapses, and dies. Albrecht reaches instinctively toward his hip for his sword, which is not there. He finds it on the ground and starts to go after Hilarion, then stops, realizing it will not bring back Giselle. He falls over her inert body in grief. Hilarion is also grief-stricken; he genuinely loved her, too.

The step vocabulary in *Giselle* is quite restricted in the first act. The same steps are used again and again as a dramatic device.

Musical themes are also repeated in variant states. These repetitions, in similar but changed forms, powerfully indicate the dramatic progress. For instance, when the mad Giselle, having been betrayed by Albrecht, dances some of the steps from their early, happy moments, only now in horribly distorted form, the effect is chilling.

The second act is an eerie woodland, a dark moonlit forest inhabited by Wilis, ghosts of young women betrayed before marriage. They emerge only after dark. It goes without saying that any mortal who tries to invade this supernatural preserve is doomed to death. This act is as different from the first as night from day; the music is different, and so are the mood, the steps, and the dramatic development. There is virtually no pantomime and no realistic acting or everyday gesture, as there were in the first act; the story unfolds completely through dancing.

The first figure we see is that of a veiled woman, Myrtha, Queen of the Wilis. The dancer of this role is usually tall and commanding, for Myrtha is cold and regal. She covers space with large leaps and beats, moving with amplitude and radiating authority. In keeping with the overall style and period of the ballet, however, she is still a willowy creature whose movements are light, although they are performed with strength and resolution. In a corner, marked with a cross, is the new grave of Giselle. Myrtha summons forth her handmaidens. The large group of women moves as one; in their most effective moment, they form an interlacing pattern by hopping slowly in *arabesque* (one leg raised hip-high behind the body) in long lines across the stage. Their formation resembles a vise or net—perhaps a foretaste of the trap they will set for the mortals who attempt to penetrate their ranks. Here is is a breathtaking formal pattern; later it will appear to have powerful dramatic overtones. All kneel and slowly sway while Myrtha continues her dynamic leaps, sometimes circling in the air, as she travels all over the stage. Myrtha moves toward the grave of Giselle, calling her forth to be initiated. Submissively Giselle emerges. Myrtha orders her to dance, and Giselle, almost in a frenzy at being liberated from the grave, agitatedly turns, then leaps wildly around the stage for a brief moment before disappearing.

Albrecht enters, deeply sorrowful. The stage has emptied; he searches for Giselle. He finds her grave and lays lilies on it.

Her vision appears; he turns to grasp it; but it is gone. There is a touch of the "mad" music from Act I. Now she reappears; he kneels abjectly and she approaches, taking a long, slow *arabesque*. Alternating flowing, sustained movements with large jumps, they dance together. He lifts her high so that she appears to be floating off into the distance. They are rapturous. In a passionate outburst of music, she throws lilies into the air and they rush off the stage. Now Hilarion has found his way in, and the Wilis go to work. They join hands in a circle, imprisoning him. He staggers, exhausted, and slumps to the ground. The women form a long diagonal line as Hilarion begs and grovels before Myrtha. He is buffeted down the length of the line as the women point implacably toward the lake. He is done in. Next, Albrecht comes to beg. Again the Wilis line up, but Giselle intercedes and shields him from Myrtha. The music is dramatic. The Wilis are supposed to dance intruders to the point of exhaustion and death, but Giselle has decided to keep dancing herself so Albrecht can have a few seconds to rest. She begins a solo *adagio* (a series of slow, legato movements), then, to tender music, he joins her. Her movements are no longer agitated, as they were when she had just emerged from the grave; they are, however, robust and vigorous. She and Albrecht now have complete trust in each other. At the end of their joint dance, they kneel, reaching skyward. Giselle does another little solo, mostly with small jumps; Albrecht leaps, and there is another passage of supported *adagio*. Albrecht again has virtuoso measures, featuring *double cabrioles* (a leap in which one leg is held in front of the body and the other leg comes up to meet it while the dancer is in the air), multiple *pirouettes* (turns on a single foot), and huge leaps, but at the end he collapses. Once more they dance together; Albrecht again collapses, but he is not yet dead. The music sounds desperate, but finally a bell rings heralding the dawn. The Wilis' power is broken. Giselle, by her endurance and devotion, has saved Albrecht; the music is hymnlike. But Giselle must withdraw to the other world. Tenderly, they bid a subdued and resigned farewell, and she disappears into thin air. Dawn breaks, and Albrecht sinks slowly to his knees as the curtain falls. He would probably rather be dead. It is a similar dilemma to that of *La Sylphide*— the hero is left alone in the real world to cope with life, rather than dying a heartsick and exalted death that might have put an end to his misery and conflict. The Romantics thus revealed a cruel (or pragmatic) streak by leaving their heroes in suspension, so to speak, with their problems and yearnings unresolved.

Giselle became popular instantly. Only five years after its premiere in Paris, it was performed in America (which had nothing resembling the European opera-house tradition as a showcase for ballet) and was taken all over the world in the 19th century. Obviously, even though the ballet was "handed down," many, many changes have occurred, and we do not know precisely how much of the present choreography is original. With such a long history, numerous interpretations of the leading roles were bound to emerge. For example, is Albrecht a cad who is just playing with the emotions of a young girl, or did he start out in a lighthearted manner and then fall truly in love, to the point where he was unable to control his actions? Giselle has been portrayed as a weak innocent or, with equal validity, as a more earthy peasant.

Although dance technique has developed greatly since the days of Romanticism (harder toe shoes permit more sustained work on pointe; ballerinas today jump higher, lift their legs higher, and in general have a far wider range of technique at their command), most Giselles of our time attempt an approximation of what we believe to be the Romantic style, striving particularly to achieve the quality of thistledown lightness. Great *Giselles* of this century have included Natalia Makarova, Alicia Markova, Alicia Alonso, Yvette Chauviré, and Galina Ulanova.

Video: GVV, HOME, KUL, PAR, PI-A, RCA.

PAS DE QUATRE

Choreography by Jules Perrot, 1845; choreographed recreation by Anton Dolin, 1941; music by Cesare Pugni.

During the Romantic age, ballerinas were worshiped, even idolized. They earned vast sums of money; admirers responded to their charms with such extravagant gestures as drinking champagne from the toe slipper of Fanny Elssler (1810–1884) and drawing her carriage triumphantly through the street. Understandably, such adulation led to the growth of king- (or queen-) sized egos and temperaments; it is also not surprising that intense rivalries developed among those of the very highest rank (as well as in their entourages). So it was something of a miracle (or a managerial *tour de force*) when four of the superstars agreed to appear on the same stage at the same time in a little display piece designed to show off the best features of each. This is exactly what happened in the celebrated *Pas de Quatre*, which was given but four times with the original cast. (Queen Victoria and Prince Albert were in the audience for the third performance.) The *Pas de Quatre* united the talents of Marie Taglioni (the first Sylphide), Lucile Grahn (1819–1907, the first Sylphide in Denmark, in Bournonville's choreography), Carlotta Grisi (1819–1899; the first Giselle), and Fanny Cerrito (1817–1909). Of the top luminaries then performing, only Fanny Elssler was missing. The *Pas de Quatre* sent critics into a frenzy.

The choreographer (who was also responsible for parts of *Giselle*) had the exquisitely difficult task of presenting each ballerina at her best, yet making sure that none of them outshone the others. There was another pressing problem—it is generally conceded that the place of honor in most programs is the end and so, naturally, each ballerina wanted to be last. Taglioni, the most famous, was actually given the final spot without much protest by the others, and the manager, Benjamin Lumley, resolved the rest of the difficulty by suggesting that the order be determined by age, starting with the youngest. This caused the other three to giggle and turn coy—suddenly all wanted to go first! But it was decided that Grahn would lead, followed by Grisi, then Cerrito, and, finally, Taglioni.

In 1936, the ballet was staged for an English company; and in 1941, in America, by Anton Dolin (1904–1983) for Ballet Theatre (now American Ballet Theatre). Dolin's is the version most often seen here. It can be safely said that the steps are not the same as the original, since no notation was left behind. The only clues we have are reviews and pictures of the day.

In any case, the essence of the Romantic style is gossamer lightness, delicacy, and decorous, beautiful small poses. In addition, in Dolin's ballet, the ballerinas are exceedingly polite to one another. These mannerisms (and manners) are more important to a convincing presentation of the piece than is "authentic" choreography. The steps are not of exceptional difficulty, but they call on all areas of classical technique: slow movements, large and small jumps, fast footwork, fluid changes of position, and, of course, floating, billowy arm and shoulder movements. (By the 1840s, the core of today's highly virtuosic ballet technique was already in place, although the best evidence suggests that everything was smaller in scale and less brilliant in effect than at present. Dancing on pointe for more than a few seconds at a time was not possible in the soft shoes worn then.)

Many of our sources about the Romantic ballet are visual. Dolin made ample reference to the lithographs of the day, and many of the poses in his ballet look familiar to those who are well acquainted with contemporary prints. The opening grouping is taken directly from a lithograph of 1845. The ballerinas, in filmy costumes of pale pink, are all on stage, with Grahn, Grisi, and Cerrito in a circle around Taglioni, who stands on pointe in the center. The first measures of the dance are slow and gracious; the four ballerinas step daintily. They link arms and walk forward together on pointe, bow to each other, jump lightly in a circle, and end in another circular pose, heads cocked demurely to one side, looking out at the audience. From time to time, one of them assumes a characteristically Romantic pose: the index finger of one bent arm (with elbow lowered) points to the chin, the other arm curves across the body.

In Grahn's variation are *arabesques,* a little skip, some beats while turning backward, and many *bourrées* (tiny steps from pointe to pointe, traveling around the stage) in a circle. After a series of soft beats, she ends kneeling. Grisi enters, picks her way forward on pointe, then does some backward turns in *attitude,* peeking coyly over her shoulder. After tiny little jumps from foot to foot, with arms waving from side to side, she concludes with a series of *fouettés* (a difficult step, in which the dancer rises on the ball or toe of one foot while the other propels her around with a whiplike motion, that was undoubtedly not in the original version), and a *pirouette.* The third variation is in a waltz tempo with delicate jumps and curlicued arms. This dance is slightly more muscular than the others (that is, more dynamic) and ends with a leap off the stage. Taglioni's dance, to dreamy music, is the essence of softness (and is said to be based on many lithographs). She rises to *arabesque,* does a small jump to the side with slightly bent knees (which gives a dainty effect), then a series of somewhat complicated beating jumps, ending in a kneel.

Eleanor d'Antuono, Natalia Makarova, Marianna Tcherkassky, and
Karena Brock in *Pas de Quatre,* American Ballet Theatre.

The rather bouncy *coda* unites the four ballerinas. Again they join arms in a circle, this time facing outward, for some *bourrées* and little jumps and filigree pointe work.

Choreographically, this ballet is only a bauble, but as a period piece it has charm and grace. It is a lovely vision of another era in dance. Ideals then were perhaps not the same as those of today, but Romanticism has left us lasting images of beauty, which we still treasure.

Video: KUL.

CLASSICISM

With the end of the Romantic era, ballet was in general decline in Western Europe. In contrast, just at that time it was beginning to flower in Russia. Mid- to late-19th century Russia saw a period of refinement of an already existent tradition. Since the late 18th century, European ballet masters, particularly French, had worked in Russia, transporting the French academic dance to hospitable Slavic soil. French ballet masters, frustrated by the lack of opportunities at home, came to Russia and there began to develop the full-length story ballet with its use of dance and mime, highlighted variations for soloists, and *divertissements* (or entertaining dances) for the entire *corps de ballet*. When Marius Petipa (1818–1910) arrived in Russia from France in 1847, he found a large ballet school at his disposal, as well as a seasoned, enthusiastic audience. Continuing where his predecessors left off, Petipa ushered in a "golden age" of ballet. He served as ballet master of the Russian Imperial Ballet until 1903, producing over 60 ballets. Most notable and durable among them are *Don Quixote* (1869), *La Bayadère* (1877), *The Sleeping Beauty* (1890), *The Nutcracker* (1892; choreograpy by Lev Ivanov), *Swan Lake* (1895; choreography by Petipa and Ivanov), and *Raymonda* (1898).

An exploration of the music of Marius Petipa takes us back to the days when Leningrad was St. Petersburg and the dancers and ballet masters of the Imperial (Maryinsky) Theater were servants of the Csar. The theater, and the Imperial Ballet School which served it, were firmly entrenched institutions of Tsarist Russia. Once accepted to the state-supported school by audition at the age of eight, the live-in students were virtually cloistered from the outside world and carefully bred for their future careers. They received room and board and intensive training in academic subjects as well as ballet. Upon graduation, some 10 years later, the select students were guaranteed employment for the rest of their lives, first as dancers in one of Russia's professional companies, then, when they grew old, at a job backstage or teaching. The school was a highly structured, successful cultivation of dancers capable of performing in such challenging ballets as the full-length works of Marius Petipa.

The reign of Petipa is considered the era of Classicism in ballet. Both the ballet of the Romantic period and of Petipa's period are classical ballet, in that both are based on the *danse d'école* (or academic vocabulary). However, it is the later period, toward the end of the 19th century, that is referred to as the age of Classicism. This term refers to style and structure as well as technique, for at this time, technique and structure reached a highly formal state of development.

Petipa brought the ballet to its full stature as a ceremonial and glittering affair played to an aristocratic, conservative public. A lightweight story provided the pretext for four or five leisurely acts spun out over a full evening. In addition to plenty of virtuosic dancing, the ballet offered a grand spectacle, resplendent with pageantry and elaborate costumes, the whole embellished by specially commissioned orchestral scores.

Broadly speaking, Petipa's ballets were divided between danced and mimed interludes (which did not overlap). The mime sections, when everybody stopped dancing, consisted of stylized gestures of the hands and arms that had specific meanings. For example, passing a hand around one's face meant "you are beautiful," while rotating both hands over one's head meant "let's dance." These mimed gestures communicated developments in the plot to the devotees of the ballet, many of whom took special lessons in their decodification. (Only one-third of the audience came from the general public; the majority of the seats were reserved for members of the imperial household.)

Each act of a Petipa ballet contained a *pas d'action*, some character *divertissements*, and a *ballabile*, or ensemble dance for the *corps de ballet*. A *pas d'action* is a danced interlude directly amplifying the ballet's story. The prima ballerina, always spotlighted in Petipa's ballets, often danced the *pas d'action* as a solo variation or as an *adagio* (a slow, sustained duet with a male partner who served as her *porteur*). The Rose Adagio in *The Sleeping Beauty*, in which the Princess dances her coming of age with her suitors, and the White Swan Adagio in the second act of *Swan Lake* are good examples of a *pas d'action*. *Divertissements*, by contrast, are dances inserted for sheer entertainment or technical display — a kind of "dance number" only tenuously related to the ballet's story line. The national dances in Act III of *Swan Lake*, the wedding celebrations in *The Sleeping Beauty*, Act III, and the series of dances in *The Nutcracker*, Act II, are *divertissements*. Central, too, to the Classical ballet are the ensemble variations composed for the *corps de ballet*, for whom Petipa is said to have worked out the dance patterns on a large chessboard. While the *corps* might dance in either a classical or character (more folk-oriented) style, its main function was to provide the frame and necessary stage setting for the dances of the soloists. (Noteworthy exceptions are the fuller roles the *corps* plays in *Swan Lake* and *La Bayadère*.) Another indispensable hallmark of the Petipa full-length classic was the spectacular Grand Pas de Deux, a special duet for the prima ballerina and her partner, which served as a highlight at the end of the evening-long ballet. Its purpose was to showcase virtuoso classical technique; variations and stylistic flourishes were added to fit the setting of the particular work.

Petipa's ballet is "classical" in style as well as in structure; his language was strictly that of the *danse d'école*. He used the codified steps and turned-out legs of academic dance, and he constantly referred to the five basic positions. The demands of his choreography inspired progress in the dancer's technique. Gone were the fleeting balances, soft lines, and low leg extensions of the Romantic era, and in their place, Petipa demanded sustained balances, high extensions, strong pointe work, fast and sharp turns, and high jumps with brilliant beats. His dances were symmetrically designed and showed off strong, straight lines. Petipa also enlarged the possibilities of *adagio* dancing. The art of partnering (also called "double work")—in which the man supports the woman in the sustained movements of *adagio*, in addition to balances, turns and leaps of heightened virtuosity—was also greatly developed in Petipa's time. The partnered *adagio* displayed the ballerina, who, supported by her cavalier, balanced on pointe and slowly raised her free leg, bending her body in all directions. (Partnering has become even more spectacular during this century in Soviet Russia; today's Soviet dancers are known for their flamboyance. It is not uncommon for a Soviet ballerina to leap halfway across the stage into the waiting arms of her partner, or for the man to throw her high in the air while she does a double flip, then to catch her, with breathtaking timing, as she nears the ground.)

While remaining within the confines of the *danse d'école*, Petipa's genius lay in his extension of this technique and his ability to devise endless variations using a relatively limited vocabulary of steps. At the end of Petipa's long career, the young revolutionary Michel Fokine (1880–1942) would object to his conservatism. But in his heyday, Petipa reigned supreme, his reputation certainly overshadowing that of his assistant, Lev Ivanov (1834–1901), who, according to many accounts, may have been restless to experiment with new ideas.

Ivanov is an enigmatic figure in the history of dance. Considering that he choreographed the most memorable portions of *Swan Lake* and all of *The Nutcracker*, surprisingly little is known about him. (The second and fourth acts of *Swan Lake* are his, and these include the passionate White Swan Adagio and some poetic patterns for the *corps de ballet*.) During his lifetime he received little credit for his work; Petipa's name was usually on the program, or at best, it was Ivanov "in collaboration with" Petipa or another choreographer. Perhaps because it was far more exotic to be a foreigner than to be a native Russian, Ivanov was kept in the background. Or perhaps some aspect of his personality was responsible. In any case, after his death his contribution was recognized, and in our day, he is mentioned virtually in the same breath with Petipa in connection with the great age of Classicism in Russia.

It need hardly be said that the Russian Classical ballets set a world standard that has never been superseded. A century after their creation, its three most famous productions are still the ballets most frequently performed. Indeed, for some people, "ballet" means *Swan Lake*, *The Sleeping Beauty*, and *The Nutcracker*.

LA BAYADÈRE
(Act II, "The Kingdom of the Shades")

Choreography by Marius Petipa, 1877; music by Ludwig Minkus.

La Bayadère in its 3-act version is still performed in the Soviet Union, and a full-length production was mounted by American

Ballet Theatre in 1980, but the ballet was entirely unknown in
the West (except when given here by the Kirov Ballet company
during the 1960s), until the act known as "The Kingdom of the
Shades" appeared in two restagings, one by Rudolf Nureyev
in London, the other by Natalia Makarova in New York. Both
of these Russian dance superstars had been members of the Kirov
company before defecting. Both (independently of each other)
restaged the work from memory—a method still used, even in
this age of technology, video, and a viable dance notation script,
to teach dance works to others and to pass choreography down
through generations.

The complete ballet tells the story of Nikiya, a bayadère
(Indian temple dancer), who is in love with Solor but badly
treated by him. Her rival for his affections arranges that she
receive a basket with a venomous snake hidden inside it. She
is bitten by the snake and dies. Solor, repentant, dreams that
he visits Nikiya among the other bayadères. At his wedding to
a woman he no longer loves, angry gods destroy the temple,
killing everyone. In a vision, Solor and Nikiya are reunited.

Act II, "The Kingdom of the Shades" is Solor's dream. It
is a stunning vehicle for the *corps de ballet*. Not only does the
corps frame the action and provide weight and mass to complete
the stage picture, it participates actively in the dancing as well.
In many older ballets, the *corps* merely "filled out" the stage by
standing about in decorative poses. In *La Bayadère*, its movements, as performed by a seemingly limitless number of young
women (actually, there are about 25), and its large costumes
(wide tutus and hanging "sleeves") that add an even greater
dimension, result in particularly rich-textured designs. The lush
patterns formed by this *corps*, both in motion and in repose, often
make it appear as if the stage is covered with a thicket of dancers.
The floor space is often completely dominated by the *corps*, which
is never less than an integral part of the total design. When
executed by a well-schooled group of dancers, moving as though
with a single breath, the effect is mesmeric. Although dance
historians consider Michel Fokine (in *Les Sylphides*, 1909) and
George Balanchine (in *Serenade*, 1934, and *Symphony in C*, 1947)
to have pioneered the full participation of the *corps de ballet*, it
is clear that this ballet is a major forerunner.

La Bayadère demonstrates another important attribute of
Petipa's, in addition to his brilliant handling of the *corps de ballet*—

Ivan Nagy and Cynthia Gregory in *La Bayadère* (Act II), American Ballet Theatre.

his ability to create entire dances from a very few steps. The ballet
has been called an excellent example of "symphonic choreography." In the first movement of a symphony, a theme is
introduced, then varied, restated, and recapitulated in different
ways throughout the movement. In *La Bayadère*, something similar is done. Petipa's extraordinarily small number of basic steps
appears in various guises but can be traced to a few roots. He
is able to adapt this core vocabulary to groups (*corps de ballet*)
and to solos performed by Solor and Nikiya and by three soloists
(the featured players, all women, called the Shades), even though
all of these dances require different movement styles and techniques (some are slow, some fast, some peppy, some thoughtful, etc.). Thus, all the steps appear related to one another,
presenting an unusual unity and coherence in dance design.

One of the most important of these basic steps is the *arabesque*; its variations include supported *arabesque relevé* (in which
the dancer rises from the full foot onto pointe and back down
again); *arabesque* with a turn; *arabesque* with a jump; a larger jump,
called *cabriole*, which has almost the shape of an *arabesque* in the
air and which can also be performed with the legs in front of
the body, like an *arabesque* in reverse. The *cabriole* is usually
executed as a solo jump, but in *La Bayadère*, it is also part of a
supported *adagio*, with the man lifting the ballerina while she
assumes a *cabriole* shape in the air. Another step closely related
to the *arabesque* is the *attitude*, in which one leg is also behind
the body, but this time bent, not straight (this is a very important step in the Rose Adagio from Act I of *The Sleeping Beauty*).
Many variations of the *attitude* occur. Another characteristic step
interspersed throughout *La Bayadère* is a tiny run on pointe, performed at various times by the entire *corps de ballet* in unison,
by some of the soloists, and by the ballerina.

Petipa's embroidery on these steps is enormously varied, so
that the relationships are not over-obvious; in fact, they are not
really discernible except on close analysis.

There is another distinctive stylistic feature of *La Bayadère*—in
many instances, Petipa does not use the traditional *épaulement*.
In classical dance, the torso is rarely presented straightforward
toward the audience; the body is usually turned slightly on the
diagonal, with one shoulder a bit forward, and the head also
turned slightly in the same direction as the forward shoulder,
with the eyes gazing out to one side of the audience. This body

carriage—that is, the relationship of the head to torso to arms and legs—is referred to as *épaulement*. In *La Bayadère,* the dancers look into, instead of past, one rounded arm—into the crook of the arm when it is both raised and lowered. This gives a very particular look to their movements, as though their heads are cocked to one side. Both Solor and Nikiya look upward into their rounded arms, endowing some of their movements with a feeling of yearning or searching.

The audience has an inkling of the importance of the *corps de ballet* from the very first moments. When the curtain rises, revealing a dimly lit stage, we see in the back a slanted platform, like a wedge. A woman steps out, into an *arabesque* position, with her supporting leg bent. She then steps forward into another *arabesque.* Right behind her, another woman performs the same step, then another and another. One by one, slowly winding in a snakelike pattern toward the front of the stage, the *corps de ballet* emerges, all executing the same slow, deep *arabesques.* At last, all 25 have entered, and they are now deployed in rows of five over the stage. All raise their arms slightly, then all together they raise one leg slowly, first in second (side) position, then stepping again into *arabesque.* Seeing an entire *corps de ballet* perform such *adagio* movements together is most unusual—in fact, quite overwhelming. Although the *corps* will take a very active part in the remainder of the ballet, it now serves as background or frame for the ballerina, her cavalier, and the three Shades.

After the *corps* has finished its dance (each woman kneeling on one knee), the Shades enter, leaping playfully in an *attitude* position, with arms joined. This is echoed by the *corps de ballet,* also in groups of three, and recalls a famous lithograph of the Three Graces. The music then becomes more dramatic and Solor rushes in. Everything about him is exotic, larger than life, rather wild and exaggerated. He is wearing a turban with a feather, and with giant leaps, often with arched back, he covers the stage, searching urgently for Nikiya. She is revealed behind a scrim (gauze curtain). He kneels and, to a solo violin, Nikiya enters. Leaping softly, ending in the same *arabesque,* she touches him on the shoulder from behind. Their brief *pas de deux* is based on *adagio* movements. They leave the stage and again the corps fills it, this time standing in two double columns, again in *arabesque,* with heads bent to the side, a beautiful example of a circular fram-

ing for the *divertissements* to follow. The Shades dance separate
variations, all of them tricky in timing and coordination. Here
again we see the *arabesque*, both in *relevé* and in leaps, as well
as the tiny running steps on pointe. Their dances alternate large,
"generous" movements with perky small ones. Solor's dynamic
variation includes the *cabriole*, with beats, behind and in front
of his body, then virtuoso leaps in a circle, sometimes with a
spin in midair. Nikiya will later perform different leaps, but also
in a circle.

After these variations are concluded, Solor and Nikiya enter
with a scarf made of yards of chiffon. Each holding one end,
they perform an *adagio* in the manner of a Grand Pas de Deux,
except that he does not physically support her, since they are
separated by the length of the scarf. But the illusion of support
is clearly there. Nikiya performs the same *arabesques* in *relevé* that
we have seen earlier in one of the variations of the Shades. The
slow rise and fall through the foot is incorporated in many of
her movements. Properly done, there is no jerking, only sustained *legato*, as though she is melting through the foot. Nikiya
varies the *arabesque relevé* in yet another manner by turning while
she is doing it. The entire *adagio* of Solor and Nikiya is based
on smooth, slow movements.

The music becomes more lively again, and the Shades enter,
followed by the *corps de ballet*. Here they perform *arabesques* at
a brisker pace, and the same little running steps on pointe that
we have seen before. Nikiya and Solor enter; this time he supports her in *cabriole*, which, as noted, is a variant again on the
arabesque. Rather than hopping in a spritely manner, however,
Nikiya, with Solor's help, is able to skim the air with her steps
and sustain them for a period of time. In the final pose, Nikiya
is supported by Solor in *attitude*, framed by the *corps de ballet*.

Video: HOME, KUL.

THE SLEEPING BEAUTY

Choreography by Marius Petipa, 1890; music by Peter Ilyich Tchaikovsky.

The Sleeping Beauty, a crowning jewel of Marius Petipa's career, is often considered the finest achievement of the Classical ballet. It is a grandiose and refined blending of the traditional mime, expressive *pas d'action,* and spectacular *divertissements* in a lavish theatrical setting. Tchaikovsky was delighted with the invitation to write the music for a ballet based on Charles Perrault's well-known fairy tale. A baby princess, condemned at her christening by an evil fairy to prick her finger and die on her 16th birthday, is saved by the gift of the good Lilac Fairy, who declares the princess will only sleep until awakened by the kiss of a prince. The fairy tale, replete with a king and queen, fairies both good and evil, a beautiful princess and dream prince, magical stage effects, and courtly splendor, lent itself perfectly to the full-evening ballet that was Petipa's pride.

Although different productions have cast the kingdom of King Florestan and his Queen in varying centuries, it is really a storybook kingdom set in the realm of the imagination. In the Prologue, the hall of the palace where the christening is about to take place is resplendent with color, and imposing with its high ceilings and great stone archways. The master of ceremonies, pages, heralds, ladies in waiting, and finally the King and Queen all promenade into the royal setting, looking most distinguished in their elaborate dress. Next, the fairies of the kingdom join the scene of courtly pageantry with the Lilac Fairy, six cavaliers, and maids of honor entering last. All dance in honor of the King and Queen and baby Aurora, about to be christened. Each of the fairies dances her own solo, presenting a gift to the Princess. The dances, of no real dramatic significance, are an example of Petipa's use of the well-timed *divertissement.* Just as the Lilac Fairy finishes her dance, a strange and frightening rumble is heard. Its meaning soon becomes clear—the master of ceremonies has forgotten to invite the evil fairy Carabosse! The grotesque old woman, her face a white mask, her long dress black and tattered, enters in a huge black coach drawn by four ugly rats. Stepping down, she gesticulates with her hand and threatens with her stick that they will have to pay the price for their omission. In mime, she delivers the ominous curse—the Princess will prick her finger on a spindle and die. The master of ceremonies is in disgrace, the King and Queen are in despair. But the Lilac Fairy has not yet given her gift. She steps forward and assures the royal court that on her 16th birthday the Princess will indeed prick her finger, but then fall asleep for 100 years. Carabosse speeds off in a rage while the others surround the infant's cradle as if to protect her from further harm.

Act I opens at Aurora's 16th birthday party. Brightly clad peasant girls dance a *divertissement* with flower garlands. Holding the arched garlands overhead, they dance in multiple circles, weaving in and out to a waltz tempo. All await the arrival of the Princess Aurora. The ballerina-princess bursts on the scene, dancing a brief and vivacious solo in the manner of a carefree young girl. She is then ceremoniously introduced to the four princes who have come to seek her hand. The Rose Adagio, the famous *pas d'action* expressive of a young girl's blossoming into womanhood, is about to start. Aurora begins the *adagio* standing in *attitude:* one leg is raised and bent behind her, one curved arm is raised overhead. Some have read in this pose, which Aurora repeats often, a kind of gentle questioning or youthful uncertainty. One after the other, each of the suitors turns and displays her while she maintains the *attitude* pose. She releases the hand of the suitor supporting her and, raising both of her arms overhead, balances momentarily, as if tentatively testing her abilities. She then takes the arm of the next prince and begins the sequence again. After a brief interlude in which the Princess dances alone, she returns to accept a rose from each of the suitors (hence the title Rose Adagio). She pirouettes slowly and accepts each rose; one prince supports her while the next offers his flower. At the end of the *adagio*, she returns to her *attitude* position, and supported in turn by each prince, she again releases her hand and balances for a little longer each time. Finally, as she frees her hand from the clasp of the fourth prince, the curved *attitude* straightens into a sharp, *arabesque* extension. She retains her balance, poised confidently on one toe, as if she has visibly come of age before the eyes of the adoring suitors. The Princess continues dancing a joyful solo until her attention is suddenly distracted by a strange woman dressed in black who offers her

Martine van Hamel (left) in *The Sleeping Beauty* (Prologue),
American Ballet Theatre.

an unfamiliar object. Before anyone can stop her, Aurora seizes
the dread spindle. The unwary Princess pricks her finger, grows
weaker, and falls to the floor in a swoon. Just as those assembled lapse into despair, the Lilac Fairy steps forward. Waving
her wand soothingly, she reminds them that the Princess will
only sleep, and she casts everyone into deep slumber along with
her. The Lilac Fairy summons a forest of thorns, thickets, and
enormous shrubbery to grow around the sleeping court.

Act II takes us to a neighboring kingdom 100 years later.
Prince Charming and his lord and lady friends are out for a hunt.
The cheerful retinue amuse themselves with dances and games,
but the Prince is tired of everyday diversions and stays behind
to wander about alone. Suddenly the Lilac Fairy floats in on a
boat with gossamer sails. She offers to show the melancholy
Prince a vision of Aurora. The Prince is utterly enchanted by the
sight of the Princess dancing lyrically and romantically amidst
a tableau of fairies and nymphs, bathed in a bluish light. He pursues her but can only hold the Princess in his arms for a moment
before she eludes him and disappears. She is after all, only a
spectral image conjured up by the Lilac Fairy. The Fairy offers
to take the Prince across the lake, through the dense and tan-
gled forest, to the castle where the real Princess lies asleep. The
Prince approaches the canopied bed set on a high platform and,
as the music heightens, he plants the awakening kiss. Aurora
greets him.

The final act ushers us into a sumptuous hall, graced with
statuesque columns and a circular gold staircase crowned by a
blue sky. It is here that the royal wedding of Prince Charming
and Princess Aurora will take place. A full series of celebratory
divertissements is performed by the inhabitants of fairyland. Puss
'n Boots, Bluebeard and his wife, Goldilocks and a Bear, Little
Red Riding Hood and the Wolf all dance. A highlight is the *pas
de deux* of the soaring Blue Bird and his Princess. First dancing
together and then separately, they compete with each other spinning and fluttering in sparkling flight, sometimes jumping so
high they seem virtually suspended in the air. The man's variation, in particular, which features many beating jumps while he
arches his body backward and forward (*brisés volés*), is one of
the most famous and demanding in the international repertory.
The Blue Birds' dance ends with the female lifted on the male's
shoulder. The celebration then climaxes with the Grand Pas de

Deux danced by the Prince and Princess. They are regal, formal, and confident dancing together. Prince Charming supports his bride's *pirouettes* and displays her long extensions and secure balances. The Prince jumps and spins during his solo, and the Princess spins on pointe with even surer mastery than she showed in the Rose Adagio. Finally, Aurora whirls into the Prince's arms and dives toward the floor; the Prince catches her around the waist and supports her in the famous inverted pose known as the fish dive. All join the bride and groom for a spirited *mazurka,* and the Lilac Fairy, standing in their midst, bestows her blessing on the happy couple.

The Sleeping Beauty was the first of Petipa's classics to be seen in Western Europe. Under the title *The Sleeping Princess,* it was presented by Serge Diaghilev (1872–1929) in London in 1921. In 1939, it was remounted in Great Britain and has been considered the foundation of the Classical ballet repertory in that country ever since. It has now been adopted worldwide, and performance of the leading role remains a kind of initiation rite for aspiring ballerinas.

The Sleeping Beauty is a supreme demonstration of the challenge of Petipa's style—steel pointe work, sharply accented spinning turns, soaring leaps, high extensions, brilliant *batterie* (beats in the air), daring lifts—and, in addition, it gives a fairy-tale plot lavish stage treatment. However, its production actually checked a growing tendency toward shapeless extravaganza in 19th-century ballet, adhering closely to the principle of choreographic symphonism: meaning that, like the composition of a symphony, it had a certain formal structure. *The Sleeping Beauty* was choreographed in strict association with Tchaikovsky's music. There are themes developed and resumed throughout the ballet, and each act is a unity unto itself. Tchaikovsky willingly took instruction from Petipa as to the length, tempo, and character of each musical sequence (as he would also do in *The Nutcracker*). The themes—a young girl's coming of age and the triumph of good over evil—are developed dramatically and musically during the course of the ballet. Each of the three acts includes an *adagio* for Princess Aurora, the first celebrating her girlhood, the second her falling in love, and the third her marriage. In these *pas d'actions,* Petipa makes fuller use than previous choreographers of the dramatic potential of the Classical ballet, as, for example, when Aurora's curved (questioning) *attitudes* become sharp (exclamatory) *arabesques* and her balances grow steadily surer.

A large number of companies have productions of *The Sleeping Beauty* in their repertories—the Royal Ballet, American Ballet Theatre, the Kirov, and the National Ballet of Canada, among others. *The Sleeping Beauty* is one of the few full-length Petipa ballets to survive, and despite slight variations in dances, costumes, and scenery, it remains a vibrant illustration of Petipa's dance poetry and theatrical invention.

Video: CVC, HBO, HOME, KUL, PI-A, SPECT.

THE NUTCRACKER

Choreography for first production by Lev Ivanov, 1892; music by Peter Ilyich Tchaikovsky. (Many subsequent versions.)

The Nutcracker for Christmas—every child's dream come true! This "Christmas confection" has been delighting young and old alike for 100 years. Although now it is perhaps the most widely performed ballet in America, it did not become a tradition here until the last 35 years or so. The first full-length production in the United States was created in 1944 (by Lew Christensen for the San Francisco Ballet), the second in 1954 (by George Balanchine for the New York City Ballet). Now there are productions all over the country, and all over Europe and Canada as well.

The Nutcracker is the third of Tchaikovsky's great ballets, coming after *Swan Lake* and *The Sleeping Beauty* (although the choreography for *Swan Lake* as we know it was actually done some years after the others). Tchaikovsky elevated the writing of ballet scores to a serious art, where previously it had been hackwork composed to formula. Obviously, he did not consider writing for dance an inferior occupation, although he was a successful composer in other, possibly more prestigious, forms (unlike most other ballet composers). Nevertheless, it was the librettist and intended choreographer Marius Petipa, and not the eminent composer, who called the tune, so to speak. (Illness forced Petipa to assign the choreography to Lev Ivanov later.) Petipa gave Tchaikovsky highly detailed instructions. Here is a portion of his scenario (the opening scene of the ballet), with Petipa's very specific musical requirements. Tchaikovsky managed to stay within these strictures and to write glorious music at the same time.

1. The President and his wife and guests decorate the tree.
   (Delicate, mysterious music, 64 bars.)
   Nine o'clock strikes; at each chime of the clock, the owl on the top of it flaps its wings. Everything is ready and it is time to call the children.
   (All this takes place during the 64 bars.)
2. The fir tree is burning brightly, as if with magic.
   (Modulated music, 8 bars.)
3. The door is thrown open.
   (Noisy and happy music for the children's entrance, 24 bars.)
4. The children stop, full of amazement and delight.
   (A few bars for the children. Tremolo.)*

Tchaikovsky was particularly proud of his use of the newly invented instrument, the celesta, for the variation of the Sugar Plum Fairy. The most thrilling section of the score is surely the "tree-growing" music, and there is a lovely passage in the second act, the Grand Pas de Deux of the Sugar Plum Fairy and her cavalier, with its harp *arpeggios* (broken chords). Excerpts of the music have long been familiar as the *Nutcracker Suite*, but they cannot compare in sweep or beauty to the complete score.

The ballet was greeted with restrained rather than overwhelming enthusiasm at the premiere in St. Petersburg. The Csar was pleased, however, and the ballet had enough popular appeal to enter the permanent repertory in Russia. It remained unknown to the West for many years.

The story of *The Nutcracker* is derived from a rather macabre tale of E.T.A. Hoffmann, a German storyteller with a pronounced leaning toward black magic and witchcraft. Like all good fairy tales, *The Nutcracker* contains some grisly touches, most of them somewhat modified for the purposes of the ballet. But some

---

*Quoted from Clement Crisp and Mary Clarke, *Making a Ballet* (New York: Macmillan, 1975); in turn quoted from Cyril Swinson (ed.), *The Nutcracker* (London: A. & C. Black, 1960), trans. Joan Lawson.

shadows and cobwebs remain. As a stage vehicle, *The Nutcracker* is a mixture of mystery and enchantment, nightmares and romantic dreams.

There are wonderful opportunities for miraculous theatrical effects—the Christmas tree that grows to a height of 40 feet; the floating bed on which Mary, the little heroine, is carried out of her living room and into the snowy night; the sparkling forest filled with snow; the Kingdom of Sweets, overwhelmingly glittery and gooey, with candies and desserts flowing onto the stage.

In the Imperial Ballet School in St. Petersburg, the formal training for the students included appearances with professional dancers in ballets on the great stage of the Maryinsky Theater. Most ballets had roles for children, and *The Nutcracker* is no exception. In fact, in this ballet, children are not just colorful bystanders; some of them are leading characters.

Unlike *Swan Lake* and *The Sleeping Beauty*, sections of which are roughly the same throughout the world, *The Nutcracker* exists in many different versions. George Balanchine's production, which incorporates some of Ivanov's original dances, will be described here. Balanchine danced some of this choreography as a child in St. Petersburg.

The ballet takes place on Christmas Eve in Germany, in a middle-class home, around the beginning of the 19th century. Herr and Frau Stahlbaum are giving a party for their children, Mary and Fritz, and some young friends. After the familiar overture, we see the two youngsters peeking through the keyhole into the living room to catch a glimpse of the adults trimming the tree. (The door they look through is actually a scrim, or gauze curtain, which can be made opaque or transparent by adjusting the lighting.) Excitedly, they jump up and down, and through the scrim we can see the glowing tree. The children race into the living room to look at the presents; other children and their parents enter. Grandparents arrive. A march is played for the boys, then a formal ballroom dance for boys and girls.

Things are well under way when another guest makes an appearance. This is Herr Drosselmeyer, a strange old gentleman who is Mary's godfather. Although kindly, Herr Drosselmeyer is also mysterious, and his presence injects a sinister note into the proceedings. He is accompanied by his handsome Nephew, who is just Mary's age. The Nephew bows politely. Herr Drosselmeyer has brought three huge presents. They are life-size dolls. The dolls then dance—first Harlequin and Columbine together, then a Toy Soldier in a stiff-legged military march. Drosselmeyer gives Mary her gift—a nutcracker. She loves it—so much so that Fritz becomes jealous, marches through the circle of little girls cradling their dolls, grabs the nutcracker, and smashes it. Mary is distraught, but Drosselmeyer bandages the broken jaw with a large handkerchief, places the nutcracker in a doll's bed, and puts it to sleep under the tree. It is time for the Grandfathers' Dance, and then the party is over. The children depart with their parents; Mary and the Nephew linger, hating to say goodbye. Finally everyone leaves, and the stage darkens.

Soon it is midnight. Mary appears downstairs in her nightgown. She seeks out the nutcracker and cradles it in her arms. Then she falls asleep on the couch. In the darkness Drosselmeyer is seen. How did he get in? He fixes the nutcracker's jaw with a screwdriver and removes the handkerchief bandage, then tiptoes away. Mary awakens, just in time to see the lights on the Christmas tree flashing. She gets up to look around, and suddenly Herr Drosselmeyer is revealed atop the grandfather clock, flapping his arms and scaring her to death. There is a rumbling noise—what next? A giant mouse. Mary hides behind a curtain. Other mice scamper across the stage. They are larger than she is. As Mary watches, terrified, the entire room becomes transformed. Wind blows the curtains (although the windows had been shut, since it is the middle of winter), and most astonishing, the tree begins to rustle and move, then to grow—higher and higher—until the tip is practically out of sight. Lo and behold, the toy soldiers that were under the Christmas tree are suddenly the height of real-life children. The windows become enlarged, the whole room grows, and, as a final touch, the tiny doll's bed, on which the nutcracker was lying, becomes life-size, and the nutcracker is now a little boy.

The mice attack, led by the seven-headed Mouse King. The Nutcracker leads the division of soldiers in the battle against them, but the mice are clearly winning. Almost all of the soldiers have been removed from the stage. Mary is completely involved in the battle. She takes her shoe and throws it at the Mouse King. As he turns around to see what hit him, the Nutcracker runs him through. With pomp and ceremony, the Mouse King expires. The Nutcracker slices off one of his crowns and holds it high. To thundering music, the Nutcracker is revealed as Drosselmeyer's Nephew, now dressed as a Little Prince. He places the crown on Mary's head, then leads her, with one foot bare, out into the resplendent night, where the Snowflakes dance. A boy's choir is heard accompanying them. Balanchine devised many light leaps and whirling patterns for the Snowflakes; they truly appear blown by the wind. As the snow starts to fall more heavily, the Prince leads Mary deeper into the forest.

Act II takes place in the Kingdom of Sweets. All the inhabitants gather to greet the arrival of Mary and the Prince, but first the Sugar Plum Fairy dances the daintiest of variations, to the tiny chime of the celesta. The walnut boat draws near, and she greets the small visitors, asking them how they came. Motioning for the audience to stand aside, the Prince begins the story, using traditional mime. Rolling his hands around each other like a muff, he says, ''This is what happened.'' He tells how he led the battle of the mice, how Mary threw her shoe at the Mouse King, how he cut off his crown and gave it to her, and how they went off in search of adventure. The Sugar Plum Fairy is enraptured. She sits the youngsters down in front of a tray of sweets and orders all of Candyland to entertain them. First comes the snappy Hot Chocolate, five couples dancing a Spanish-style variation. Next, a sinuous Arab woman undulates in a sultry manner, striking some tiny finger cymbals and performing back bends and splits. At the beginning of Tea, two Chinese girls enter with a large lacquer box. Out bounds a veritable Chinese jumping jack. At the climax of the number, he leaps in a split again and again. Then the acrobatic Candy Canes take over. (Balanchine retained this dance from the original Ivanov.) The leader—a small, springy man—doubles himself over and leaps repeatedly through his hoop, which seems barely large enough to accommodate him. Balanchine danced this role in Russia. Six lively teenagers dance with him.

Marzipan is represented by a ballerina and four women whose dance stresses little steps on pointe and precision in tiny jumps on pointe and beats. Mother Ginger, played by a tall man made immeasurably taller by stilts, comes lumbering onto the stage wearing a huge hooped skirt. When she has made her way to the center, eight small children emerge from her skirt. The four little boys are Polichinelles—Punch-like characters with humps in their backs and stomachs. Balanchine has given them

Snowflakes in *The Nutcracker*, New York City Ballet.

engaging, childlike movements, and when they have finished their dance, all crowd back under Mother Ginger's skirt as she inches her way off.

Now the ballet takes on a kind of glow. It is time for the famous Waltz of the Flowers. Balanchine added a new role here, that of the Dewdrop, the ballerina. Silvery, delicate—it is a prized part. The flowers form lovely patterns and the Dewdrop sparkles and flies in and out of their formations. At last comes the Grand Pas de Deux for the Sugar Plum Fairy and her cavalier. Majestically they enter as the music swells. The climax of their dance is a long balance held by the Fairy. With a crash of cymbals, she is caught by her partner, then lifted high in the air while her feet beat back and forth; she pirouettes many times and finishes in the famous fish dive, a spectacular ending that graces several of the grandest *pas de deux* in the repertory (that of *The Sleeping Beauty*, Act III, for example). It is generally considered that the Sugar Plum Fairy and her cavalier represent Mary and the Prince when they grow up. Now the children must be off. As the candies and foods gather to bid them goodbye, they mount a sleigh, which rises into the sky.

In some versions of the ballet (although not Balanchine's), there is a final scene showing Mary at home, waking up from her dream—for, of course, it *was* all a dream.

Although differences among various productions are many, the most significant occurs in some Soviet versions (not in the original Russian), and this has been carried over in the productions choreographed by Rudolf Nureyev for the Royal Swedish Ballet (later also presented by the Royal Ballet of London) and by Mikhail Baryshnikov for American Ballet Theatre: the children are actually played by small adult dancers. This gives a real potential for a love interest, not a vicarious one as in the Balanchine version. In these productions, the Sugar Plum Fairy and her cavalier are omitted, and the Grand Pas de Deux is danced by Mary (called Clara in both productions) and the Nutcracker Prince. Baryshnikov added an unusual touch—his Grand Pas de Deux is actually for three—Clara, the Prince, and Drosselmeyer. In Baryshnikov's version, it is the kindly Drosselmeyer who spins the fairy tale for Clara (not her own fantasies). In the *pas de trois* (dance for three), he is helping her to wake up, to make the transition back to reality without getting hurt—because she is still too young to live happily ever after with her prince, although at 10 or 12 she is not too young to dream of storybook romances.

All the participants in Baryshnikov's ballet are adults, and all the characters in Clara's real life are also in her dream, although transformed into something else. There is even a puppet show in Act I in which a fairy-tale princess is wooed by both a Mouse King and a Prince; to the delight of all the young spectators, she chooses the Prince. Nureyev's strategy is similar: all of his characters are adults, and to reinforce the dream idea, the same dancer plays Drosselmeyer, the Mouse King, and the Prince. The *divertissements* of the second act (which do not take place in the Kingdom of Sweets but in Clara's room) are performed by her own dolls come to life.

Because of the many different productions, one cannot speak of the choreographic stamp of *The Nutcracker*, as one can of other classics such as *Giselle* or *Swan Lake*. Every choreographer has free rein. The story, too, as we have seen, can be greatly altered, particularly in focus. It is only the sequence of dances that remains the same. It is perhaps strange that *The Nutcracker* has become such an enduring favorite. In many versions, there is virtually no starring role (the Sugar Plum Fairy does not appear until halfway through the evening), and there is little (if any) character development. Moreover, the second act is merely a string of *divertissements*, colorful perhaps but not profound. Some observers have seen in Mary's encounter with the Nutcracker a little girl's first intimations of sexuality. This is most clear, of course, when the children are older and danced by adults. But mostly, *The Nutcracker* is like a great big Christmas present— pretty, delightful, carefree, without conflict, and, above all, meant for pure enjoyment.

Video: HOME, IEI, KUL, PAR, PI-A, SPECT.

SWAN LAKE

Choreography by Marius Petipa and Lev Ivanov, 1895; music by Peter Ilyich Tchaikovsky; scenery and costumes for 1895 production by M. Botcharov and M. Levogt.

The most popular Classical ballet of all, *Swan Lake,* was a great disappointment at its first performance. Tchaikovsky's enduring and now celebrated score was given poor choreographic treatment by a certain Julius Reisinger in Moscow, and the ballet seemed to have little future. Several years later, the success of Tchaikovsky's scores for the ballets *The Sleeping Beauty* (1890) and *The Nutcracker* (1892) prompted the director of the St. Petersburg Imperial Theater and his ballet master, Marius Petipa, to consider a remake of *Swan Lake.* Ironically, the composer died while the ballet was in early rehearsal and he never saw the 1895 Petipa-Ivanov version that, with some variation, has survived to today as a beloved classic.

Swan Lake tells the story of a Prince who falls in love with a Swan Queen, a woman transformed into a bird by Von Rothbart, an evil sorcerer. She heads an entire flock of Swan Maidens, strange composite creatures condemned by Rothbart to be swans from dawn to dusk and women from dusk to dawn, until rescued by a man's undying love. Enthralled by the Swan Queen Odette's beauty, the Prince swears his eternal love at the enchanted lakeside. Later, at a party for his 21st birthday, the Prince is urged to pick a wife from among the visiting princesses, but he declines, remaining faithful to the image of Odette. The sorcerer, Rothbart, suddenly appears and tricks the Prince into declaring his love for Odile, an exact double of Odette whom he has fashioned with black magic. Realizing his fateful mistake, the Prince rushes back to the lake, but it is too late; the swan-woman is doomed by his unwitting betrayal. Odette plunges into the lake to drown, for now it is only death that can release her from the spell. Prince Siegfried follows her, and his suicide finally destroys the sorcerer's power. The Swan Maidens are set free, and the lovers are seen reunited in death.

The dramatic elements of this ballet—the redeeming power of ideal love, the conflict between good and evil, the play of supernatural forces, the portrayal of a dual woman—one aspect the innocent, pure Odette, the other the seductive Odile—all give the ballet tremendous audience appeal. However, a ballet cannot succeed on the basis of a theme alone. It is the choreographic inspiration of *Swan Lake* that has assured its long life.

Swan Lake was the combined achievement of Marius Petipa and his assistant Lev Ivanov. (Petipa contributed Acts I and III, Ivanov, Acts II and IV.) Act I is a fine illustration of Petipa's working formula. In Prince Siegfried's garden, guests have gathered to celebrate the young man's 21st birthday. Those assembled display their manners and costumes, and some boys and girls dance short *divertissements* in solos and trios. The Queen enters regally and, using traditional mime, gestures that her son Siegfried must soon marry (she points to her ring finger). Despite the serious note she has injected, after her departure all the guests gather to dance a *divertissement* with a spirited polka rhythm.

The second act of *Swan Lake* opens at the magical lakeside and casts a different spell. Ivanov embellished upon the Petipa approach—he carried further the dramatic potential of the classic vocabulary, harmoniously integrated the dancing of the *corps de ballet* with that of the principals, and found full inspiration in the construction of the musical score.

It is here, while hunting with his friends, that the Prince first encounters the Swan Queen. She is at once frightened and passionate, a full-blooded woman trapped in the body of a fluttering bird. The actual steps she dances are remarkably simple—mostly quick *bourrées* (tiny steps) on pointe and rapid runs leading into posed *arabesques.* But Ivanov breathes life into his strange creature in the movements of her arms rippling behind her, an expressively arched torso, and the trembling beats of her pointed feet. Her composite nature is dramatized by such touches as the posing of the head and neck to suggest at once a swan nestling in her downy shoulder and the ardor of a real woman. When she first sees the Prince she is terrified and uses the traditional mime to express "you-me-no-shoot." But her feelings are also meaningfully communicated by her entire body, her feet running frantically, her torso twisting, her arms undulating agitatedly as she explains her fate and begs for safety.

Siegfried promises not to hurt her and they disappear into the forest. Just then, Odette's entire retinue of enchanted swans appears at the lakeside, moving toward the front of the stage in a serpentine line. They are met by a group of huntsmen, the Prince's friends, who aim their bows at the frightened birds. Odette rushes in and, standing in front of the others, spreads her arms out protectively. The huntsmen realize their mistake, bow in apology, and leave. The Swan Maidens then dance in unison, waltzing in a three-column formation that ends with their gathering at either side of the stage. Now the Prince and Odette begin the famous White Swan Adagio. Odette rests on one knee, the other leg stretched before her; bending low she encloses her arms around her like wings. Siegfried extends his arm to her; she rises and allows him to support her in a deep, low *arabesque*. She falls forward into his arms, and he catches her at the last moment. They repeat this movement as if to stress their growing mutual trust. As Odette and Siegfried walk toward the lake, the swans all assume an *arabesque* pose and turn in little hops, as if to echo and complement the lovers' duet. The Prince and Swan Queen reappear among the *corps;* he lifts her high in the air. In an *arabesque* pose, she hops softly down the diagonal line which the Swan Maidens have formed across the stage. Siegfried follows, and when she reaches the end of the line, he lifts her and carries her to the other side of the stage. After supporting her *pirouettes* and balances, he holds her arms as if calming her fluttering wings and gently rocks her from side to side. Odette now stands on one pointe, her right foot beating rapidly against her left ankle. After some slow *pirouettes*, she balances with her left leg extended to the side before falling once again into the Prince's arms. With the end of the *adagio*, the lovers leave the stage. Four Cygnets, or young swans, appear to dance a lively variation. Joined in a line by their crossed arms, they dance brightly in unison. Two more Swan Maidens dance joyously in celebration of Odette's new-found love. However, the dawn is breaking and the Swan Maidens cannot stay. The romantic mood is shattered by the appearance of Rothbart. Odette returns; her movements grow frantic as her feet carry her away and her arms reach longingly for the Prince. With a rustle of white downy "wings," she disappears with the other swans, and Siegfried has no choice but to return to the castle with his friends.

Petipa's Act III ushers us into the great hall of the castle, where guests in sumptuous attire have gathered to celebrate Siegfried's birthday. The Prince is introduced to six visiting princesses, his prospective brides, but can scarcely feign any interest as he waltzes with each one. Other *divertissements*—Spanish, Hungarian, and Polish in style—are performed. Suddenly, the trumpets sound a flourish and a new couple is introduced. To the crash of cymbals a bearded knight enters with a beautiful woman dressed in black. The prince has no way of knowing it is really Rothbart and his diabolical daughter Odile. He rushes toward them—the woman looks exactly like his beloved Odette. Now the second famous *pas de deux*, known as the Black Swan, is about to begin.

Following the established *pas de deux* formula, the Prince and Odile first dance together. In an illustration of Petipa style, the Prince partners Odile, who dances with cold polish, points of steel, strong balances, and direct movements. Siegfried supports and underscores her spinning *pirouettes* and lunging *arabesques*. Odile then adds a softer note to her turns and balances. Remembering that she is impersonating Odette, she adds some arm movements distinctly reminiscent of the Swan Queen. The Prince then dances alone, jumping high, beating his feet, and turning in the air to express his joy at rediscovering Odette. Next, dancing alone, Odile grows bolder in her cunning seductiveness, balancing confidently on a single toe. After the Prince dances again, Odile, in her second variation of the *pas de deux*, performs the famous 32 *fouettés*, fast whipping turns supported on one foot, to crown her victory over the benighted Prince. She ends with dazzling *piqué* turns, whirling on pointe into the Prince's arms. Finally the Prince kneels before her as she tosses her proud head and stretches into a victorious *arabesque*. At the moment the overwhelmed young man pledges his love to her, the room darkens ominously, and there is a crash of thunder. The Prince, realizing he has been betrayed, rushes off in despair. Odile and Rothbart disappear in a cloud of smoke.

Act IV takes us back to the lakeside, where the swans, their arms aflutter, their feet pattering, are grouped around the Swan Queen. Siegfried begs forgiveness, but Odette can do nothing; all is lost. With Rothbart threatening them in the background, the grieving Swan Queen can stay no longer, and she rushes into the lake. Siegfried follows her, and it is only then that Rothbart is destroyed and the Swan Maidens are freed.

The demanding choreography of *Swan Lake* has always allowed for individual interpretation within its structure. The dual role of Odette-Odile provides one of ballet's greatest challenges.

Maria Calegari (center) in *Swan Lake*, New York City Ballet.

In addition to meeting its technical demands, the ballerina must address certain questions—in what proportions will she be bird-like or womanly? Timid or ardent? And how strident can Odile be and still remain convincing as Odette? The Prince's role is, of course, subordinate, but it has been enlarged in some productions, most successfully in those of Rudolf Nureyev (1964) and Erik Bruhn (1967). In Bruhn's staging, the dramatic focus is considerably shifted by having the Prince's mother and the evil sorceress (a Rothbart-like character) portrayed by the same woman.

In its nearly 100 years of life, *Swan Lake* has undergone many changes; variations have been omitted and restored, and the ending has varied from production to production. Although the lovers usually meet a tragic fate, on occasion Rothbart is defeated by the power of love, and Siegfried and Odette are united in life, not death (a "happy-ending" version is currently in the repertory of Moscow's Bolshoi Ballet). *Swan Lake* has also lent itself to one-act treatment, set entirely at the lakeside and made up largely of choreography from Act II. This condensed version is in countless repertories throughout the country and throughout the world. *Swan Lake*, despite metamorphoses and retouchings, has retained its essential identity along with its great appeal for generations of audiences.

Video: HBO, HOME, KUL, PAR, PI-A, VAI.

THE CLASSICAL
PAS DE DEUX

The Grand Pas de Deux of Classical ballet is one of its most showy, exciting attractions. A special duet for the ballerina and her cavalier, it first appeared as a brilliant feature of Petipa spectacles. While it is unlikely that Petipa himself originated the Grand Pas de Deux—it was probably imported by his virtuosic Italian stars—he nonetheless elevated it to an important highlight of the full-length ballet. (*Pas de deux* literally means "dance for two"; the Grand Pas de Deux is usually the duet for two leading dancers that concludes or climaxes the act or the evening.)

The Grand Pas de Deux starts slowly and builds up to an exuberant, whirlwind finish. The ballerina and her partner first dance together, then take turns doing two or three solo variations, and finally return to dance the *coda*, or ending, with each other. The beginning is an *adagio*, a section that is slow and regal, allowing for the display of the ballerina by her partner. Each of the separate variations accelerates in speed and heightens in technical virtuosity as the ballerina and cavalier both show off and compete with each other. The *coda* is then a breathless, triumphant climax for the two stars.

The Grand Pas de Deux was a perfect vehicle for the ballet of the Classical era. It was an opportunity to exhibit the developing art of *adagio* partnering. Virtuosic lifts were also becoming fashionable in the Russian technique, and the *adagio* and *coda* of the *pas de deux* afforded much opportunity for displaying the ballerina borne aloft. In Petipa's day, it was the ballerina who received most of the attention, and it was up to the male to support her smoothly and unobtrusively. In later periods, outstanding male stars have rechoreographed the man's variations for use as personal vehicles. This has shifted the emphasis between male and female virtuosity in the *pas de deux*.

Individual dancers have left their mark on the development of these display pieces. In Petipa's time, a series of Italian ballerinas stimulated the fireworks of the *pas de deux* by their technical proficiency and, in some cases, near-acrobatic tricks. One of these ballerinas was the Italian Pierina Legnani (1863–1923), who arrived in St. Petersburg in 1893 with the unrivaled ability to perform 32 consecutive *fouettés* (whipping turns). Petipa incorporated her *fouettés* as a crowning *tour de force* in the Black Swan Pas de Deux of *Swan Lake*, Act III. Other ballerinas, particularly the overlooked Russian stars, were provoked by jealousy into unlocking Legnani's secret. (Actually, she would "spot," or whip her head around at the very last minute of the turn, to focus in the same place with every revolution, thus avoiding dizziness.) Eventually, the ability to do *fouettés* became virtually standard for a leading female dancer and an accepted part of the virtuosic vocabulary of the *pas de deux*.

Originally, the *pas de deux* was a highlight of the story ballet and always had some stylistic touches relevant to the ballet's plot. Some of the well-known *pas de deux* are closely linked to the ballet's story, while others are more frankly technical exhibition pieces. The particular qualities of the Black Swan Pas de Deux are derived from the story: it is an expression of the wicked Odile's attempts to bedazzle the Prince and convince him she is really the Swan Queen. Other famous *pas de deux* are more abstract. The *pas de deux* of the Blue Birds and that of the Prince and Princess in Act III of *The Sleeping Beauty*, as well as the Grand Pas de Deux for the Sugar Plum Fairy and her cavalier in Act II of *The Nutcracker*, are, for example, essentially displays of virtuosity to bring an evening-long ballet to a rousing finish.

Most *pas de deux* can be performed separately—that is, on their own, as effective virtuosic vehicles outside the context of the "parent" ballet. Certain well-known *pas de deux*—such as *Le Corsaire*, *Sylvia*, and *Don Quixote*—are performed almost exclusively as separate show pieces.

Video: VAI.

LE CORSAIRE

The full-length *Le Corsaire*, first choreographed in 1856 and restaged by Petipa in 1865, has been lost. However, in 1899, inspired once again by the legendary Legnani, Petipa added to the ballet a special *pas de deux*, to music by Riccardo Drigo. In the 1930s, after the complete ballet had been dropped from the repertory, the famous Russian dancer Vakhtang Chabukiani (b. 1910) rechoreographed the *pas de deux* to emphasize male virtuosity. In the 1960s, another legendary Russian, Rudolf Nureyev (b. 1938), again revived the *pas de deux*. His version, close in spirit to Chabukiani's, was also a vehicle designed to display the male dancer's soaring elevation. The *pas de deux*, as performed by Nureyev and his partners, most notably Margot Fonteyn (b. 1919) and Lupe Serrano (b. 1930), retained some touches of the original Eastern setting, with its story of an abducted slave girl and the dashing pirate who saves her from the harem. The male's costume, probably inspired by Chabukiani, consists of baggy trousers and a headband, while the female wears the traditional tutu.

The *pas de deux* opens with the man rushing dramatically onstage, running into an *arabesque* pose, one hand outstretched, the other touching his shoulder. The female enters with tiny *bourrée* steps on pointe. He kneels as if to behold a vision. In the *adagio* duet, standing behind her, he supports the ballerina as she steps forward into a lunging *arabesque* and then lifts her in this pose. At the end of the *adagio*, he lifts her very high and regally carries her off. For his first variation, the man reenters far upstage. He propels himself into gravity-defying, spinning jumps, tucking his legs under him and landing in an *attitude* pose. After fast turns on one foot, with the other leg straight out to the side (known as turns *à la seconde*), he then throws himself into barrel or flipping turns, executed as he revolves around the stage in a circle. The ballerina's variation emphasizes a feminine kind of virtuosity—rapid pointe work, tricky balances, and lightning-fast turns. She leaps into a side split, landing on one foot while fully extending the other leg high to the side. Then, balanced on one pointe, she extends her free leg in all directions. Her partner next soars onto the stage in a long high leap in which

Laura Brown and Paul Russell in *Le Corsaire*, Dance Theatre of Harlem.

he seems, for a moment, to linger in the air. He ends his variation with more flipping turns. The ballerina, as if spurred by his feats, whips off a series of rapid turns, concluding with a succession of *fouettés*. Her partner, at still greater speed, whirls into more turns *à la seconde*. As his turns grow faster, she appears to spin into his arms. In the brief *coda*, he supports her *pirouettes* and then stretches out on the floor, one arm extended as if in tribute to her as she balances triumphantly on pointe.

Video: KUL, VAI.

DON QUIXOTE

A full-length Petipa ballet to the music of Ludwig Minkus, *Don Quixote* was first presented in 1869. Tenuously based on the adventures of Cervantes's errant knight, it provided a setting for Petipa-style Spanish dances. Mikhail Baryshnikov staged this evening-long work for American Ballet Theatre in 1978, but previous to that, it was little known outside the Soviet Union. The famous *pas de deux*, however, has been a popular concert piece for years.

The costumes are bright red and black brocade, and the Spanish touches—a rose in the ballerina's hair, hands on hips, an exaggeratedly arched upper back—are still intact. In the *adagio* section, the cavalier slowly turns his señorita as she maintains an *attitude* position. She then balances alone on pointe, one hand on her hip, the other gesturing broadly. He next lifts and exhibits her proudly. Back on her feet, she falls in swooning backbends over his arm. The *adagio* ends with the ballerina in a very high lift, held far above her *porteur's* head. They leave the stage and the male returns for his first variation, full of spinning leaps, high jumps with beats in the air, and fast turns *à la seconde*. The ballerina returns with a black fan, waving it coquettishly. Hands often on her hips, she displays intricate and quick pointe work. The man reenters to execute the barrel or flipping turns while circling the stage. Next, his partner balances on one leg and gaily kicks the other in all directions before whipping off more quick turns. As the pace quickens, the man repeats his turns *à la seconde*. She spins toward him at a breathless speed and they finish

Natalia Makarova and Fernando Bujones in *Don Quixote*,
American Ballet Theatre.

together, kneeling on the floor, each with one hand on hip and the other curved high, their heads and backs arched proudly.

Video: HOME, KUL, PI-A, VAI.

SPRING WATERS

Twentieth-century ballet choreographers often compose dances for two that are called *pas de deux*, although they may not follow the traditional "*adagio*-variations-*coda*" formula. Often a duet that emphasizes virtuoso features, but in which the couple may in fact dance together throughout, is called a *pas de deux*. Soviet choreographers have contributed a great deal to the spectacular aspects of partnering in duets.

In Asaf Messerer's (b. 1903) *Spring Waters* (to music by Sergei Rachmaninoff), a ballerina is supported in lunging *arabesques*, launched into leaps and thrown into the air to spin repeatedly before being caught by her partner. In one particularly breathtaking section, the ballerina hurls herself across the stage and, in a horizontal position, is caught by her partner at the last second near the ground. The dance ends with the ballerina perched high in the air, standing tall, held aloft by her partner, who uses only one hand to support her.

The Grand Pas de Deux emphasizes the traditional distinction between male and female qualities. The man is strong, supportive, and gallant in his partnering, gravity-defying, aggressive, and daring in his variations. The ballerina is an object of admiration, beautifully sculpted, poised, superbly balanced, and flexible in her *adagio*, light flirtatious, quick and agile in her variations. The *pas de deux* is actually a highly stylized version of the courtship dance between a man and a woman, a sparkling theatrical variant of one of the oldest and most enduring dance forms in the world.

Video: HOME.

Natalia Makarova and Ivan Nagy in *Spring Waters*,
American Ballet Theatre.

COMEDY BALLETS

Comedy ballets in the traditional mode are stories of love with happy endings. Elaborate, full-evening works, they are not necessarily funny (although they may contain humorous episodes); rather, they are lighthearted and fun. They are also distinguished from the more grand Classical ballets in that their characters are ordinary people, not royalty, ancient heroes, or gods. The people in comedy ballets are usually country rustics. There is often an out-and-out buffoon (Alain in *La Fille Mal Gardée* is an example of this) and at least one juicy "character" role. Such a part, usually an older person (not a love interest), is more acted than danced, with a great deal of attention to human foibles (ticks, hiccups, fat stomachs, odd gaits in walking, and so on). Dr. Coppélius in *Coppélia* is one of the great character roles in the ballet repertory. Another is Herr Drosselmeyer in *The Nutcracker*. Much of the plot is made clear to the audience in broad pantomimic gestures worthy of the music hall.

Because comedy ballets do not treat noble themes, but do concern "real" people, types and styles of dancing appear that were not considered seemly in the more high-minded tragic stories. In particular, *demi-caractère* dancing—the classical style with touches of theatricalized folk and perhaps social dance mixed in—is a feature of the choreography for both the *corps de ballet* and the leads. The more earthy folk style—still choreographed for the theater, of course, but requiring the dancers to wear boots and long skirts and pants rather than toe shoes, tutus, and tights—is called *character dancing*. This has a place both in the traditional comedy ballets and in the great classics.

The romantic female lead in a comedy ballet is called a *soubrette*, meaning that it is a role intended for a young, gay ingenue who is basically carefree and who will eventually live happily ever after. This type of part contrasts with the time-honored tragic roles, such as Odette or Giselle. In the hierarchy of values in the Classical ballet, the tragic heroines are usually considered the ultimate challenge. A great Swan Queen may be known as the leading ballerina of her generation virtually on the strength of that role alone. It is such touchstone roles, along with the display *pas de deux* of the age of Classicism, that require the most beautiful "line," the most sensitive phrasing, the purest classical style, and the most beautiful physical proportions. Just a rank below come roles like Swanilda (the heroine of *Coppélia*), which do not demand quite the same fineness of movement, but can be enormous fun and give the performer a wonderful chance to reveal an infectious personality. It is quite possible for a gifted ballerina to be outstanding in both the great comic and the great tragic roles.

LA FILLE MAL GARDÉE

Choreography and libretto for first production by Jean Dauberval, 1789; music for first version a potpourri of French popular tunes and airs. (Many subsequent versions to various scores.)

La Fille Mal Gardée is the oldest ballet in the international repertory—or, to be more accurate, it may be the oldest active ballet scenario. Jean Dauberval's (1742–1806) engaging story has provided the basis for numerous productions over 200 years, although the original choreography has probably disappeared completely, as has much of the music. The title may be translated, somewhat awkwardly, as "The Ill-Guarded Girl" or "The Unchaperoned Daughter." In Russia it is called "Vain Precautions," but in the English-speaking world it is virtually always known by its French name.

The ballet, a village love story, received its first performance not in a world capital but in the provincial city of Bordeaux, perhaps because its subject was quite a daring departure and might not have had a chance in "establishment" Paris. What was novel about the ballet was that its leading characters—indeed, all its characters—were peasants, not nobles or royalty or gods, and this was completely unconventional for ballet at the time. These rustic folk were treated more or less realistically—the heroine churns butter, her mother spins, the villagers go on a picnic and get caught in a rainstorm. Thus, it is one of the earliest ballets to deal with everyday life. The choreography combines folk movements with classical ballet and passages of mime. With the French Revolution under way at the time of the ballet's premiere (on July 14 of the same year, a mob in Paris would storm the Bastille), the fact that peasants were the subject may have made it unusually acceptable. (Of course, these were storybook peasants, not the exploited laborers and serfs who were rising up throughout real-life France.) In any case, during an early performance, a leading dancer interrupted the show to propose a toast to the non-noble, nonecclesiastical citizens of France—the so-called Third Estate. The ballet was first seen in London in 1791 and in New York in 1794.

Legend has it that Dauberval got the idea for the story when he saw an engraving in a store window showing a distraught young girl whose mother, having discovered her daughter's tryst with her sweetheart, is roundly dressing down the young man, who is fleeing the scene. Here is the scenario he produced: Lise and Colas, country folk, are in love, but Lise's mother, the Widow Simone, wants her daughter to marry Alain, who is undoubtedly richer but certainly not as handsome, and something of a dimwit as well. When Alain comes calling with his father, Thomas, intending to ask the Widow for her daughter's hand, Lise and Colas are discovered in the bedroom, where Lise has been sent by her mother, supposedly to keep her out of trouble. The lovers beg the mother to change her mind and allow them to marry each other. This she does, to the general joy of the assembled company, with the exception of Alain and his father. The ballet is a comedy, a bright slice of life, full of affection, tenderness, and mischief. The original music was a collection of popular tunes, believed to have been arranged by a member of the local orchestra. Since then, there have been many scores, some using snippets from the original with modern additions, some using other music entirely.

A list of choreographers who have set the work reads like a roll call of the most famous dance designers of two centuries. To begin with, Dauberval was a pupil of Jean Georges Noverre (1727–1810), the most influential theorist and ballet reformer of the 18th century. Others who have created productions include

Jules Perrot (1810–1892; Perrot was responsible for parts of *Giselle*), August Bournonville, the most famous name in Danish ballet, Marius Petipa and Lev Ivanov, who also choreographed *Swan Lake*, and Bronislava Nijinska (1891-1972), sister of Nijinsky. The most recent version—considered by many a comic master-piece of the 20th century—is by the English choreographic gen-ius Sir Frederick Ashton (1904–1989). An impressive number of the most noted ballerinas in history have performed the title role, including Anna Pavlova.

Since Ashton's version is the one most commonly available to the Western world at present (it is in the repertories of several European companies, the National Ballet of Canada, and the San Francisco Ballet), that is the one that will be described in detail here. Despite the ballet's origins, Ashton's production is frankly a portrait of the English countryside. He has written: "There exists in my imagination a life in the country of eternally late spring, a leafy pastorale of perpetual sunshine and the humming of bees; . . . my beloved Suffolk, luminous and calm . . . the thrill of arrival in the country and the days of contemplation and distant, endless staring and dreaming." No doubt whatsoever about where he drew his inspiration.

Ashton was also directly influenced, however, by Ivanov's Russian version. The famous Diaghilev ballerina, Tamara Kar-savina (1885–1978), who had been trained in Russia, had long been a resident of England, and Ashton consulted with her. Indeed, she was able to reproduce exactly some of the mime sequences she knew in her youth. Ashton's musical score was devised by the music director of the Royal Ballet, John Lanch-bery, who combined bits of the original version with music of Ferdinand Hérold, Gioacchino Rossini, Gaetano Donizetti, and connecting passages he wrote himself, to suit the action as Ashton visualized it. This was a collaboration (such as that of Marius Petipa and Tchaikovsky on *The Nutcracker*) in which the choreographer provided the composer with a very detailed and specific list of requirements—describing the ballet almost moment by moment.

Ashton rather daringly opened his full-length evening with a *divertissement* for a rooster and four hens—daring because such a broad stroke might have backfired and created the wrong mood. But, in fact, the peckings and scratchings are nothing short of hilarious and establish just the right tone of merriment for the events to come.

Lise enters, clearly lovesick. She cannot find Colas but, as a token of her affection, leaves a ribbon tied in a lover's knot; he later finds it and attaches it to his staff. This is the first of many uses of ribbons in the ballet; Ashton has incorporated them into the choreography and also invested them with a poetic significance—they represent both gaiety and attachment. Indeed, when the two sweethearts are finally allowed to dance together (after Lise's mother has scolded her and ordered her to churn the butter), they form a cat's cradle of entanglements with the ribbon, which is an integral part of the dance design. He spins her out along the ribbon and winds her up in it again. (A word about Lise's mother, the Widow Simone. This is a comedy role, traditionally danced by a man. It is also more than clear that, at bottom, she has the tenderest feelings for her daughter and her welfare.)

Farm girls enter and urge Lise to play. After more reprimands from Lise's mother, Thomas and Alain pay a visit for the purpose of courtship, arriving to a pompous march. Lise is at first dismissed, then returns to watch Alain struggling clumsily through his paces to some unfortunate (and ridiculous) bleats of piccolo and tuba. Poor Alain! He's not a villain, he's just not bright, and his Dutch-boy hairdo and pigeon-toed walk don't help him much either. For reasons unknown, he clutches a red umbrella. Ashton's steps for him are a clever equivalent of a stutter. His courting dance comes to a rousing conclusion with—a somersault! It is time for all to set off to the harvest picnic, and here Ashton creates another memorable image—the village girls, grouped together, simulate the wheels of a cart with circling ribbons. Somehow Alain winds up as the "horse," with a ribbon for a bridle, which says more than any words could about his place in this ballet. This "parade" to the fields, complete with chickens, takes place in front of a forecurtain, covering a complicated scene change going on behind.

At the picnic, the harvesters relax while Alain and Lise, the "official" couple, dance the expected *pas de deux*. Ashton humorously incorporates Colas into the proceedings—making it a *pas de trois*—unnoticed by Alain, who is busy concentrating on his role as a noble partner. If it were not already clear, the affection between Lise and Colas would here be obvious, as they exchange pantomime kisses while she is supposedly dancing a love *pas de deux* with her suitor. Alain, determined to make an impression (but succeeding only in making a fool of himself), seizes a flute as though intending to lead the assembled company in a dance. But, of course, he plays the instrument out of tune and, when it is snatched from him, throws a tantrum.

In one of Ashton's typically skillful changes of pace, he brings on the fireworks in a Grand Pas de Deux. Colas dances exuberantly, bounding into the air, landing bunched over near the ground, then exploding upward—all in exquisite classical positions. In an inventive construction, Lise's friends make X's (kisses) with ribbons; Lise, in the center, grasps the ribbons in one hand and is circled by her friends, still holding the ribbons themselves. She is thus delicately supported and turned on a single pointe as the ribbons radiate outward like the spokes of a wheel. Colas then runs in to lift her and the ribbons softly drop away, leaving the couple to provide their own support for each other. This dazzling *pas de deux* is the technical highpoint of the evening; the huge leaps, spins, and dainty footwork have been called "a veritable manifesto of virtuosity." In their dance together, Colas lifts Lise a full arm's length above him, in the manner of the spectacular Bolshoi dancers. Throughout the work, Ashton combines just this type of sensational display with the fleet, small-scale foot movements associated with the Danish school, his own decorous inventions, and mime sequences from prerevolutionary Russia, some of which, undoubtedly, derive from various versions in France. (Lise's hanging the ribbon on the tree in Act I has been traced back to the first Paris production of 1803 and may, of course, be earlier still.)

In another inspired change of pace—because more virtuoso dancing would only weaken the striking measures of the *pas de deux*—Ashton now inserts a humorous clog dance for Widow Simone and some friends from the village (a bumptious number performed in wooden shoes), then a joyous maypole dance, with yet more ribbons. All is brought to an abrupt end when a thunderstorm causes everyone to run for shelter. Poor, dear old Alain is swept off his feet into the air when his umbrella is inflated by a burst of wind.

As the second act opens, Widow Simone is trying to keep Lise gainfully occupied with spinning, but she nods off to sleep,

Eleanor d'Antuono and Fernando Bujones in *La Fille Mal Gardée*
(Jean Dauberval-Dimitri Romanoff), American Ballet Theatre.

after trying to stay awake by keeping time with a tambourine for Lise to dance to. Colas appears in the window; he opens the upper half, lifts Lise off her feet, and swings her to and fro. The music combines love themes with a touch of Widow Simone's tambourine dance. Harvesters noisily enter to collect their pay and, in another folk touch, perform a stick dance (a legacy of the English Morris dancers). Colas seizes the opportunity to sneak in with the others, unnoticed, and hides among bales of hay. All leave, and, in one of the most heart-warming sections of the ballet—a pure mime passage dating back at least as far as Ivanov (1885)—Lise touchingly imagines her married life with Colas and the children they will have, only to be embarrassed when he reveals himself hidden in the hayloft. They exchange scarves, again as tokens of love. But panic follows when they see the Widow Simone approaching. Where will he hide? She frantically looks about—even opening a drawer to see if there is a corner of space for him there.

Colas escapes to the bedroom, while Lise looks furiously busy sweeping as her mother returns. But the Widow is not exactly stupid; she notices Lise's new scarf and, as fate would have it, locks her in the bedroom to get her out of the way. Just at that moment, Alain and his father arrive again, this time with the marriage notary. Serious business is at hand, but it is presumably a happy moment for Alain, and his doleful tuba melody from the first act is replaced by one on the same theme, but written in a joyous manner for the piccolo. His "stuttering" mannerisms have not left him, however, as he mounts the stairs, only to discover Lise and Colas embracing each other in the bedroom. In a muddle of anger, confusion, contrition, pleading, softening, and ultimate tenderness on the part of Lise's truly devoted mother, the marriage contract is torn up, Thomas and Alain take their disgruntled leave, and Lise and Colas receive her mother's blessing. For the final *pas de deux*, Ashton has wisely not tried to rival the sparks of the first act. True enough, Colas leaps beautifully and lifts Lise high, even throwing her into the air in a bravura manner, but there are also moments of quiet tenderness, where the movements are low to the ground. At one moment, Lise approaches Colas, presumably preparing for an exciting lift—but then she merely snuggles up against his arm. It is a glowing ending to the sunniest of love stories.

Ashton's full abilities are revealed in his inventive dance designs and in his skillful formal construction—his alternation of lyric and comic, boisterous and tender. Moreover, he has given characters individual and appropriate movement qualities, beautifully balanced—the young lovers are classical, in the springtime of their emotions; the farmers mix classical with more blunt-toed folk idioms and project a real feeling of closeness to the earth and devotion to manual labor. Simone, Thomas, and Alain are cut from other cloth, deriving from traditions of English pantomime and music hall. The chickens, of course, are in a class by themselves. But perhaps what gives Ashton's pastorale its particular luminosity is his essential sympathy toward his characters; there is just not a mean streak anywhere. Even Alain is made a lovable fool, and in the end, Simone's true love for her daughter overshadows her crosspatch demeanor. The lovers are clearly dancing off to a radiant future.

Video: HOME.

COPPÉLIA

Choreography by Arthur Saint-Léon, 1870; music by Léo Delibes.

Coppélia is the most famous comedy ballet of all time. It was composed in a period between the height of Romanticism, marked by *Giselle,* and the flowering of the Russian school of Classicism, which featured *Swan Lake, The Nutcracker,* and *The Sleeping Beauty.*

For several centuries—since the time of Louis XIV—France had been the leader in the dance world. *Coppélia,* choreographed in 1870, came at the end of that dominance. Very soon afterward, within 20 years, Russia would be the center of Classical ballet, and in the United States today, many of the ballets performed, as well as the manner of teaching ballet steps, derive from Russian models and methods developed between 1880 and 1890.

Coppélia is a sparkling, fun-filled tale, providing many opportunities for joyous dancing and two wonderful roles—the dotty old scientist, Dr. Coppélius, and the rambunctious young girl

Swanilda. (At the time of the ballet's premiere, dancing as a profession for men had reached a very low ebb in public estimation; things were so bad that the leading male role in *Coppélia*—a youth named Franz—was actually danced by a woman in men's clothing. The role was made as brief as possible and contained no virtuoso dance passages.)

Coppélia was composed as a full-evening, three-act ballet, but the original third act was soon lost, and choreographers ever since have been faced with the problem of how to end the ballet. Some, like George Balanchine, have created an entire new third act, adding music from other Delibes compositions. Others have more or less tried to ignore the fact that the third act is missing, and give the lovers just a few seconds to get together before ringing down the curtain. We may be sure that a traditional Grand Pas de Deux never existed, because of the fact that the hero was first danced by a woman.

Although created in France, most versions of *Coppélia* seen today (Acts I and II, that is) derive from Marius Petipa's reconstruction of Arthur Saint-Léon's (1821–1870) choreography, mounted in St. Petersburg in 1884. Like a number of ballets from Russia, *Coppélia* reached the West thanks to Nicholas Sergeyev (1876–1951), who fled the October Revolution taking with him notebooks of the great classics in notation. (He also staged *The Sleeping Beauty, Swan Lake, Giselle,* and *The Nutcracker* in the West.) *Coppélia* was first seen in America as early as 1887, and Anna Pavlova made her United States debut dancing the lead in this ballet in 1910.

There is no doubt that part of *Coppélia's* durability and charm is due to Delibes's rich, melodious score, one of the finest ever written for dance. (Incidentally, it is believed to have introduced the *czardas*, a Hungarian folk dance, to the ballet stage.) The story was taken from a Gothic tale by E.T.A. Hoffmann and was also used by Jacques Offenbach in his opera *Tales of Hoffmann*. It is not surprising to find touches of the macabre in a primarily light-hearted tale—menacing elements were a specialty of Hoffmann's and they add to the mystery and enchantment of all fairy stories.

In a town in Galicia, Swanilda loves Franz. As the ballet begins, Swanilda, a charming young girl, comes out of her house. Just across the square, in the house of the mysterious Dr. Coppélius, she sees another young girl sitting outside on a balcony, reading a book. Swanilda greets her, bowing with a smile. Coppélia, the other girl, does not move. Swanilda does a little dance; again no response. Shrugging her shoulders, Swanilda goes on about her business—and her main business is dancing. She is clearly a young woman in love, and she pours out her feelings in a full-blown melody. But there is a slight cloud on the horizon. She has noticed that Franz, her sweetheart, has shown an interest in the young lady on Dr. Coppélius's balcony. She hears him approaching and hides.

Franz comes along, a good-natured peasant fellow (without the winsomeness of Swanilda), and sure enough, begins to show off in front of Coppélia. Nothing happens for the moment, and Franz glances over at Swanilda's house, clearly unable to make up his mind which of the two has captured his heart. Suddenly Coppélia moves—a rather stiff little bend forward—then is quickly snatched away. Swanilda goes off in a huff but soon returns, chasing a butterfly. As it alights on the ground, she captures it, but Franz takes it away and pins it on his blouse. Upset already, Swanilda is brought to tears by this display of cruelty. She angrily accuses Franz of unfaithfulness. Villagers distract her with their dancing. The Burgomaster enters with the news that a Festival of Bells will be held in the town and that dowries will be presented to a number of young couples. Will Swanilda marry Franz? Shaken by his behavior but still unsure, she trusts to an ear of wheat to tell her whether Franz really loves her. During the soulful Ear of Wheat Adagio, danced by Franz and Swanilda with other couples, Swanilda shakes the wheat. If she hears a sound, Franz loves her, but she hears no sound. Franz protests, but Swanilda is convinced that their engagement is over. He leaves angrily, and Swanilda begins a wonderful dance with her eight friends, one of the pure-dance highlights of the work. She finishes triumphantly as though nothing has disturbed her. Villagers dance a *czardas*; then, as night falls, all leave the stage.

The door of Dr. Coppélius's house opens, and the doddering old man comes out into the night. In some productions, he is rather grotesque and sinister, in others, he is more a comic fuddy-duddy. In any case, he brandishes a giant key, locking his door with a flourish. As he leaves, he is accosted by a band of young men and in the scuffle, unnoticed, he drops the key. Some time later, Swanilda and her friends discover it. Though

Patricia McBride, Shaun O'Brien, and Peter Martins in *Coppélia* (Alexandra Danilova-George Balanchine, after Petipa), New York City Ballet.

frightened, they decide to enter Dr. Coppélius's house to find out just who this odd (and stuck-up) Coppélia is. Shaking with fear, the girls urge each other on, unlock the door, and go in. Franz, meanwhile, is also determined to see Coppélia. He brings a ladder and leans it against the balcony. Just at that moment Dr. Coppélius returns, frantically searching for his key. He chases Franz away, then sees, horrified, that his front door is wide open. He rushes in, and Franz returns, intent on gaining access.

Act II takes place inside Dr. Coppélius's shadowy workshop, filled with life-size dolls of all kinds. Still quaking, the young girls enter, looking around in wonder. Swanilda goes behind a curtain in search of Coppélia, then leaps out again in fright. Her friends insist that she go closer. Summoning up her courage, she approaches Coppélia behind the curtain. This time she stays a little longer, then emerges with a delighted look on her face. She struts around mechanically, indicating that Coppélia is only a doll! How amusing! And how ridiculous Franz now seems! Then one of her friends accidentally leans on some kind of button or switch, and the dolls of Coppélius's workshop appear to spring to life. (In some productions, the girls, realizing that all these life-size creatures are only dolls, run around winding them all up.) In the midst of this disorder, Coppélius enters. Of course, he is absolutely horrified; the workshop is completely out of control. He chases the girls out, not noticing that Swanilda is hiding behind the curtains that conceal Coppélia.

Coppélius hears more noise—it is Franz coming in through the balcony window. In response to questioning by Coppélius, Franz says that he has come to find the woman he loves. Coppélius has an idea. Changing his approach from a scowl to a smile, he engages Franz in conversation, then offers him a drink. After a few of these drinks, Franz is completely knocked out, and Coppélius sets to work. Consulting a reference book, he looks for the secret formula that will help him transfer the living force from Franz to his most prized possession. He brings her out—of course, it is Swanilda in Coppélia's clothes. Coppélius works his magic spells and is completely delighted (and astounded) when the doll takes on some aspects of life. She moves very stiffly, one part of her body at a time. She blinks, she raises her shoulders, she tries out her arms and legs. Coppélius is ecstatic. Swanilda is having a wonderful time. She can't wait until Franz wakes up so she can show him how he was deceived. But then she begins to move a little more wildly, no longer taking her "orders" from Coppélius. He throws her a black mantilla and she performs a Spanish dance. Wearing a Scottish sash, she does a nimble heel-and-toe number to bagpipe music. But she is getting restless. Will Franz ever wake up?

Coppélius, after his acute joy at her animation, is becoming exasperated by her naughtiness. She stamps on his book, then crashes into the toys. Franz now stirs, and Swanilda gleefully (and with a superior air) rolls out the doll Coppélia, completely lifeless. Franz is instantly persuaded that Swanilda is the girl for him, while Coppélius collapses in despair. He did not create a living thing, after all. Although he is essentially a comic character (and has deluded himself ridiculously), we can almost feel sympathy for his enormous disappointment.

While the choreography for the final act has been lost, the libretto has been preserved. It tells of the Festival of the Bells, which takes place along with the wedding of Franz and Swanilda. First the dejected Coppélius is given money by the Burgomaster, then comes a series of *divertissements*—solos for Dawn, Prayer, and Spinning (three women), and a dance for Discord and War, among others. As a climax, many later choreographers have created a Grand Pas de Deux for Franz and Swanilda. The ballet ends joyously.

Coppélia has been greatly loved since it reached the West and, if anything, is now more popular than ever. Although the ballet can be enjoyed simply as a delicious entertainment, it also hints at deeper themes. The role of Dr. Coppélius can take on an almost tragic dimension—he has virtually fallen in love with his "daughter" and is "crushed to discover that he did not endow her with the miracle of life." A most astute observer of the dance, Lincoln Kirstein, has written that the ballet's essential consideration is whether "the artist is responsible for creating work with independent or eternal life"—a serious question for creators in any art, in any age.

Video: KUL.

TRADITIONAL BALLETS
OF THE
TWENTIETH CENTURY

The ballet in one act (introduced by Michel Fokine and Serge Diaghilev) has become the characteristic form in the 20th century, and more and more, abstract (or plotless), often reductive, dances predominate among experimental choreographers today. However, the lush appeal of the full-evening 19th-century classics is still strong—*Swan Lake*, *The Sleeping Beauty*, and *The Nutcracker* remain the most frequently performed ballets in the world. Moreover, there are many choreographers who continue to produce works in the same vein. Indeed, the Russians and the English have created a number of them. *Ivan the Terrible*, *Tales of Hoffmann*, *Mayerling*, *Sylvia*, *Spartacus*, *Eugene Onegin*, and *Ondine* are just a few 20th-century works modeled on 19th-century concepts. These multiact ballets all have stories and unfold at a fairly leisurely pace throughout the evening. Passages of pure dance alternate with mime, although in the 20th century, formal mime has become less common than ''acted'' sequences. There is a sense of spectacle, enhanced by opulent sets and costumes, and frequent magical effects. The cast is large. For variety, there are usually some comic, or ''character,'' roles and bits of comedy as well as drama. Love is virtually always a central theme, and this means that there is at least one opportunity during the evening for a Grand Pas de Deux as well as for lyrical episodes. The music is very often written specifically for the ballet—this is the case with the two most widely performed of the contemporary ''traditional'' ballets, *Romeo and Juliet* and *Cinderella*, both of which have scores by Sergei Prokofiev.

ROMEO AND JULIET

Choreography for first production by Ivo Psota, 1938; music by Sergei Prokofiev; scenery for first production by V. Skrušny.

Sergei Prokofiev's *Romeo and Juliet*, a full-length ballet score written in 1935, has inspired many balletic versions of the well-known story. The music, which can be considered a 20th-century classic, is the most widely used ballet score since those composed by Tchaikovsky. The score provides the ballet with a musical libretto, complete with a sequence of episodes, crescendos of action and emotion, and a separate musical motif for each of the main characters, as well as a recurring, swelling melody expressive of the love of Romeo and Juliet. The score unfolds in a Prologue, three acts, thirteen scenes, and an Epilogue, following the structure of Shakespeare's tragedy of the star-crossed lovers.

The ballet premiered in Czechoslovakia, but the first important Soviet version was choreographed by Leonid Lavrovsky (1905–1967), who presented it in Leningrad in 1940. Sir Frederick Ashton, John Cranko (1927–1973), Kenneth MacMillan (b. 1929), Michael Smuin (b. 1938), and Yuri Grigorovich (b. 1927) are among the many who have mounted their own productions. (In 1943, Antony Tudor [1908–1987] also composed a *Romeo and Juliet*, but to a Frederick Delius score rather than to Prokofiev.) Choreography, staging of the dances, dramatic emphasis, character portrayal, costumes, and sets have varied with each choreographer's treatment. Nonetheless, all follow the familiar story, strongly supported by Prokofiev's music.

Scene 1 opens in the marketplace or main square of Verona, an Italian Renaissance city. Servants, shopkeepers, and ordinary people mill about. Before long, a quarrel breaks out between servants of the house of Montague and servants of the house of Capulet, traditional rivals. Young men from each of the feuding houses rush to join the sword-fighting melee, until the Prince of Verona steps in to halt the fighting and forbid further disturbances.

Scene 2 takes us inside the Capulet house, where a youthful Juliet plays with her nurse until her mother, Lady Capulet, interrupts her with the announcement that Paris has asked for her hand in marriage. Juliet is reluctant to accept the fact that she is no longer a child. That evening, the Capulets are hosting a grand masquerade ball and the guests are about to arrive. Meanwhile, the gay music attracts Romeo, a son of the house of Montague, and his mischievous friends, Mercutio and Benvolio. They disguise themselves and sneak into the Capulet house. At the elegant ball, the guests dance in a formal, Renaissance style. The young Juliet has just been presented to Paris, and as she dances, Romeo and his friends enter the room. Romeo is enchanted by her and, despite the danger, approaches her in the dance. She is visibly transfixed by him as well. Tybalt, Juliet's fiery-tempered cousin, recognizes the intruders, but the elder Capulet prevents an outbreak of violence. That night, the love-struck Juliet wanders out to her moonlit balcony. Romeo appears in the garden below and they pledge their love in a romantic *pas de deux.*

Act II brings us outside to the bustling marketplace. Juliet's nurse pushes her way through the jostling crowd to deliver a letter from her charge to Romeo. Romeo reads its contents—Juliet has consented to be his wife, and they must secretly wed at the cell of Friar Laurence. After rushing to their meeting at the chapel, kneeling together before the good Friar, the young lovers are united in wedlock. On the way home, they pass through the raucous marketplace where the people have been drinking and the mood is querulous. Among the revelers is the angry Tybalt, who challenges Mercutio to a duel. Romeo begs them not to fight, but it is too late, and in the course of the fray, Tybalt viciously stabs Mercutio in the back. Watching his best friend die and witnessing Tybalt's swaggering insolence breaks Romeo's self-control, and he kills Tybalt in revenge. People rush in to mourn their kinsmen, and Romeo is forever banished from Verona.

The next scene unfolds at dawn in Juliet's bedroom. In a tender *pas de deux,* the lovers embrace. Later, Paris is again presented to the distraught Juliet. To her parents' indignation, she refuses the marriage. In desperation, she rushes off to Friar Laurence, who suggests she drink a sleeping potion that will make her appear lifeless. She will be buried in the family tomb where Romeo can join her, and they can then escape together. Back in her bedroom Juliet fearfully contemplates the phial of poison but decides to drink it. In the morning, the nurse discovers her

Robert LaFosse and Leslie Browne in *Romeo and Juliet*
(Kenneth MacMillan), American Ballet Theatre.

dead. Amidst much lamenting, Juliet is brought to the family tomb. Romeo, as is well-known, does not receive the correct message. When he descends into the burial vault he believes his beloved Juliet to be really dead and stabs himself in despair. Juliet, awakening slowly, shivers in the dark vault, then sees her loved one lying lifeless and kills herself. Over the bodies of their dead children, the Capulets and Montagues vow to end their feud.

Prokofiev's music for *Romeo and Juliet* provides a pretext for a wide spectrum of dance styles. The ballet, in fact, showcases the whole gamut of possibilities in ballet dancing, from mime to comedic character dance and Classical *pas de deux.* The crown scenes in the market call for colorful milling about, a vigorous *tarantella* (an Italian folk dance), and character dancing in duets, trios, and variations for the *corps*. There is much stylized dueling and fighting. The indoor scenes at the Capulets require extravagant pageantry and provide an opportunity for dignified court dancing. The minor characters, such as Juliet's nurse, Romeo's friends, and Friar Laurence, develop their personalities through mime and movement. The more intimate scenes, such as Juliet's soliloquies and the balcony and bedroom scenes, call for pure classical ballet style. The maturation of Juliet is also expressed in classic dance, as her use of pointes becomes stronger and her movements ripen from those of a lighthearted adolescent girl to those of a passionate woman.

The different treatments of this ballet reveal interesting variations in emphasis in national and personal style. The Soviet Lavrovsky's version is grandiose, slow-moving, and obvious in intent. (A film of Lavrovsky's production was released in 1954, starring Galina Ulanova.) Lavrovsky was concerned with a very close translation of Shakespeare into dance. As he explained his approach, "the depths of passion and ideas, and the intensity of feeling conveyed by Shakespeare's tragedy, demand the fusion of dance with mime. In ballet, words are absent and the effect of every phrase of mime must correspond with the spoken language of the stage characters." His literal treatment results in a great deal of mime and tends to give the ballet a somewhat static feeling. The Soviet *Romeo and Juliet* is also characterized by a specifically Russian dramatic style, which tends to be more flamboyant than the English or American. Ulanova's performance as Juliet is famous for the beauty of her technique as well as for her histrionics—the impassioned flinging of capes, the breathless runs, and (for us) the exaggerated lift of her upper body.

John Cranko's version for the Stuttgart Ballet in 1962 is less literal in its approach. He consequently achieves an exciting flow and theatrical rhythm. He keeps the crowd scenes particularly lively, and his ballroom scene is especially successful. Although Cranko's choreography is not always technically demanding, he moves the *corps* masterfully and uses many lifts and innovative steps that look difficult and have great theatrical flair. He also excels in portraying individual characters; Mercutio's death scene is more detailed in Cranko's version than in any other. Cranko, a South African trained in England, who directed the Stuttgart Ballet before his unexpectedly early death, enjoyed working on full-length ballets. His *Romeo and Juliet, Eugene Onegin,* and *The Taming of the Shrew* catapulted his two leading dancers, Marcia Haydée and Richard Cragun, to international stardom.

Kenneth MacMillan's *Romeo and Juliet,* choreographed for the Royal Ballet in 1965, is a good example of English dramatic style—clear and direct, but more restrained and subtle than the Russian. MacMillan's *Romeo and Juliet* is distinguished by a special emphasis on the character of Juliet. We see her first as a frivolous child playing with a doll, then as a young woman surrendering to the throes of her first love. She matures as the events of her life close in on her, struggling with decisions and responsibilities. MacMillan's version is also famous for its *pas de deux,* with a particularly haunting one in the tomb when Romeo dances with a "dead" Juliet.

Sir Frederick Ashton's mounting of the work, originally created for the Royal Danish Ballet and revived by the Festival Ballet (now the English National Ballet) in 1985, is the gentlest of the versions choreographed to Prokofiev's sometimes bombastic score. He omits most of the boisterous street activity: There are no pranksters or prostitutes in his Verona, and very little fighting. Ashton's work is a delicate one, marked less by grand passions than by good manners. His choreography, as always, is infused with a courtly classicism.

A completely different approach is demonstrated by Antony Tudor. His is not a spectacular full-length ballet filled out with episodes of swordplay, Renaissance court dance, and special *pas de deux.* Danced to selected works of Delius, it is condensed into one act with nine scenes. The action is intensely focused on the lovers, and events seem to flow out of one another without preliminaries, giving the ballet the inevitability of tragedy. It is more Tudor's stylization than elaborate pageantry that gives the ballet its Renaissance feeling. His dancers assume period poses with their feet just slightly turned out and their weight tilted back. During Romeo and Juliet's first duet at the ball, some of the other guests sit at a table with their backs to the audience, which gives the same flat, friezelike appearance as in the backgrounds of some Renaissance paintings. Eugene Berman's set, with its winding roads, archways, pillars, and porticoes, helps too to create a Renaissance feeling of space. Tudor also borrows some of the theatrical devices from the Elizabethan stage. The servants from the house of Capulet watch the entire play from different positions, help with some of the scene changes, and at one point form a wall separating a tableau of Juliet and her nurse weeping over Tybalt on one side and Romeo seeking Friar Laurence's help on the other. Tudor, who did not wish to interrupt the flow of the ballet with a *pas de deux* or other special "dance numbers," turned the balcony scene into a rapturous encounter between the two lovers rather than a Grand Pas de Deux. They dance separately; Romeo below leaps and turns, while Juliet, on the balcony, curves and stretches her body in response. In the bedroom scene, Juliet rises to dance happily. She rushes toward Romeo; he lifts her, but must immediately leave. Tudor achieves a special poignancy in the tomb scene. When Juliet awakens, she sees Romeo about to die. With his remaining strength, he pulls himself up and lifts her before falling. She spins around frantically. With his last ounce of life, Romeo rises again and holds her in his arms before collapsing. Juliet rises suddenly on her pointes, as if to surge upward toward the finality of death— and stabs herself.

Tudor's ballet is not structured in the manner of those using the Prokofiev score, with its very specific demarcation of scenes. The Delius music provides no thematics, hint of plot, or even musical counts to follow. It is impressionistic and supportive, giving a very particular emotional tone and background to the ballet.

Video: HOME, KUL, ORION, PA-I, VAI.

CINDERELLA

Choreography for first production by Rostislav Zakharov, 1945; music by Sergei Prokofiev; scenery and costumes for first production by Pyotr Williams. (Many subsequent versions.)

Cinderella is an ideal theme for treatment as a full-length ballet, for this enchanted love story has all the right ingredients: a hero and heroine, mock villains (the stepsisters), touches of the comic and grotesque, magic, and a happy ending. Many choreographers have been drawn to it. During the last century, versions were produced in Russia and France; later (1938), even Michel Fokine tried his hand at it. The first realization of the Prokofiev score, by Rostislav Zakharov (1907–1984), occurred in Russia, where there have been at least two more stagings since. The great English choreographer Sir Frederick Ashton created a *Cinderella* for the Sadler's Wells (now the Royal) Ballet in 1948, which was historically important as well as a delightful entertainment—it was the first full-length classic ballet created in that country. The English—Ashton in particular—have found such loving, "old-fashioned" spectacles especially congenial, and the Royal Ballet has since become famous for them. Kenneth MacMillan, then chief choreographer for the company, has created several, and the late John Cranko, an alumnus of the Royal Ballet, brought this type of "opera-house" ballet to Stuttgart, where it helped establish the style of his new company, which later gained worldwide fame.

In the United States and Canada, there are many productions of *Cinderella*, and new ones continue to appear. No single version has become a standard, as has the Petipa-Ivanov *Swan Lake*, for example. Almost all use the Prokofiev score, which establishes the basic structure.

As the familiar tale begins, Cinderella's two ugly stepsisters are sewing a scarf in preparation for a ball to which they have been invited. In many productions, the stepsisters are played by men, and this makes their attempts to be dainty and graceful particularly comic. The neglected Cinderella—a beautiful young woman—sits by the hearth in rags. Their father reads

Magali Messac in *Cinderella* (Peter Anastos-Mikhail Baryshnikov), American Ballet Theatre.

nearby as the sisters argue over who will wear the scarf. Cinderella looks wistfully at the portrait of her mother over the fireplace. She does a little dance with the dustpan, then the broom, then dares to try on her sisters' scarf, yearning to wear something luxurious. She has a tender rapport with her father. The sisters continue to squabble as a beggar woman knocks at the door. Only Cinderella pays attention to her, offering her food; the others are much too busy. The old hag leaves and couturiers and others bring in the fancy clothes, shoes, and jewelry the sisters will wear to the ball. With great ceremony, the ungainly pair squeeze themselves into the clothes. The dancing master arrives to teach them the rudiments of graceful movement, and then they are off to the ball. Alone, Cinderella takes the broom and pretends it is a handsome partner. She dances dreamily, performing with grace the steps her sisters just struggled with. In the course of her dance, the beggar woman returns, but is amazingly transformed into a ravishing young woman, dressed in a classical tutu. After her light, bouncy variation, the fairies of the Four Seasons appear, each dancing a solo and each bringing a glamorous article of clothing to replace the rags Cinderella is wearing. When finally a pumpkin is changed into a coach, Cinderella's transformation is complete, and she goes off to the ball, but not before the Fairy Godmother (the former hag) warns her to be home by midnight.

In Act II, richly dressed couples dance in a festive hall. The stepsisters have their turn, with laughable results, and in their own variations, make attempts at some "real" ballet steps— turns, beats, *adagio*, formal arm movements (*port de bras*). One of them even flirts, peeking out from behind a huge fan; the other is lifted—more or less—by a partner, who shows visible signs of strain. Other guests take over the floor. A jester performs an animated dance; then, with a flourish of trumpets, the Prince and his retinue enter. To delicate music, Cinderella arrives in her coach, accompanied by a large group of fairies. Daintily she *bourrée*s forward in her sparkling slippers. The Prince approaches her; she shyly withdraws but is persuaded to dance a waltz with him in which the fairies join. There is more dancing by the guests. The stepsisters try to butt in, but are rebuffed. After Cinderella's small solo, the Prince offers her an orange, the most precious fruit in the kingdom. He also gives oranges to the sisters, who immediately argue about whose is larger. The Prince and Cinderella dance a tender but grand *adagio,* and there is more panoply in a large waltz with all the guests. Twelve o'clock sneaks up unexpectedly, and Cinderella, hearing the hour strike, dashes away, leaving the Prince completely bewildered. In her haste, she has dropped her glass slipper.

Act III shows Cinderella back home, dozing on the hearth. She reminisces about the ball—or was it just a dream? But in the pocket of her ragged dress, she finds one glass slipper. Again she waltzes with the broom, reliving the most enchanted moments. The stepsisters lurch into the room. They had a good time at the ball, too, only their feet hurt, and they hobble about. The jester arrives to announce the Prince's party, searching the kingdom to find the beautiful girl whose foot fits the glass slipper. The sisters, naturally, are sure one of them will be a perfect fit, and there is quite a ceremony of shoe trying. The first sister's foot is much too large; the second sister actually manages to jam the shoe halfway on, but in demonstrating the fit, she skids and falls. Cinderella rushes to her aid, and as she bends over, the other slipper tumbles out of her pocket. The Prince reaches over to get a better look and Cinderella shyly turns away. The Prince announces she will be his bride, and the Fairy Godmother appears to bless the union. In the final scene, a glade by night, Cinderella and the Prince, accompanied by the fairies, dance an *adagio* to dreamy music.

Video: VIEW.

EARLY BALLET REBELS

THE LEGACY OF DIAGHILEV

Ballet has never been the same since Serge Diaghilev—it was he who introduced a new era of theatrical dance to the Western world. Diaghilev was a young Russian of good lineage who could not quite find a place for himself in official artistic circles. He was not a creative artist, but rather an unfailing discoverer of talent in others, a brilliant catalyst for artistic innovations and collaboration. Tired of local government bureaucracy, Diaghilev began to export Russian art to the West. Next, he turned his distinctive abilities to organizing a touring ballet and opera season in Paris, engaging some of the most talented performers in Russia. When, on the evening of May 19, 1909, the curtain rose for the first time on the Diaghilev "Saison Russe," a startled Parisian audience saw ballet bathed in the vibrant colors of major artists and danced to the music of distinguished composers. The Diaghilev Ballets Russes introduced several short works on an evening's program, ballets whose subjects were often of an unprecedented daring, danced in an unrestricted variety of styles, free from the formulas of Petipa's classics. For 20 years, performing mostly in Paris, London, and Monte Carlo, the Ballets Russes was a breeding ground for major innovative ideas in all the arts.

Diaghilev could not have achieved this without the availability of outstanding talent. A nucleus of extraordinary Russian dancers—Vaslav Nijinsky (c. 1889–1950), Tamara Karsavina,

Adolph Bolm (1884–1951), Anna Pavlova—provided the magnetic center attracting other artists. Equally important was the presence of a choreographer with fresh, forward-looking ideas: Michel Fokine.

MICHEL FOKINE

*F*okine's works were the mainstay of the prewar (1909–1914) Ballets Russes repertory and provided the kind of "twentieth-century" ballets appropriate to Diaghilev's total vision.

An outstanding male dancer, Michel Fokine (1880–1942) graduated from the Imperial Ballet School in St. Petersburg in 1898. The school, like its affiliate theater, stood for the preservation of the status quo and was frankly suspicious of experimentation. Fokine could not accept the notion that respect for tradition meant the suppression of new ideas. He found the structure and aesthetic within which Petipa worked stifling. Why, he demanded, should the ballerina always appear in a tutu and pointe shoes regardless of the period or character portrayed? Why rely on stilted mime gesture rather than allow the dance itself to be expressive? Why, he challenged, were the dancers entirely limited to the steps and postures of the *danse d'école* even when such conventions served no purpose?

New ideas and a spirit of reform were in the air, despite official disapproval. In 1904 Fokine made public a letter to the administration of the Imperial Theater stating his principles for the "New Ballet." He insisted that ballet not rely on ready-made steps or combinations but rather treat each subject individually and expressively. He then declared that dances should never be inserted arbitrarily into a ballet just as *divertissement* or entertainment; the ballet should instead be an integrated whole. Fokine also opposed the "stop action" use of mime sequences and urged that meaning be expressed through the dancers' entire bodies. Next, he called for the integration of the *corps de ballet* with the soloists, rather than its relegation to an ornamental background. Lastly, Fokine wrote of an alliance of music and the visual arts on an equal basis with the dance. Impressed by the beauty of museum figures in nonballetic poses and undoubtedly also inspired by the St. Petersburg visit of the dance revolutionary Isadora Duncan (1877–1927) in 1905, he began to put some of his ideas into practice at the Maryinsky.

But Fokine was able to fully liberate his ballets from the conventions of the past only when he became choreographer for Diaghilev's Ballets Russes in 1909. Although several were conceived in Russia, his acclaimed ballets were the result of his reforms put into practice on a Western stage, and many of the dances created during that period remain staples of ballet repertories the world over. What is more, Fokine's approach primed ballet for the enormous experimentation and innovation that was to follow.

It would be misleading, however, to conclude that before Fokine ballet was never expressive or that a *corps de ballet* was never more than a pretty picture frame. One has only to think of Ivanov's second act of *Swan Lake,* Petipa's expressive use of Classicism in the Rose Adagio from *The Sleeping Beauty,* or his handling of the *corps* in *La Bayadère,* to realize this is not so. Even though Petipa and Ivanov were greatly limited by convention, the seeds of certain developments can be found in their work. If Fokine rejected their legacy, he was also greatly inspired by it and admits repeatedly in his memoirs that the classical dance remains the basis of all his work. And after a very brief time, ironically, Fokine, the great reformer, was considered too conservative, and by 1912 he had fallen out with Diaghilev. Although he remained active as a choreographer until his death in 1942, his lasting works were all created during his few short years with Diaghilev.

Diaghilev went on to foster the careers first of Vaslav Nijinsky, then Leonide Massine (1895–1979), Nijinsky's sister, Bronislava Nijinska, and, finally, George Balanchine (1904–1983), thus decisively demonstrating his "nose" for talent and, in the process, influencing the aesthetic outlook of the worlds of theater, fashion, and even interior decor.

After Diaghilev's death in 1929, Balanchine eventually developed a major school and company of his own in the United States, while creating one of the most vibrant strains in 20th-century dance. Other dancers and choreographers who had worked with Diaghilev dispersed to form companies and schools of their own all over the world. Ballet, as we shall see in the following pages, developed in many directions. The new-found latitude—to lean toward the experimental or modern, or to rework the old with a new vision—is all part of the lasting legacy and open-ended heritage of the Diaghilev Ballets Russes.

THE DYING SWAN

Choreography by Michel Fokine, c. 1905; music by Camille Saint-Saëns.

The Dying Swan is ballet's most famous solo and will forever be associated with its first interpreter, Anna Pavlova. Pavlova was trained at the Imperial Ballet School along with Fokine and Nijinsky and became a prima ballerina before leaving Russia. She danced briefly with Diaghilev, but from 1911 until her death in 1931 she toured the world with her own company. The legendary Pavlova awakened an appreciation for dance in diverse audiences in countries near and far and can be credited with doing more than any other single individual to bring classical ballet to world attention. Pavlova's repertory (unlike that of the other great disseminator of ballet in the first quarter of the century, Diaghilev's Ballet Russes) tended to be conservative and noncontroversial, perhaps even a touch sentimental. She was nonetheless indefatigable in her devotion, and the poetry of her dancing left thousands of people who had never before seen ballet with an indelible and haunting memory.

Pavlova, in contrast with the more robust dancers of her day, was slender, long-limbed, and fragile. Her delicate physique and soulful quality evoked the ideal of the Romantic ballet with its evanescent visions and ethereal sylphs. *The Dying Swan*, a solo about a beautiful creature expiring and gasping for life, perfectly suited her talents, physical type, and personal style. *The Dying Swan* came to be synonymous with Pavlova, a vehicle that she performed throughout her career. Indeed, it is said that just before her death, the last words uttered by the great dancer were, ''Prepare my swan costume.''

No more than two minutes long, *The Dying Swan* was choreographed especially for Pavlova by her childhood friend,

Galina Ulanova in *The Dying Swan*, Bolshoi Ballet.

Michel Fokine. He was at that time playing Saint-Saëns's *The Swan* on the mandolin, and when Pavlova asked him to compose a solo for her, they both immediately agreed upon the suitability of the music and theme. The dance was composed in only a few minutes, with Fokine demonstrating and Pavlova following his improvisations. At the end, Fokine added such details as the fluttering arms and broken wrists. The dance begins with tremulous steps on pointe and a slow circling of the stage. Reaching with her long neck, her quivering arms stretched behind an arched torso, the exquisite swan creature strains toward life and flight, but her strength is ebbing away. She slowly sinks to the earth, her arms still fluttering behind her. Growing fainter, she glides forward and sinks down; bending helplessly over an outstretched leg, she succumbs and dies.

Fokine speaks of this dance as one that satisfies the eye but also penetrates the soul. He describes it as "creating a poetic image—a perpetual longing for life of all mortals." He pointed, too, to the historical importance of this short dance. It stood for him as a bridge between the old and the new dance. Like the "old" dance, it demands a high degree of technical mastery and uses toe shoes and a traditional costume (with tutu and down feathers reminiscent of *Swan Lake*). Like the "new" dance, the choreography demands that the dancer be expressive with her entire body, and it uses technique to appeal to the emotions of the spectator rather than for display.

Video: KUL, PI-A, VAI, VIEW.

LES SYLPHIDES

Choreography by Michel Fokine, 1909; music by Frédéric Chopin.

Michel Fokine was interested in accurate reconstruction of historic or "period" styles. He was drawn to the idea of choreographing a kind of nostalgia piece recreating the *ballets blancs* ("white ballets") of the early 19th-century Romantic era. Partly to repudiate criticism that he had rejected toe dancing in the interest of reform, Fokine decided to create his own version of the Taglioni-inspired Romantic ballet. He choreographed *Les*

Sylphides in pure Romantic style, infusing it with the pristine delicacy, softness and lightness, ethereality, and demure restraint of an earlier day. He was especially attracted to the period's expressive use of pointe work to suggest the skimming and hovering of bloodless creatures whose feet barely touch the ground. Inspired by lithographs of Romantic ballerinas, Fokine had his reconjured Taglionis (four soloists and twelve *corps* members) impeccably costumed in period style, from their long, white gauze shirts and fitted, décolleté bodices to their gossamer wings, parted hair, and little chaplets.

The ballet, first performed for a 1907 benefit at the Imperial Theater, was originally called *Chopiniana*, since it was danced to a suite of Chopin piano pieces. This early version vaguely evoked scenes of the composer's life, suggesting that the lone male dancing among the supernatural creatures was Chopin. When the ballet was premiered in Paris in 1909 as *Les Sylphides*, it was an entirely abstract essay of a dreamy youth yearning and soaring his way through a vision of ethereal Sylphides.

Fokine said that he had never read an adequate verbal description of *Les Sylphides*. Perhaps this is because the special mood of the ballet, with its synthesis of music, motion, and design, is untranslatable. *Les Sylphides* is an atmospheric ballet; it physically incarnates a poetic vision, inspiring a yearning for ideal beauty which seems momentarily attainable and then sadly lost. Without defined characters or specific *mise en scène, Les Sylphides* is a danced ode to beauty that is unique in effect.

The seemingly effortless flow of the dances accompanied by Chopin waltzes, nocturnes, and *mazurkas* belies a meticulous choreographic structure. A short prelude is heard before the curtain rises on a nocturnal woodland with a tableau of white, winged Sylphides, some reclining, others standing in clusters around a youthful Poet. There is a Sylphide on each side of him leaning her head on his shoulder. The symmetrical tableau becomes animated as, to the strains of the nocturne, the sylphs lightly skim the floor on toe, dissolving the opening scene and creating new groupings. Their rounded arms, when not fluttering, are curved softly toward their bodies, their shoulders held in a gentle *épaulement* angle. The Poet dances with one seemingly weightless Sylphide, lifting her and supporting her in *arabesque*. Another sylph enters and runs under the arch formed by the couple's arms. All the while, the *corps* of Sylphides dips

Karena Brock, John Prinz, and Marianna Tcherkassky in *Les Sylphides,* American Ballet Theatre.

and sways; scooping the air with rounded arms, they move from parallel lines into a semicircle and back to straight lines as if to receive the next soloist. To a gay waltz, another sylph dances alone, running with tripping steps, turning in *attitude*, lifting her hand to her mouth as if calling on some mischievous spirits before running off.

In silence, the *corps* next forms a three-sided square for the *mazurka*, in which a Sylphide leaps and hops through the poised white frame. She leaps across the stage in repeated wide *jetés* (leaps) while the *corps* echoes her movements with undulating arms waving first to the right, then to the left. Now to the melody of a slower *mazurka*, the Sylphides regroup, locking interlacing arms. The Poet enters, leaping and step-hopping in breathless exuberance. He kneels before the ecstatic vision and reaches one arm forward beseechingly before running off. As the *corps* regroups itself into three clusters of four Sylphides, a soloist dances to a slower waltz, dreamily sweeping the air with her arms, posing briefly in *arabesque*. She dances as if she is in a private reverie and pauses, hand to ear, to listen to distant voices.

To the next waltz, the Poet enters holding a Sylphide high in the air. She slowly floats down and they dance an *adagio* duet. As the music quickens, she runs away; he follows with one curved arm raised in longing. The *corps* has subtly shifted from a linear shape to a reclining pose, their fingers lightly touching their cheeks. The final Valse Brillante is exhilarating—the *corps* dances in unison as the Poet and soloists skip and soar through the scene. The group of Sylphides dips and bends with rounded arms. They turn toward the back of the stage and, fluidly regrouping, end the ballet with the opening tableau.

Les Sylphides is entirely self-contained, devoted to musicality and style rather than stage spectacle. While it uses the vocabulary of the *danse d'école* exclusively, there is not a moment of virtuosity displayed for its own sake. (The necessity to sustain the mood, balance, and musicality of the piece makes it, nonetheless, a great technical challenge.) Even the male dancer jumps and soars without obvious preparation or any of the mannerisms of the *danseur noble*. Fokine urged the interpreters of that role: "Do not dance for the audience, do not exhibit yourself, do not admire yourself. On the contrary, you have to see the ethereal Sylphides. Look at them while dancing. Admire them, reach for them. These moments of longing and reaching toward some fantastic world are the very basic movements and expressions of this ballet.''

In *Les Sylphides*, the *corps* merges, blends, and harmonizes with the soloists. Their regroupings, sometimes in silence between dances, add to the flow and continuity of the ballet and further distinguish it from the applause-seeking *divertissement*-type work. The result is a visualization of Chopin that Balanchine would later claim (along with Ivanov's *Swan Lake*) as inspiration for his own plotless ballets. To this day, *Les Sylphides* remains one of the most frequently performed works in the ballet repertory.

Video: HBO, HOME, KUL, PI-A, SPECT.

THE FIREBIRD

Choreography by Michel Fokine, 1910; music by Igor Stravinsky; scenery and costumes for first production by Alexander Golovine and Léon Bakst.

The group of Russian artists working with Diaghilev wanted to add a ballet with a national, folkloric theme to their repertory. Fokine was pleased to discover that the legend of the firebird, one particularly suited for dance interpretation, had never been used before in the theater. He composed the libretto, based on tales of a magical bird, by piecing together several Russian legends.

The next task facing Fokine and his collaborators was to find the right music. Diaghilev urged that they listen to the music of a little-known young composer, and they heard a piece called ''Fireworks'' played by an unenthusiastic orchestra to a cool audience reception. Nonetheless, both Diaghilev and Fokine were most excited by the music of Igor Stravinsky and commissioned him to write the music for their new ballet. *The Firebird* was, of course, the first of many ballet scores by this prolific composer, recognized by many as this century's greatest musical genius.

The theme of *The Firebird* is one typical of many Russian legends—a naive, good man is victorious over one who is evil and powerful. A handsome and guileless Ivan Tsarevich wanders into the kingdom of the evil Koschei. As Ivan roams about, recoiling from the sight of petrified monsters, the sinister forest is suddenly illuminated by the entrance of the Firebird. Ivan tries to capture the Firebird, but when he succumbs to her pleas to be set free, she rewards him with a magic feather and promises that if he is ever in trouble he need only wave the feather and she will come to his aid. After the Firebird disappears, the door to Koschei's castle opens and twelve Enchanted Princesses emerge to perform a dance with golden apples. Ivan dances with the prettiest of them all, Princess Unearthly Beauty, until the maidens suddenly withdraw in fear and run back to the castle, warning him not to follow. But the enamored Ivan ignores the warning and pounds the gates of the castle with his sword. An alarm awakens Koschei's entire monstrous kingdom followed by Koschei himself, who sets about to turn the young intruder into stone. In the midst of the confusion and danger, Ivan waves his magic feather and the Firebird arrives to rescue him by dancing the entire grotesque retinue into complete exhaustion. Koschei's evil soul is then symbolically destroyed by the dramatic smashing of a huge egg. The last scene takes us to Ivan's court where his marriage to Princess Unearthly Beauty will take place.

Fokine was very pleased to collaborate on *The Firebird* because of the opportunity it afforded him to use expressive movement, integrate the *corps'* dancing with that of the principals, and work in close association with other artists. We are immediately aware of Fokine's style as Ivan enters Koschei's castle, walking in a manner more natural than that of a typical *danseur noble*. The duet with the Firebird expresses the struggles of a captured bird to be free, her yearning and capacity to fly even while restrained. Fokine's intention was ''arms [that] would now open up like wings, now hug the torso and head, in complete contradiction of all ballet arm positions.'' The Firebird's dance, while technically demanding, was to be ''without *entrechats, battements, ronds de jambes,* and, of course, without a turnout and without any preparations''—in short, unencumbered by all the conventions of the *danse d'école*. (It is interesting that by our own standards the Firebird's movements look rather typically balletic and even static. This is a good example of the phenomenon that ideas that

Cynthia Gregory and John Meehan in *The Firebird* (Michel Fokine), American Ballet Theatre.

seem innovative in their day can easily look conventional a few years later.)

Fokine's approach to choreography is well illustrated by the Princesses playing with the golden apples. They dance barefoot with natural, fluid grace in a refreshingly informal and folksy style. Their dance blends smoothly with the duet of Ivan and his chosen Princess. At one point, two circles of maidens surround each of them separately as they reach out to one another, forming a tableau reminiscent of a Russian wedding dance. The monsters of Koschei's kingdom, who burst on the scene after the Princesses' departure, certainly bear little resemblance to a conventional *corps de ballet*. They squat, crawl on all fours, hug their knees, and roll malevolently from side to side, turning themselves into comical and grotesque shapes, all the while leaping and spinning with considerable, if subtle, virtuosity. The entire *corps* effects the "dance to exhaustion" climax, kicking and stamping their feet, slapping their thighs, jumping and turning in the vigorous manner of a Russian folk dance. Fokine said of *The Firebird*, "For this ballet, I completely excluded the stereotyped hand pantomime and ballet gesticulations for the development of the plot on the stage and expressed the story with action and dance."

The Firebird provided an opportunity to unify "creative music and creative choreography." Fokine and Stravinsky worked together in close cooperation. During long afternoons, Fokine improvised the roles while Stravinsky interpreted Russian melodies for him on the piano. Later, they refined and selected the dance and musical sequences. (This, for many, is an ideal, if difficult to realize, method of working and avoids the problems involved in choreographing to precomposed music.) The scenery and costumes were designed by Golovine and Bakst who provided a most sinister-looking castle, a dense forest, and a handsome tree of golden apples as well as vibrantly colored costumes.

The Firebird remained in the Ballets Russes repertory for the rest of the company's life—almost 20 years. In 1954, with the help of the first Firebird, Tamara Karsavina, the ballet was reconstructed for the Royal Ballet in London. It is now in the repertory of American Ballet Theatre as well. George Balanchine composed his own *Firebird* in 1949, also to Stravinsky.

A major difference between the Fokine and Balanchine versions is that Fokine's Firebird moves slowly, sedately, deliberately, without virtuosity; Balanchine's creature of fire darts like a flame—mercurial, athletic, dazzling. (Some years later, however, when he did another production of *Firebird,* he gave his ballerina almost no dancing at all.) Balanchine also omitted the golden apples and the egg, although his basic story is the same.

LE SPECTRE DE LA ROSE

Choreography by Michel Fokine, 1911; music by Carl Maria von Weber; scenery and costumes for first production by Léon Bakst.

Late at night, a young girl returns home dreamily from a ball. It was perhaps her very first ball and she is lost in romantic reverie. The rose she presses to her chest embodies the spirit of the man who gave it to her as they whirled to the rhythm of a waltz. She sinks into an armchair; as she falls asleep, her fresh memories conjure up the rose-cavalier, who soars into the room to dance with her. The ballet *Le Spectre de la Rose* ("The Spirit of the Rose") is quite literally a danced poem. It is a ballet version of Théophile Gautier's poem about a rose who tells a young girl, on whose breast he has been worn all night, that his rose spirit will continue to dance with her until dawn.

The ballet is actually a romantic *pas de deux,* creating, in the seamless flow of the dance, the impression of a dream come to life. The curtain rises on the young girl's boudoir, empty, expectant. The high ceiling, white walls paneled in pink, tall French windows, and careful positioning of a curtained bed, armchair, draped table, sofa, and a bird cage give the room a cozy, formal look. The young girl strolls into the bedroom and as she unties her evening cape, we see that she is clutching a rose. She turns with an invisible partner, reliving the tender feelings of the ball. Exhausted, she sinks into her armchair, allowing the precious rose to slip to the floor as she falls asleep. With a surge of waltz music, the spirit of the rose leaps in through the window. He dances a continuous legato waltz, whirling and leaping around the room. When the music grows a bit softer, he gently lifts the

Mikhail Baryshnikov in *Le Spectre de la Rose,* American Ballet Theatre.

sleeping girl from her chair and continues to waltz with her effortlessly. She dances with little tripping steps, her eyes closed as
if awake in a dream. The "imaginary" cavalier leads the girl back
to her chair and, as if ecstatic to simply be in her presence, proceeds to dance alone—rushing to and fro, waltzing, leaping, and
turning. Pausing momentarily to bid farewell to the sleeping girl,
he runs across the stage and disappears with a soaring leap out
the window. The young girl awakens slowly. The pleasant memories of the ball and the dream mingle as she picks up the fallen
rose and presses it to her breast.

Short, simple, and tender, *Le Spectre de la Rose* was one of
the most popular ballets of the Diaghilev repertory. Tamara Kar-
savina, who danced the role of the young girl, brought to it all
the requisite sweet yearning and shy emotion. Vaslav Nijinsky's
role as the Spectre was created as much by, as for, him. Left
to a lesser artist, the idea of a man dressed as a rose, dancing
around first by himself and then with a somnambulent girl, could
easily look ridiculous. In this role, as in many others, it was not
enough to dance the steps. Nijinsky transformed himself into
a rose essence, not a dancing flower but a human embodying
and exuding the lush aura of a rose. He changed the use of the
arms so they were curved like Art Nouveau flower stems, his
head curled to the side as if he were inhaling his own perfume.

The actual steps of the ballet are those of the classical ballet—
waltzes, *tours jetés* (leaps with a turn in the air), *arabesques*, and
turns. But, as we have learned, in Fokine's hands, steps are never
displayed for their own sake. The familiar combinations are transformed into the elements of a poetic idea. The ballet is a *pas de
deux*, with a duet for the couple and a long solo for the male,
but there is no element of competition. Fokine described the male
role: "He is in no circumstance a ballerina's partner. The arm
positions in this ballet are the opposite of the correct arm positions of the old ballet. The arms live, speak, sing, and do not
execute positions."

Nijinsky's final leap through the window caused quite a sensation and gave rise to fantastic claims about its height. Fokine,
with his usual deprecation of virtuosity, downplayed the leap,
insisting it was not higher than slightly over a foot.

A role in a ballet can never be performed the same way by
different dancers. When a role is closely associated with a certain dancer, especially the one for whom it was created, it is often

difficult to accept another dancer's interpretation. Nijinsky dancing in *Spectre* is an example of the identification of a particular dancer with a role, and that association, along with the nature of the role, has made it difficult for others attempting the part. Nonetheless, *Le Spectre de la Rose* has been revived for the Joffrey Ballet, American Ballet Theatre, the Festival Ballet of London, and a number of other companies.

PETROUCHKA

Choreography by Michel Fokine, 1911; music by Igor Stravinsky; scenery and costumes by Alexandre Benois.

Petrouchka was the first thoroughly awkward and lonely character to "star" in a ballet. The evanescent creatures of the Romantic ballet and the somewhat sturdier, if still fanciful, heroines of Petipa's dramas are familiar ballet personas. In the Ballets Russes, the preeminence of performers such as Nijinsky, Bolm, and Fokine refocused attention on male dancing. The vigorous strength of the men dancing in *Prince Igor* (1909), the demonic sensuality of Nijinsky's Favorite Slave in *Schéhérazade* (1910), and the androgynous lyricism in his portrayal of the Rose, had already done much to revolutionize the conception of the male in ballet. Withal, ballet had never featured a leading man who was simply a vulnerable, pathetic, misunderstood soul. Petrouchka, the Russian equivalent of a Punch or Guignol, is a puppet with a human heart, described by Benois, who was coauthor (with Stravinsky) of the scenario, as "the personification of the spiritual and suffering side of humanity." We meet Petrouchka at a Russian street fair along with two other puppets, a mechanical Ballerina doll and a brutish Moor. Petrouchka, who longs to escape his puppet body and yearns for the love of the Ballerina, is abused and rejected. Nevertheless, at the ballet's end, his spirit lives on in defiant and perpetual hope.

Petrouchka's movements are expressive of the character's particular, introverted state. Petrouchka's hallmark is his "turned-in" stance—his arms, legs, and shoulders fold in toward a limp torso. This was conceived by Fokine in explicit contrast to the proudly exhibited turned-out posture nearly synonymous with the image of a ballet dancer. Petrouchka is shy and tortured—his head drops, his shoulders sag, his arms dangle. He is frustrated and desperate—when he dances, his movements are angular, convulsive, and jerky. Petrouchka (first danced by Vaslav Nijinsky) was not given a single step from the *danse d'école* to help him appear more attractive. Nijinsky's success in *Petrouchka* was due to his ability to portray dignity in despair and his credible transformation into an endearing puppet spirit.

The first scene of the ballet is a Russian street fair; the public square in wintertime teems with an assorted colorful crowd. There are people of good manners walking arm in arm, soldiers and officers looking for fun, street vendors hawking their goods, children riding a carousel in one corner, grooms, coachmen, peasant men and women keeping in constant motion to stay warm. Toward the back of the stage, we see a large fair booth with a blue curtain drawn across the front and a sign on the top of its frame announcing (in Russian) ''Living Theater.'' The multicolored crowd bustles about the fairgrounds with realistic movements, creating an impression of lively spontaneity. A dancer holding a triangle in one hand begins to show off her ability to turn repeatedly on one foot. Across the way, another dancer begins to compete with her, and the groups amuse themselves by watching and applauding the contest.

Suddenly, two drummers step out from the vicinity of the blue-curtained booth and the swelling orchestral music is cut off. The crowd looks on with curiosity as drum rolls announce Charlatan, a man with a tall, pointed hat who pokes his head out of the blue curtain. Charlatan steps out and charms the crowd with a magic flute; the people sway as one to the music. When the blue curtain snaps back, we see three motionless puppets, each one suspended on a high armrest. The Moor puppet is huge and boldly dressed, his giant white mouth and white eyes set in a coal-black face. The Ballerina, with her china-doll face and bright red cheeks, looks equally empty-headed and, like the Moor, ready to be wound up. They provide a sharp contrast to the limp and lifeless Petrouchka, his body crumpled like a forlorn rag doll. At the Charlatan's command, the three puppets snap to life. They step down from their perch to join in a hectic dance, tapping out a lively rhythm with their feet. Strangely, despite Charlatan, the puppets seem to have a little drama of their own going on. The Moor flirts with the coy Ballerina and

Petrouchka flies into a feet-stamping rage. Charlatan puts a stop to the scene and, as the puppets return to their dance, the curtain falls.

The second scene shifts indoors to poor Petrouchka's barren cell, where a portrait of Charlatan hangs menacingly on the wall. Petrouchka lies on the floor and shakes as if his whole body were convulsed with sobs. He rises and stabs his stiff arms spasmodically into space, gesturing toward the outside world as the woodwinds play his theme. When he stands still, his knees buckle and turn in, his arms crisscross his awkward body in shame. Suddenly, the Ballerina bursts on the scene, prancing about on pointe, stiffly but with spirit, while she plays a cornet. When Petrouchka flops up and down with jumps of joy, she feigns horror and leaves. Finally, in desperation, Petrouchka flings himself against the black walls and searches for an opening. As his musical theme is heard again, Petrouchka finally succeeds in punching a hole in the wall.

Next we move on to the sumptuous and colorful quarters of the vain Moor. Self-satisfied and thoroughly absorbed, the Moor plays with a coconut. When he discovers that he cannot break it with his scimitar, the dimwitted giant begins to worship it. Now the Ballerina pays the Moor a flirtatious visit and waltzes gaily around the room. The clumsy Moor tries to imitate her movements. Just as the Moor plops the Ballerina down on his lap, a distraught Petrouchka bursts in waving his arms frantically. The Moor chases the intruder around the room, kicks him out, and pulls the Ballerina back onto his lap.

The final scene takes us outside again to the bustling fairgrounds. Evening is approaching, and the crowd seems to have swelled. A group of nursemaids dance until they are interrupted by a plodding dancing bear. Some coachmen then provide a rousing Russian peasant dance. They are joined by swaggering drunks, lively gypsy girls, and the entire high-spirited crowd, which dances in unison as the snow begins to fall, creating a most festive scene. The merrymaking is suddenly interrupted by the appearance of Petrouchka running in terror through the crowd, the Moor in hot pursuit. He strikes Petrouchka down with a single blow as the heartless Ballerina covers her ears in mock horror. Petrouchka, lying on the floor, gestures a few last times to the concerned crowd that has gathered to watch him die. Charlatan pushes his way toward Petrouchka and lifts up

Denise Jackson and Rudolf Nureyev in *Petrouchka,*
The Joffrey Ballet.

the inert body, showing the assembled crowd that Petrouchka is really only so much sawdust. (Hidden by the crowd, the dancer has indeed been replaced by a puppet.) The people shrug and disperse, leaving Charlatan alone on stage. As if out of nowhere, Petrouchka's woodwind fanfare is heard—could it be that he is not dead? Charlatan looks up at the top of the booth and sees Petrouchka (or is it only his aspiring, rag-tag spirit?) once again stabbing his arms into space in a gesture of defiance and hope. Charlatan is horrified at the sight and slinks out of view as the curtain falls.

The ballet *Petrouchka* originated with Stravinsky's idea of writing a piece for piano and orchestra in which the solo instrument would be attacked by the others, fight back, rally, and end defeated. This grew into the idea of telling the story of a puppet struggling against fate. This time, Fokine was called in to compose the dances after the music, scenario, and stage design were completed. While he confessed the difficulty of working with Stravinsky's complex and often-changing rhythms, Fokine still considered *Petrouchka* ''one of the most complete demonstrations of [my] application of ballet reforms.'' The crowd gives the impression of an improvised mass, but on closer inspection, one notices the careful design—everyone is occupied with an activity appropriate to his character and station. The manipulated movements of the puppets were designed to contrast sharply with the freewheeling meandering of the human fairgoers. The slow-witted, extroverted Moor moves heavily, displaying his self-satisfaction with his turned-out posture. The mindless Ballerina dances stiffly, every movement empty, mechanical, and precise.

Petrouchka was revived for the Royal Danish Ballet in 1925 and for Ballet Theatre in 1942. It is currently in the repertory of the Royal Ballet, the Joffrey Ballet, and American Ballet Theatre, among others. The role of Petrouchka provides a rich dramatic challenge for a male dancer.

VASLAV NIJINSKY

When Fokine abruptly left the Ballets Russes in 1912, the source of the tension seemed to be Diaghilev's interest in furthering the choreographic career of Vaslav Nijinsky, his favorite both on and off the stage. Nijinsky was the amazing prodigy of the Imperial Ballet School, only a few years younger than Fokine. A dancer of both legendary physical prowess and extraordinary dramatic gifts, he enchanted audiences with his ability to transform himself into the roles he danced.

While Nijinsky's merits as a choreographer have been widely debated, his originality and iconoclasm are beyond dispute. Going much further than Fokine in discarding ballet tradition, Nijinsky began anew to analyze the possibilities of human movement. In his three major ballets, he hardly used a single step from the *danse d'école*. His first choreographic essay was *L'Après-midi d'un Faune* (1912), an eight-minute living frieze recalling archaic Greece, in which the basic step was a kind of dissected walk. Subjecting the dance to a strict adherence to period style (as he saw it), he had his dancers move with their torsos facing front and their heads and feet in strict profile. The ballet was angular, stark, abrupt, and minimal. It was thoroughly intense but never pretty. *Jeux* (1913), Nijinsky's second ballet, was just as forthright in its rejection of attractive, palatable dancing. Again, there is not a single recognizable ballet step; a young man and two women curl themselves into a variety of odd, unflattering poses. The contents of both ballets were as unprecedented as their form. The first ballet, which was about a narcissistic faun— Nijinsky—awakening to sexual consciousness, ended with an abrupt jerk of the faun's pelvis as he stretched out on a nymph's discarded veil. *Jeux*, a tale of three-way flirtation at a tennis game, began and ended in an odd manner—with a ball bouncing across the stage. Furthermore, with its overtones of decadence and cynicism, it is considered the first ballet to comment on the psyche of modern man.

Nijinsky's next project was *The Rite of Spring,* an archaic ritual of ancient Russia awaiting spring, danced to Igor Stravinsky's specially commissioned score. What he had begun to do in his previous works, Nijinsky now launched into full-scale. Academic ballet abandoned, his dancers were turned in, awkward, and deliberately weighted down in their heavy costumes. They shivered spasmodically, and, huddled in slow-moving, concentric circles, they shook convulsively and stamped the ground. In its extreme rejection of ballet aesthetics, *The Rite of Spring* triggered a riot at its Paris premiere.

The extent of Nijinsky's influence on the development of ballet is somewhat debatable. (Nijinsky tragically declined into insanity and none of his works has fully survived. Both *Faune* and *Sacre* have been reconstructed and performed by the Joffrey Ballet.) While others may not have been directly inspired by Nijinsky's work, his ballets undoubtedly broke the ground for new ideas. His radicalism, even if consciously rejected, planted fertile seeds of experimentation.

LE SACRE DU PRINTEMPS
(The Rite of Spring)

Choreography by Vaslav Nijinsky, 1913; music by Igor Stravinsky; scenery and costumes for first production by Nicholas Roerich. (Many subsequent versions.)

In Russia, after the long frozen winter, spring erupts in a sudden, rushing torrent that seems to cause the whole earth to crack. The idea for *The Rite of Spring* came partly from the composer Stravinsky's childhood memories of this, "the most wonderful event of every year." With the help of Nicholas Roerich, an artist and anthropologist who designed the ballet's costumes and sets, a scenario evolved. The composer, writing in his autobiography of its inception, recalled that he "saw in imagination a solemn pagan rite: sage elders seated in a circle watched a young girl dance herself to death. They were sacrificing her to propitiate the god of spring.'' In the ballet, young boys and girls celebrate the renewal of the earth with vigorous, pounding tribal dances, competitive ritual games, and pairing off. An elder consecrates the ground, signaling an even more intoxicated celebration of the earth. A sacrificial virgin is chosen from among a group of maidens. She dances herself to death as a human offering to the god of spring. Stravinsky, in later years, would claim that although his music could support a choreographic story line, the ideas came from the music and not the music from the ideas.

To the dismay of the composer, the May 1913 premiere of the score, accompanied by Vaslav Nijinsky's choreography, was one of the stormiest nights in modern theater history. The audience erupted in such an avalanche of protests, whistling, stamping, and shouting that, loud as the music was, the dancers could not hear it. The reasons for the riot were probably complex, but the awkward, sometimes grotesque and frantic look of Nijinsky's dancers and the unfamiliar sounds of Stravinsky's score provided a perfect catalyst for the tumultuous demonstration.

In the opening scene, seizures of movement break out among the isolated groups crouching about the stage. The Elder, led in by a group of sages, consecrates the ground with his taut and distended body. Recharged, the tribespeople dance in adoration of the earth with increased passion, shrinking with awe, exploding in ecstasy. In the second scene, a line of maidens files in, their drooping heads resting on their hands, their elbows tight against their waists, their toes turned in as if in self-protection. The Chosen Virgin, emerging from their group, assists and leads the ensemble in celebrating her own sacrifice. Men and women, divided into five groups, leap and stamp savagely, jump high with extended arms and legs, and run sideways with bent knees, their heads lying on one shoulder. One hand raised stiffly, twisting around grotesquely, and trembling uncontrollably, the Chosen Virgin leaps with ever-increasing, asymmetric frenzy, flinging herself into a lifeless collapse.

Nijinsky's *The Rite of Spring* was performed only seven times in all and was long considered lost to posterity. But the idea of dancing to this music, despite the considerable problems it poses, has continued to fascinate choreographers.

Although the score, considered by many to have inaugurated a new musical era, no longer shocks audiences the way it once did, devising dances to it remains a formidable challenge. Stravinsky's rhythmic system—bar after bar is in a different time signature—demands intricate, precision dancing. Although choreographers have felt free to accept, modify, or reject the original scenario, the raw, pounding power and primeval feeling of Stravinsky's score virtually directs the choreographer to compose something atavistic and vigorous for a large ensemble. The music seems to dictate a kind of "primitive" dance, with bouncing crouches, ground stamping, trembling limbs, and preying jumps. This type of dancing can easily look monotonous, or even artificial, especially on the lightweight bodies of ballet dancers. Stravinsky, who was most unhappy about Nijinsky's version and, at best, lukewarm about subsequent efforts, came to believe his score was best left to the concert hall.

Léonide Massine composed a second, less controversial version for the Ballets Russes in 1920 (Martha Graham [b. 1894] would later dance the virgin in his ballet). The next relatively widely seen production was that of Maurice Béjart (b. 1927), which premiered in January 1959, and was brought to the United States in 1971. Béjart, at that time the director of the Belgian company Ballet of the Twentieth Century, attempted to breathe some fresh air into the European ballet scene. Innovative, ambitious, sexual, and showy, Béjart combines a classical base with excursions into modernism. Béjart explained that for him the surge of spring is "an immense primordial force . . . which suddenly bursts forth, kindling new life in all things." He equated the rebirth and fertility of spring with the union of man and woman. Béjart discarded the idea of a prehistoric people actually awaiting spring and the sacrifice of a chosen virgin. Instead, the ballet is a kind of massive fertility ritual, culminating in a celebratory orgy led by a chosen boy and girl. The first part is a group dance for the men, strong, vital, full of crouches, jumps, bounding leaps, and bent knees, pumping to the fierce pulse of the score. Next is a languorous, sensual dance for the girls. The ballet culminates in the mating scene, where erotic gestures alternate with classical steps. At the end of the riotous spectaculars, the men bound off the stage through an enormous arch.

Kenneth MacMillan's *The Rite of Spring* premiered at Covent Garden, London, on May 3, 1962. Although MacMillan retained the scenario of a sacrificial virgin, his setting was not prehistoric Russia. Instead, his ballet is set in an abstract, primeval time and space, possibly as allusive to the future as to the past. The curtain rises on an immense slab of rock, which looks like a survivor of some eerie apocalypse. The dancers, depersonalized in red, brown, and yellow leotards and identical wigs, are set against the brown, desolate backdrop. MacMillan shows the grim impersonality of the mass caught up in a driving ritual. He uses a mixture of styles—his own brand of the frenzied, stamping, primitive movement suggested by the music, as well as some classical steps and allusions to jazz. When the virgin is chosen, she collapses into a tangle of arms and legs. She begins her dance by stepping through the bodies of other dancers lying and undulating on the floor. During the sacrificial scene, a round gold ball begins to glow and grow larger and larger until it fills most of the backcloth. At the ballet's end, the body of the virgin is tossed high into the air.

Glen Tetley (b. 1926) premiered his version in 1974, and it was later performed by American Ballet Theatre. His ballet is massive, full of rushing groups of dancers, repetitive pounding, and strained, twisted shapes. The mood is that of an agonizing, impersonal, athletic ritual, the significance of which is not specified. The work begins with a single male figure performing a long solo full of yearning, growing, falling, and recovering movements. Twelve couples dressed in unitards execute a heated mating dance during which the single male spots a female dancer who rivets his attention. As he starts to approach her, a group of men pick him up lengthwise and toss him about. Mysteriously inert, possibly expired, he is carried off stage. The woman and another man dance a duet which is solemn and contorted. The first male soloist returns and is manipulated by the men into various vertical and diagonal, presumably phallic, positions. After the ensemble forms another mass, he is freed to make his way through the crowd and emerges from between the legs of the couple who danced before. He is then left alone to dance with desperate, breathless, punishing movements. The ensemble comes back to perform an orgiastic, ever-accelerating circle dance. Meanwhile, the solo male fastens himself into a harness that is actually a trapeze, and, astonishingly, this takes him flying up and out straight toward the audience as the curtain falls. In Tetley's ballet, we have all the sound and fury of archaic ritual, and

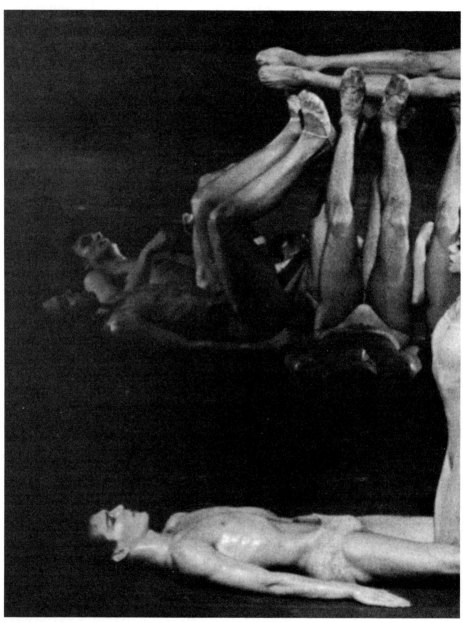

Clark Tippet, Martine van Hamel, and Charles Ward in *Le Sacre du Printemps* (Glen Tetley), American Ballet Theatre.

allusions in the male soloist's role to ideas of death and rebirth or even to a Christ-like, sacrificial figure.

John Neumeier's (b. 1942) *The Rite of Spring*, created in 1972, also opens with a single male, but from the beginning he lies inert on the floor as both men and women file by in silence. They dance around him with the look of alert, cautious young animals, seeming to hear some strange sounds in the distance and focusing toward some faraway presence. Building up stamps and lunges, they periodically reach out abruptly toward the prostrate figure. As the dance increases in tempo and passion, the girls are carried off by the men. The group then rushes back onstage in an agitated cluster. They hold a struggling young woman high over their heads, presumably the abducted Chosen Virgin. She disappears (as has the man who was lying on the floor), as some of the dancers begin a coupling dance and others crawl on the floor, continuously rolling their heads. With a sharp crescendo, the group trembles violently in unison. A light flashes blindingly; the music, light, and vibrating dancers work up to a screeching climax and a sudden blackout. Now in the dimly lit (post-holocaustal?) stage we see only the outlines of bodies crawling over one another in an undulating sea. The Chosen Virgin returns to end the ballet with a long solo, perhaps most remarked on for her total nudity, kept within the bounds of good taste by the semidark stage.

These treatments of *The Rite of Spring* will doubtless be followed by others, as choreographers continue to find Stravinsky's powerful score intriguing.

One of the most ambitious undertakings of recent years was the reconstruction of Nijinsky's *Sacre* for the Joffrey Ballet in 1987. Over a 15-year period, the husband and wife team of Kenneth Archer and Millicent Hodson exhaustively researched not only the original choreography but the brilliantly colored original designs and drops (extant photos of the Nijinsky production are all in black-and-white). Hodson was greatly aided in reconstructing the dances by a notated score kept by Marie Rambert (1888–1982), later a ''founding mother'' of British ballet, who was Nijinsky's assistant in 1913. In its present incarnation, with its tribal Elders trembling and shaking, the harrowing *Sacre* has been a gripping theatrical success. Although much about the production is based on informed speculation (Rambert's score was not complete), from the evidence before us it is unarguable that Nijinsky's was one of the most uncompromisingly modernist visions of the early 20th century.

MODERN BALLETS

BALLET SINCE DIAGHILEV

With the sudden death of Diaghilev in 1929, an era came to an end. Without his strong guiding hand and accomplished showmanship, his brilliant company collapsed immediately. There was nothing to take its place, although a number of troupes were formed, some lasting only a season or two, others proving more durable. But none had the artistic impact of Diaghilev's own group. Over the years, his dancers and their heirs have scattered far and wide. They are now to be found throughout the world (from South America to Australia), and, through them, the Diaghilev heritage lives on, although there are just a few Diaghilev ballets that are still actually performed.

The Ballets Russes, although it had Russian roots, developed into an international, more or less transient, European company once Russia became inaccessible because of political events. Starting in the 1930s, a different view of dance began to develop in conjunction with a marked strain of nationalism: "Real life" events and people from specific places began to be considered appropriate for treatment in dance, either in a literal or a symbolic manner. (This contrasted with the fairy-tale or exotic world of many Diaghilev and 19th-century ballets.) Also, the plotless or pure-dance ballet (sometimes called "abstract"), which was not dependent on a story or even an idea but was an exploration of movement in relation to the music that accompanied it, gained greater and greater favor with both choreographers and audiences. This concept of movement itself as the subject of a dance was virtually new. At the same time, partly for financial reasons, although also for aesthetic ones, small chamber dance groups came into existence. It became equally acceptable for ballet to be small-scale and intimate, or as grand as the opera house.

At first America and England, which had perhaps the least firm tradition of classical ballet (in America there was almost nothing), were the chief beneficiaries of these new perceptions. Large traveling repertory troupes continued to appear in both countries, but native groups were also formed, most notably the Royal Ballet (formerly Sadler's Wells) and Ballet Rambert in England, and American Ballet Theatre and the New York City Ballet in America. Although these troupes now seem "establishment" (with the exception of Rambert), all but ABT started very modestly, and all have encouraged experimentation and the development of "home-grown" choreographers. France and Germany have also had a share of experimental groups. Particularly in the United States, starting in the 1960s with the dance boom, the number of native companies has mushroomed. Foremost among these has been the Joffrey Ballet.

Moreover, since the 1930s, as traditional ideas about ballet were changing, new generations of choreographers began to work, many of whom had been schooled in, or had an affinity for, vocabularies other than that of the strictly classical dance. It was just about this time, also, that the first modern dancers, with their radically different feelings about the meaning and execution of dance, were beginning to appear. Who influenced whom will probably always be a matter for lively—often heated—debate, but the fact remains that the notion of what dance "is"—be it ballet or modern or some other form that perhaps has not yet even been named—has been drastically altered in the past 60 years. Without question, it has been enlarged and enriched immeasurably.

GERALD ARPINO

As a choreographer, Gerald Arpino (b. 1928) is a true eclectic. One of the six original dancers of the Joffrey Ballet, which he cofounded in 1956 with Robert Joffrey (1930–1988), Arpino has choreographed a steady stream of new works since the early '60s—usually at the rate of two, three, or more per year—in just about every conceivable style. He is extremely fluent—although not always deeply penetrating—in the classical idiom, but his true interest seems to lie in capturing the spirit of the times: "I tune in to what's happening; I am a topical choreographer," he has said. One is tempted to think of him as a dancemaker-journalist, picking up current issues, examining them, and then discarding them when they are no longer "newsworthy." One of his most successful such commentaries, the black *Clowns* (1968), was created at the time of the Vietnam War. Still valid on stage, it deals strikingly with nuclear annihilation in a "theater piece" that uses mixed-media, pop visual symbols, and almost no dance at all.

Many of Arpino's ballets are also in one way or another a celebration of youth, expressing the anxieties, hopes, companionship, energy, and physical sleekness of the young. Certainly this is the case with *Trinity*, choreographed in 1970, which evokes unmistakable images of the hippie generation. *Sea Shadow, Secret Places,* and *Light Rain* also come to mind as some of his most appealing "young" ballets.

With Joffrey's untimely death, Arpino, his longtime associate, became Artistic Director of the company. Thus far, he has continued Joffrey's philosophy of repertory: to present revivals of historical ballets, such as *Parade* and *Le Sacre du Printemps;* restagings of works by acknowledged masters (Tudor, Balanchine, Ashton); new ballets by contemporary choreographers, who often come from fields outside the ballet; and a continuing supply of his own, generally more transient, creations.

TRINITY

Choreography by Gerald Arpino, 1970; music by Alan Raph ("Sunday" and "Saturday") and Lee Holdridge ("Summerland")

Trinity, the ultimate "flower-power/rock" ballet, is Arpino's most effective hymn to the youth of the 1960s. His self-styled "Aquarius ballet," with its pulsating score and nonstop energy expenditure, is completely in tune with the era of flower children, beatniks, love-ins, peace marches, communal living, and the fashion for Eastern mysticism that once swept America, as young adults demonstratively rebelled against the value systems of their elders during the Kennedy years and after. The music, at times exultant, at times plaintive, is based on motifs from Gregorian chant and Renaissance church melodies. As delivered by an orchestra, an electric organ, a boy's choir, and a rock group called the Virgin Wool, it seems to recall an age of primal simplicity, acting as a potent metaphor for the attempt to get in touch with the basics of human nature embraced by many segments of the rock generation.

Arpino gives his 15 dancers movements from the virtuoso classical vocabulary—many leaps, turns, and runs across the stage—performed with an intensity that echoes the pounding of the music. He flavors these movements with gyrations inspired by disco and rock: rippling torsos, pelvic thrusts, and high kicks with heads thrown backward. The critic Deborah Jowitt has written that "the whole dance seems a taut by-play between the freedom inherent in rock and the control necessary for ballet."

The title, in addition to a possible religious association, refers to the ballet's three parts. Part I ("Sunday"), which opens with twisting leaps, is all exuberance. The blare of brass inspires ear-high kicks; an organ fanfare ushers in a more thoughtful moment in which the dancers take each other's hands. To exultant music, the dancers begin to sense the jazz rhythms coursing through their bodies. They lunge and slink, then explode into pirouettes.

In split leaps, the stage space is filled with flying bodies. Suddenly, all are lying on the floor in a circle, like the spokes of a wheel.

Part II (''Summerland'') is somewhat softer, more evocative of young love. Couples pair off. In meditative duets, the girls lean on the boys and rock against their bodies or are cradled in their arms, as their legs unfold. There are dreamy pirouettes and many slow, supported leaps. A line of boys runs across the stage, carrying girls in smooth but spectacular overhead one-arm lifts, ''as if the girls' bodies were garlands hanging from an upraised palm'' (Walter Terry). The music slows; couples embrace; they sway against one another on the floor. Their bodies make ''flying angel'' designs, then swiveling in liquid-like slow motion, the dancers disappear.

''Saturday,'' the final section, perhaps refers to the Jewish Sabbath. On a darkened stage, a single male walks forward with a flickering candle, soon joined by others who carry votive lights. Soft drumming accompanies an organ melody. The men put the candles down—then the rock beat takes over. This time, it is, if anything, more insistent than in the first movement. Legs, arms, and hands with splayed fingers dart everywhere, and soon bodies are hurtling into space. Dancing mostly solo, all engage in flashy leaps, twirls, kicks, and dashes in a near-frenetic display of rock-driven energy. After a sonic crescendo, the music becomes quiet. The dancers again lay candles on the stage and file off in diagonals; the beat, softly now, outlasts them. In the final moments, the lone man seen at the beginning returns with two candles and sets them on the floor, then recedes into the distance. Only the glowing lights remain.

The ballet was originally rehearsed to the burning of incense. In 1974, it caused a sensation in the Soviet Union, accompanied by the first American rock band ever to perform in Russia. It continues to be enthusiastically received by youthful audiences everywhere. *Trinity* was presented on the first program in the ''Dance in America'' television series in 1976. It remains a Joffrey ''signature'' piece.

Edward Morgan in *Trinity,* The Joffrey Ballet.

FREDERICK ASHTON

*F*rederick Ashton is the most important influence in the development of English ballet in our country. An exact contemporary of George Balanchine (both were born in 1904), Ashton accomplished in England what Balanchine did in America—that is, he developed a native tradition of serious dance where none had existed. Both men started their work around 1930; by the 1960s, the battle had been won. (Ashton may perhaps have been even more influential in England than Balanchine has been here—although his technical innovations are not nearly so radical—because there have been fewer choreographers and fewer accepted channels for expression in England than in America.)

In both countries in the 1930s, what serious dance there was derived from Russian sources. "Native" dance, if any could be so called, was performed in vaudeville and music hall. There weren't even any proper dance theaters. (Pavlova, Fokine, and other classical artists performed in New York's Hippodrome, between animal acts and jugglers, when they appeared here; there were simply no other facilities.) Dancing in opera houses—the traditional home of the art—was in a dismal state.

Over a period of 30 years, Ashton forged what has come to be known as the British style of classical dance, assisted initially by Marie Rambert and then, for more than 25 years, by Ninette de Valois [b. 1898] administrative director of the Royal Ballet and its predecessor companies).

Unlike Balanchine, de Valois believed—along with Ashton, whom she engaged as her principal choreographer in 1935—that the 19th-century classics, supplemented by original British ballets, should be the cornerstone of a national ballet company. Although the full-length classics—*Swan Lake*, *The Sleeping Beauty*, and others—are now regularly performed in America, they were unknown here when the British first presented them in 1949 and 1950. Ashton staged and augmented the Russian classics (which had been brought to England by a refugee of the Revolution, Nicholas Sergeyev) and created numerous works of his own. His style is characterized by a complete command of the classical vocabulary, by grace, by felicity of invention, by good breeding, reticence, and refinement. His ballets can be dramatic, passionate, sunny, or humorous but are never histrionic or in any other way extreme, either emotionally or technically. A decorous delicacy informs all his work.

Ashton's output and range are enormous, but if his most memorable contributions were to be singled out, they would be his story ballets, both short and full-length. His special gift here, in addition to choreography that is never less than eminently danceable, is his ability to recreate the atmosphere of other times and places, to evoke the social order of another day, creating individual worlds as settings for his works. His outstanding works in this vein include *La Fille Mal Gardée, The Two Pigeons, Romeo and Juliet, Ondine, Daphnis and Chloë, The Dream, Enigma Variations*, and *A Month in the Country*. In all of these, Ashton also demonstrates his essential sympathy for human nature. He seems to have great affection for all his characters, whatever their stations in life, although he has reserved his most inspired choreography for lovers. He has also done a number of plotless ballets, of which the most famous is the serene and lyrical *Symphonic Variations* (1946), perhaps the first fully realized statement of the English classical style in its purest form.

Ashton's works are performed by few American companies. The ballets described here—those most frequently seen by American audiences—do not begin to represent the range of his talents or his artistry.

Video: HOME.

FAÇADE

Choreography by Frederick Ashton, 1931; music by William Walton; scenery and costumes for first production by John Armstrong.

Façade has been called "a trifle, but a trifle of genius." Witty and satirical, without being bitter, it is a set of tongue-in-cheek *divertissements* parodying popular dance forms—folk, social, and theatrical. Music hall, vaudeville, and the revue influenced its creation. Some of the humor is out-and-out burlesque, some of it is subtle and kinetically sophisticated. The sparkling music is a perfect match.

The curtain rises to reveal a backdrop painted as the front of a house. Above the Dutch door (one with top and bottom sections that open separately) are two painted ladies, nude. In one production, there is also a clothesline with wash hanging on it. In the opening number, Scotch Rhapsody, two lassies and a lad, kilt-clad, parody Highland dancing. The male takes great delight in bumping his two female partners together. The Yodelling Song concerns a Milkmaid, three Mountaineers, a three-legged stool, and a make-believe cow. The top of the Dutch door opens, and we see the Milkmaid's face, saucer-eyed. She opens the bottom and comes downstage with her stool, ready to milk her cow. The Mountaineers distract her from his chore, and all engage in a little flirtation as well as a yodelling contest. The Mountaineers hold their noses in reaction to the Milkmaid's smelly feet and pretend to be the cow, one dangling his hand in imitation of the udder, another flapping his arm like a tail. Then they wave goodbye, leaving the Milkmaid depressed.

As she stands there, out of the door comes a lady in a skirt, straw boater, and long gloves. This lady strips to her underwear and performs a brilliant and sophisticated, ever-so-slightly naughty, gay little Polka, *sur les pointes*, one of the cleverest numbers in the show. (This dance was initially performed by Alicia Markova [b. 1910], the first great 20th-century ballerina of English birth; the role was later assumed by Margot Fonteyn, Markova's heir to all the leading classical roles and an inspiration to Ashton in his own development. He created many of his finest characters for Fonteyn.)

Paul Shoemaker and Robert Estner in ''Popular Song,'' *Façade,*
The Joffrey Ballet.

At this point, in later versions of the ballet, two couples—flappers and their boyfriends—launch into a rather mad, desperate Foxtrot, in which traces of the Charleston and the Black Bottom may be observed. In the Waltz that follows, for four young women in organdy with the empty expressions of private-school girls, the accent is on arm movements. In Popular Song, the next section, two young gentlemen, linking arms, stare at the girls, who retire to the position of observers; the boys then perform a soft-shoe shuffle from the music hall, without facial expression of any kind. (They have been described as "dutifully limp" and "deadpan.") Another later addition is the Country Dance, in which a Squire wins a Maiden away from the Yokel she had momentarily been kissing. The Squire's "business" with the shooting stick is also straight from the music hall.

Ashton's own role came in the Tango Pasodoble. He danced the role of the Gigolo, brilliantine hair and all, who attempts to seduce a highly innocent and unknowing Debutante. Wearing evening dress, he approaches her, runs his fingers down her back, and invites her to tango. The Debutante is quite unsure how to do it but gives it a good try, with the Gigolo becoming more and more exasperated. The poor dear girl is most good humored and allows herself to be endlessly manipulated, finally finishing the dance in a disheveled state, after the Gigolo has tripped over her feet and then turned her head over heels. The closing Tarantella Sevillana, led by the Debutante, unites the company.

Façade, a durable work if ever there was one, despite its frivolity, is associated with a crucial period in British dance history. It was first performed by the Camargo Society in London with a cast consisting (with one exception) of Ballet Club dancers. These two groups—the Camargo Society and the Ballet Club—were both organized in 1930 with the express intent of encouraging the development of British ballet. Diaghilev had died in 1929; although his Russian company, which had dominated the European dance world for 20 years, went out of existence immediately, it left a lingering popular suspicion that classical dance and Russian dance were one and the same thing. It was time to develop original material. The Ballet Club was organized by Marie Rambert; the Camargo Society, founded by nondancers, employed dancers from the studios of both Rambert and Ninette de Valois, the two women who would be responsible for launching, developing, and nurturing the two great companies that for many years *were* the British ballet: Ballet Rambert and what became the Royal Ballet. Ballet Rambert, now called Rambert Dance Company, continues to this day; the Camargo Society was disbanded after two years when it became clear that de Valois's Vic-Wells Ballet (which grew into Sadler's Wells and later the Royal Ballet) was well on its way. *Façade* is the earliest ballet from these important days to have survived.

LES PATINEURS

Choreography by Frederick Ashton, 1937; music by Giacomo Meyerbeer, arranged by Constant Lambert; scenery and costumes for first production by William Chappell.

Les Patineurs means "the skaters," but for some reason the ballet is always known by its French name. Created in 1937, it has been immensely popular from the start and has been performed all over the world. In many ways, it is an unusual ballet for Ashton—it has no hint of story, not even a theme, and no emotional development. It is quite simply a series of exceedingly pleasant *divertissements* to tuneful music, in a balletic imitation of skating. Ashton never belabors the skating conceit; he uses just enough gliding and skimming steps and tumbles on the ice to give the idea. And for the most part, his choreography is the purest classical dance; he has not distorted or stretched the technique to achieve the illusion of skating. When the work was created, one of the dancers in the company (Vic-Wells Ballet) had had skating experience, so Ashton had some knowledgeable advice on that vocabulary.

Les Patineurs was choreographed at a time when it was popularly believed that there were no dancers of excellence in England except those of Russian background. Ashton deliberately made a showcase for the emerging virtuosity of the British-trained dancer, although the mood of the ballet is playful rather than exhibitionistic. The music is taken from two operas by Meyerbeer, one of which actually calls for a "skating ballet" (unrelated

to the opera's five-hour story). It is a cheery score with lots of
"um-pah-pah" rhythms and bright orchestration—perfect to
dance to.

Ashton's ballet is delicate, gracious, charming, and inventive. Good manners are a keynote. The scene is a frozen pond
at night with snow-laden trees in the background, and the time
is the 19th century. The merry company wear colorful winter
outfits—the women in bonnets and calf-length skirts, the men
in caps and jackets (or long-tailed coats, depending on the
production). Four couples enter with gliding steps in a circle.
Throughout the ballet, there is much use of deep *plié* (bending
of the knee), with the supporting foot flat on the ground (rather
than on the ball of the foot, or *demi-pointe*), the free leg stretched
out behind, and the body tilted somewhat forward to give the
idea of the gliding motion of skating. Even with high jumps, the
accent is on the descent, on long, low steps to stimulate the look
of being on the ice. Two girls come on walking forward on
pointes, as skaters might pick their way across the ice on the
tips of their skates. They waver, appearing to lose their balance
as their weight tilts backward, but in a flurry of fast footwork,
they regain a fairly upright position. One boy falls; his partner
dusts him off and they go on. A flourish of trumpets heralds
the arrival of the Boy in Green (in some productions, he wears
blue), the show-off of the bunch. He bounds on with high beats,
pirouettes ending in low *arabesque* (with supporting leg deeply
bent) and then again ending on one knee, as skaters do. He spins
in the air in a fairly self-satisfied manner. Then off he goes.

In a change of mood, two lovers, dressed in white, enter as
the music becomes dreamy and sentimental. He lifts her as she
delicately opens one leg forward, then he draws her across the
stage, with only the tip of one of her toes touching the floor,
another skating maneuver. He turns her over so that she is completely upside down, with her legs making a graceful arc as they
go into a split. After two repetitions of this lovely lift, the woman,
returned to the ground and upright, raises her arm and places
her index finger straight up into the closed fist of her partner.
Standing on one pointe, she whips the other leg around, and
the momentum makes her spin. These well-known turns are
called *finger turns* and appear as a highlight in many virtuoso
pas de deux. In this dance, however, the tone is muted, not bright,
and the finger turns are not performed strictly for display. The

Fernando Bujones in *Les Patineurs*, American Ballet Theatre.

lovers leap in a circle together; then, as she descends into a very deep bend on one leg with the other leg projected behind her, he spins her around. This is not a classical ballet step, but one that is a standard feature of exhibition skating. To end the *pas de deux*, again with her single toe touching the ice, he draws her off the stage.

The rollicking music of the beginning of the ballet is heard again, and the four couples reenter zestfully. The girls hop, hop, hop on a single pointe—as one might see on skates. To lusty, bandlike music, the Boy in Green leaps on again, performing what could pass for a double axle skating jump. The skaters all grab each other by the waist and snake around in a circle in the shuffling "gliding" step. After a brief *pas de trois* (dance for three) for the Boy in Green and two girls, all exit. Two other girls dance a dainty variation ending with a double fall on the ice; then it is time for a friendly contest between two more girls. The first performs the famous *fouetté* ("whipping") turn (also a highlight of the Black Swan Pas de Deux and other display pieces); the second does *piqués* in a circle—that is, a series of spins on one toe during which the dancer travels in a pattern. On comes the Boy in Green with more virtuoso steps. He looks rather smug, but then almost loses his balance. Only some furious peddling saves him from falling backward.

For the finale, the music builds to a climax in a bright gallop. The tempo quickens. Snow begins to fall, and the skaters, again lined up holding each other by the waist, pick their way in a circle on the tips of their toes. But the lead girl wavers, and this sends reverberations all down the line. Those who tumble pick themselves up and dust off their bottoms, laughing gaily. Everyone spins, but the Boy in Green is, as always, the fleetest. As the curtain falls, he is still turning.

With *Les Patineurs*, Ashton created an endearing and substantial work, rather that a piece of fluff, which might have been easy to do with the subject matter and the music that he chose. In addition to the inventiveness of the steps and formations, Ashton sustained interest by varying the pace, by alternating brightness (almost brashness) with lyricism, and by interweaving group patterns with solos. *Les Patineurs* has been in many, many repertories since its creation. Incidentally, it is one of the earliest ballets to be televised—by the BBC in London in 1937.

GEORGE BALANCHINE

*I*n 1924, Russian-born Georgi Balanchivadze and a small group of dancers left the Soviet Union for Western Europe. Perhaps they had not really planned to leave permanently when the group set off on an official tour to Germany. None of them—not even to each other—mentioned the possibility that they might never return. All, however, somehow sensed they might be leaving their homeland for good.

Balanchine (the name he adopted for Western Europe) and his colleagues had been trained at the Imperial Ballet School in St. Petersburg, with its exacting curriculum. Although the Csar was deposed in 1917, the school continued to function throughout most of World War I and the Bolshevik Revolution—times in Russia where there was often not enough to eat and no fuel during winter. One notes with astonishment that, in the days when conditions in his country were so dire, Lenin did not dispense with dance altogether. There were even some performances, although naturally the training was not so thorough as in the opulent old days. Dancers—and everyone else—were half-starved; mere survival was everyone's foremost task. Somehow, even in this atmosphere, not only did the dancers continue their strenuous training, but Balanchine even started doing choreography of an experimental sort and obtained a public showing. "Experimental" in those days meant, among other things, dancing in bare feet, doing acrobatic lifts, and using unconventional music. Balanchine's second evening of experimental choreography was banned by the authorities; perhaps it was this, more than the state of political and economic upheaval in the Soviet Union, that made him decide to leave.

Making their way to Paris, Balanchine and the other dancers auditioned for the famed impresario Serge Diaghilev and were taken into his Ballets Russes, the foremost dance company in Europe. Not long after this, at the age of 20, Balanchine was asked to choreograph for the company. Diaghilev's group at the time had a reputation for modernism that sometimes featured style over substance, "shock tactics" over lasting artistry. With *Apollo* (1928), Balanchine's sixth work for the company and the oldest of his ballets that survives in today's repertory, Balanchine disregarded this "modernist" strain in the Diaghilev company. Instead, he went back to the classical school of dance technique, reaffirming the cardinal tenets of that training—the graceful, noble carriage of the torso, turnout in the legs and feet, arms rounded in perfect circles, feet pointed like arrows, high jumps and leg extensions.

With Balanchine, the dance—the choreography itself— became the subject, always rooted in the classical school. But there was a difference—although his dancers turned out their legs, they also turned them in; although they rose to pointe, they also shuffled about on their heels; although they rounded their arms, they also straightened them and splayed their fingers; although they held themselves gracefully erect, they also jutted out their hips and caved their torsos inward in "contractions" (a term made famous by Martha Graham); although they danced beautifully to the music, they also danced "against" it—that is, in syncopation with it, in a sophisticated and rhythmically complex counterpoint. Most of all, although the dancers were clearly the products of the most rigorous classical training, many of the steps Balanchine devised for them (all technically difficult) could not be found in any ballet "textbook." Balanchine was creating a new language of dance, based on and presupposing the old, traditional classical school. His "classicism with a difference" has been called Neoclassicism, and, in one way or another, with many variations, this approach, first seen in *Apollo*, is evident in virtually all the works he created in his prolific 60-year career.

Of his ballet *Apollo*, Balanchine himself has written: "Stravinsky's score for *Apollo* taught me that a ballet, like his music, must have a restraint and discipline. . . . I saw that gestures, the basic material of the choreographer, have family relations, like different shades in painting and different tones in music. . . . The score was a revelation. It seemed to tell me that I could, for the first time, dare not to use all my ideas; that

I, too, could eliminate . . . to the one possibility that is inevitable. . . . I look on *Apollo* as the turning point of my life.''

It is this simplicity—this daring to pare down and throw away—that is a mark of maturity in any art. Balanchine's collaboration with Stravinsky, which was to extend for almost 50 years, is one of the most profound and productive in 20th-century culture.

Video: HOME.

APOLLO

Choreography by George Balanchine, 1928; music by Igor Stravinsky; scenery and costumes for first production by André Bauchant. (Originally called Apollon Musagète.)

To the ancient Greeks, Apollo was the ideal of manly beauty. In the visual arts, he is always portrayed as noble and elegant. As a god, he was associated with the sun and also with prophecy, with arts and learning (especially music), and, as a shepherd, with flocks and herds. Of these images, Balanchine selected a young Apollo, not the majestic sun god, but a rough still unpolished boy, perhaps even a soccer player—''a wild, half-human youth who acquires nobility through art,'' as he said.

He portrayed Apollo as the leader of the Muses, the seven Greek goddesses of the arts and learning. In the ballet, these have been reduced to three. It should be mentioned that there is very little about the ballet, except for the inspiration, that is actually Greek. The costumes nowadays are usually practice clothes, not Greek tunics, Apollo does not wear the traditional laurel wreath, and Mt. Parnassus (home of the Muses) is represented by stairs.

As the ballet opens, Leto, in dramatic lighting atop the stairs, gives birth to Apollo in a series of violent contractions. The stage darkens, and the newborn Apollo appears at the bottom of the stairs. He is a full-grown man but wrapped in swaddling clothes—that is, tightly strapped in bands of cloth. Although, of course, swaddling clothes are mentioned in the Bible—the

infant Christ was wrapped in them—they were also used for
many centuries in Russia in the belief that they made the baby's
body grow straight. Two handmaidens start to undo the bandages. Apollo begins to breathe and heave, then spins, unwrap-
ping the bandages as he does so. Naked to the waist, he recoils
in fright as though blinded by the day. He reaches out almost
randomly with his hands, as if trying to get his bearings. The
handmaidens, one supported by the other so that they assume
a "wheelbarrow" formation (one of many unique Balanchine
configurations in the ballet), enter with a lute, symbol of Apollo's
mastery of music. They place it in his hands and show him how
to pluck it. He imitates their playing motions, and there is a
blackout.

When the lights come up, Apollo, now dressed in a tunic
top, has achieved young manhood. He plays his lute, plucking
it agitatedly as though trying to get more music out of it. He
steps forward—not timidly like a child, but still haltingly like a
young man testing his strength. Again holding the lute, he circles his playing arm wildly. From three corners of the stage, the
Muses enter, picking their way toward him on the tips of their
toes. They bow, then move closer and reach above him, forming a triangle with their arms. Then they bend low, each raising
one leg in back (deep *arabesque*); Apollo raises the neck of his
lute straight up into the air to complete the design. All shuffle
on their heels in a circle, each Muse cupping another's head with
her palm. At the end of this dance, Apollo gives each Muse a
"prop"—a symbol of her art—then sits back, commanding each
to perform for him.

The first is Calliope, Muse of poetry, to whom Apollo has
given a tablet. She bends sharply through the torso, and, gesturing forward from her chest (or her heart), palm to the ceiling
with fingers apart, and opening her mouth, she appears to be
calling forth speech from deep within her. She repeats the same
gesture from side to side, but with less and less conviction. She
stops. Suddenly she begins to run, now with more strength to
her movements. She will write! She appears to scribble on her
arched palm (signifying the real tablet that she has laid aside).
She shows Apollo what she has written; crushed by his lack of
approval, she leaves the stage with bowed head.

Polyhymnia, Muse of mime, lays aside her emblem—a mask.
She is far more extroverted—one might almost say aggressive—

Peter Martins, Karin von Aroldingen, Kyra Nichols, and Heather Watts in *Apollo*, New York City Ballet.

than her sister. One of her most difficult steps is a double spin on one toe ending with one leg extended behind (*arabesque*). She performs the entire variation with her finger pressed to her lips, since speaking is not allowed in mime. (This increases the technical difficulty of executing the steps.) So forceful is she that she becomes carried away and opens her mouth, simulating speech. Again Apollo disapproves and, cowed, Polyhymnia too leaves the stage.

Terpsichore, goddess of choral song and dance, the most delicate Muse of all, lays aside her lute and daintily paws the ground with her pointe, turning her body from side to side. In a filigree solo she jumps and turns. She rises to *arabesque* with circular arms, then walks around herself on her heels (a most unusual and—traditionally speaking—ungraceful step).

After she has left the stage, Apollo's solo as a full-grown man begins. With strength and breadth of gesture, large, soft leaps, and beating steps, he evokes a modern athlete as well as a god. Gone are the tentative motions of his previous solo; now, however, his dance includes some off-balance falls, suggesting that he is still struggling for mastery or equilibrium. He invokes the heavens, reaching upward, then sometimes seems troubled, as though sensing the pain of being an adult. Slowly he spins to the ground, at the end swiveling on one knee and then the other to a semireclined position, in a pose reminiscent of a classical Greek statue. From here he gestures; Terpsichore, his chosen, enters and touches his outstretched finger with her own, in a moment recalling Michelangelo's painting of God awakening Adam into life. In their tender *pas de deux*, Balanchine invented new ways for a man to support a woman. Some of the poses recall flying and swimming. He rocks her back and forth while her legs are twined around his body. She puts out her hands; he lays his head upon them. Traces of a boy remain. She balances on his back to "swim"; she sits on his knees when he is seated. From an *arabesque* position he turns her upside down in the air; then, lunging forward, he draws her along behind him. They finish—he in a forceful stance, such as a warrior might assume, she leaning her chest against his back in a deep arch. No *pas de deux* in history ever ended in such a way.

The music changes from dreamy to agitated, and two other Muses return for the *coda*. Here Balanchine calls forth several unusual images or formations. At one point Apollo seems to be the driver of a chariot and the Muses his spirited horses (this is sometimes referred to as the "troika"); at another moment, all come together and their legs appear to form the spokes of a wheel or, perhaps appropriately, a sunburst. Apollo seems to be taming wild fillies, although he is quite wild himself. He takes gigantic leaps, twisting his body in the air. Now the music evokes grandeur and majesty. Apollo, followed by the Muses, begins his ascent to godhead. As the curtain falls, he has reached the top of the (mountain) stairs, at the back of the stage, with the Muses deployed on the lower rungs behind him.

Apollo is less important for its themes (although they are compelling) than for its dance and musical invention. To understand the importance of this work, in which Balanchine used the traditional classical vocabulary as a starting point, it is necessary to be aware of the experiments of Michel Fokine and Vaslav Nijinsky, as well as some of the earlier work of Balanchine himself (experimental, acrobatic, and often referred to in the press as "grotesque"). One must also consider the legacy of Marius Petipa, choreographer of *The Sleeping Beauty* and *Swan Lake*, upon whose work Balanchine "embroidered."

During the early years of the century—specifically the 20 years preceding *Apollo*—in Paris, where Diaghilev ballets often had their debuts, the public was exposed to such "antiballets" as *Afternoon of a Faun* and *Le Sacre du Printemps*. Audiences considered these works innovative (which they were). In this atmosphere, Balanchine showed that it was equally daring and innovative to go back to tradition, and that a fresh departure from it was (and always will be) possible for artists who are truly creative.

Interpreters of Apollo through the years have spoken of the athleticism in the title role. Perhaps here—in the hands of a Russian, in the Paris of the 1920s—is the germ of that special quality in dance that is now referred to as particularly American—the sheer exultation in muscular mastery, a reckless expenditure of energy as though there were no limit to it—which Balanchine, during his long career here, did much to disseminate, and which is now recognized as an "American" style.

For Balanchine, as for many other choreographers, no ballet was ever in its definitive or final form; each performance and each cast change brought something new. He sometimes changed his works, even years after creating them. In a most striking example of this, he radically altered *Apollo* in 1979, when the ballet was over 50 years old. It seems astonishing that he could have had new ideas on a subject he had been involved with so long before. But for Balanchine, as for others, dance was a living art: he presented the ballet without Apollo's birth or youthful development; rather, it began with the entrance of the Muses and ended not with an ascent to heaven but with the sunburst pose. This changed the accent of the ballet from Apollo's growing up to a more pure-dance focus, centered on the *pas de deux* between Apollo and Terpsichore. A year later, however, Balanchine restored *Apollo's* first variation. In Fall 1989, The Miami City Ballet revived Balanchine's original version of *Apollo*.

SERENADE

Choreography by George Balanchine, 1935; music by Peter Ilyich Tchaikovsky (Serenade in C for String Orchestra); *costumes for first production by Jean Lurçat.*

   Serenade is Balanchine's first ballet composed in America. In the original cast, there were American dancers only, and all were relatively obscure (from the beginning of his stay in this country, Balanchine avoided big-name stars). In 1935, if he had wanted stars, they would all have been foreign-born, and almost all would have had Russian names, even if they had never been near Russia, for at that time it was almost impossible to have a successful career in ballet without a name that had a Russian sound to it.
   During the late 1920s, a young American dance enthusiast, Lincoln Kirstein, had fallen in love with the Diaghilev Ballets Russes when he saw the troupe during their final London seasons. Kirstein, born in 1907 and educated at Harvard, was independently wealthy and had lived a life of privilege, but was not sure what profession he would enter. After exposure to Diaghilev, however (and, after Diaghilev's death in 1929, to other troupes), he had formulated a plan, setting a goal for himself that sounded almost impossible to realize: He would create a

major ballet troupe in America. The reason this idea was so startling was that there was almost no tradition of ballet in this country and few good dancers to call on. What ballet America had seen was almost all imported, and serious dancers were generally trained abroad. The audience for dance was very limited.

In 1933, Kirstein invited Balanchine to come to America to found and run a dance academy and eventually develop a company. Balanchine, just finishing a season with his own group, was about to be unemployed. Of course, Balanchine had never heard of the young Kirstein (who was then 26) and knew almost nothing about America (except for liking Ginger Rogers's legs), but for one reason or another, he was willing to entrust his future to Kirstein and his preposterous idea. He and a colleague arrived in New York on October 18, 1933.

In January 1934, the School of American Ballet opened its doors for the first time. Balanchine, however, was used to professional surroundings, and the world of performance was his life-blood. He was not interested in waiting for several years until the dancers in his school were of truly professional caliber; he was eager to get started. So in March, he began to choreograph his first ballet in this country, tailoring it to the students he had. This was *Serenade*.

Serenade is a ballet to train dancers in ensemble performance. In this work, all of the ideas about dancing that Balanchine would later become famous for were already apparent—the primacy (or autonomy) of pure dance, or the choreography as star; the use of classical technique as the basis for further movement exploration; distinguished musical support; the full participation of the *corps de ballet*; and the deaccentuation (or complete absence) of guest stars, decor, costumes, and plot.

Serenade is a ballet of patterns, fluidly shifting from one to another. The number of dancers changes all the time and there is nothing regimented about the designs. It is something like a kaleidoscope—each slight variation reveals a whole new picture. In fact, it is the striking images made by the group that are the most memorable, not the individual steps: a long diagonal line of girls suddenly dissolves as, one by one, with a whirlwind circling of their arms, the girls break the formation and rush off into the wings, like a giant wave; plunging *arabesques* by the full

Serenade, New York City Ballet.

corps give the effect of cascading water. In a delicate waltz for a couple, the woman is barely lifted off the ground, like a breath; a woman leaps into the arms of a man, but turns backward in midair just before she is caught; a woman in an expansive *arabesque* is slowly rotated twice by a man hidden behind her so it appears she is sustaining the movement by herself; a man enters in the mysterious and evocative Dark Angel configuration, his face masked by the hand of a woman who stands behind him; later she flaps her arms like giant wings.

The opening pattern is particularly striking. As the curtain rises to Tchaikovsky's opulent music, 17 girls stand facing front with their arms raised, palms straight to the side, as though shielding their eyes from the sun. Slowly they lift their wrists, bring their hands to their foreheads, lower them across their chests, and let them fall rounded. They breathe with their arms, raise their heads up and back, and begin. The first section is a vivacious *allegro,* always with touches of lyricism. Amidst the rich *corps* patterns, often made while the women are running and rushing somewhere else, there are some solo moments. A ballerina leaps through rows of girls, then does her own little dance full of beats, fast jumps, and spins. The *corps* runs, interweaving. Moving backward, they seem to swim with their arms. Again a ballerina leaps through their midst. They whirl, and from a diagonal, peel off into the wings.

Another ballerina enters. Her movements are large and generous and she seems to fall off pointe as she abandons her center. As she leans in a giant backbend, girls rush on and support her; she bends forward; others enter. Five women leap with one leg raised, as though skipping. A ballerina turns, as all the girls enter, forming a large circle. They kneel, raising and lowering their arms on different counts. The ballerina leaps in a split, and suddenly the entire stage is turning in a circle; the girls finally melt into the opening pose, again shielding their eyes.

Another ballerina enters, as though searching for someone. There is one empty spot in front. She finds it and raises her hand against the sun. A man enters, and all the girls turn and begin to leave, each trailing one hand behind her as though skimming the surface of water. The cavalier touches the ballerina; she responds, and they begin to waltz. Of course, this is no ordinary waltz. The ballerina runs on pointe around her partner; the man lifts her airily; they run forward together. She does larger leaps with his assistance, changing direction as he carries her. As she whirls on her toes, lines of girls enter, first from one side, then from the other. The ballerina hops on her toes in *arabesque;* two girls leap as the rest of the *corps* forms a pattern resembling a waterfall. With the *corps* in a line behind, all the dancers waltz forward, raising their legs, dipping low in *arabesque,* and leaning back. Forming a V, the *corps* crisscrosses the stage in interlacing lines; and finally, with lunging movements, moving in irregular patterns, they find their way off the stage.

Four are left, with one ballerina, to begin the Russian Dance. This section, after the lyrical waltz, is again dynamic. It has more fire than the opening, but it starts slowly. Five standing women descend to a split together. On the floor in a row, each offers her hand to another. They rise and twine themselves about, forming a tight circle, to dreamy music. They pause, and suddenly the music becomes lively. The ballerina begins vigorous, animated small steps on pointe, becoming more expansive. She has many small beats, then leaps, then sustained and open movements, such as a series of full-blown *arabesques.* The four girls complement her on a slightly less demanding scale. The music becomes more passionate and sweeping, and other girls rush on as though propelled by it. The whole stage seems alive with movement. The waltz ballerina reenters and, as the girls all leap and rush into the wings, she falls to the ground.

Now the final movement of the ballet—called Elegy—begins. Here Balanchine deals with human passions for the first time in the ballet, but in a very unspecific way. Three ballerinas and a man seem to express romantic longing, rejection, despair, and resignation. As the waltz ballerina lies on the floor, the Dark Angel couple enters. They go forward; then the man embraces the fallen woman, who raises her head and blossoms. The second ballerina assumes the slow *arabesque* in promenade, and then swoops down into a kneeling position. The three march forward together, to rich, throbbing music. A third ballerina rushes in, leaping with brio into the man's arms. Two ballerinas pull him back, and other women run toward him, then past him and off the stage. Again the third ballerina enters with a daring leap into his arms. He pushes her along the ground. All three ballerinas embrace the man, seemingly in despair. Again the waltz ballerina falls to the ground. He touches her gently, and the Dark Angel flaps her wings. The two leave, as the waltz ballerina reaches desperately after them. She is alone. Six women enter to a dirgelike melody. The ballerina runs forward, shielding her eyes, then back to embrace a tall "mother figure." Four men appear. They lift her chest-high and carry her off. The "mother figure" follows, walking forward on pointe with her head back. Behind her come the six girls. The curtain falls.

In alluding to human emotions, Balanchine introduces mysteries he does not solve. He said that he merely followed the unspecified emotional currents in the music. Although there are many hints of personal feeling, there is no story in the ballet. Like *Les Sylphides*, it is truly a ballet "about" dancing.

Serenade has remained a favorite of performers since it was created, and has been danced all over the world. It does not date. As dancers have grown more accomplished over the years, they have brought new precision to it, but it is a ballet that can accommodate many levels of expertise. Balanchine's small group of student performers, called the American Ballet when it made its professional debut in 1935, eventually developed into the New York City Ballet in 1948, after many years of setbacks and sporadic progress. *Serenade* has been in the company's repertory from the first, and it is sometimes called the "signature piece" of the New York City Ballet. It is also performed by many other companies in the United States and Europe.

CONCERTO BAROCCO

Choreography by George Balanchine, 1941; music by Johann Sebastian Bach; scenery and costumes for first production by Eugene Berman (now commonly presented in practice clothes).

Concerto Barocco, to some exalted (yet lively) music of Bach, is one of Balanchine's most refined compositions. The ballet has no plot, no characters, and virtually no pretext of any sort. Two ballerinas are associated with the two solo violin parts, but there is not always an exact correspondence. There is also a *corps de ballet* of eight women and, in one section, a male dancer.

The ballet has been compared to a cathedral for its architectural clarity, its beauty, and its observance of ordered form. A cathedral is made up of interlocking parts—nooks and crannies, aisles and chapels all flowing into one another. It is also a hallowed place, but, although Bach's music is sublime and some of Balanchine's images are piercingly beautiful, there is nothing reverential about this ballet. It brims with life and vigor, just as the music does, at times keeping a jaunty beat, at other times projecting a passion under tight control.

Bach wrote in a contrapuntal style—that is, he wrote music in which two or more of the melodic lines sound simultaneously, weaving in and out of each other, with the melody going from voice to voice. (This contrasts with music of a later century, where melody is most often only in the higher voices, and the bass line provides a harmonic accompaniment.) With Bach, note plays against note, melody against melody. Bach's music is also characterized by an unusually strong, regular musical beat (in common with much music of the baroque era). Balanchine seems to have found a sort of visual and kinetic equivalent to this kind of music. *Concerto Barocco* is primarily an ensemble ballet, simulating the equality of musical voices. Even the two ballerinas are dressed in the same costumes as the *corps*, and their patterns and steps play in and out of the *corps* formations. In this, *Concerto Barocco* bears some relation to *Serenade,* in which the soloists sometimes step out of the ensemble, and at others melt into it.

In movement quality and general atmosphere, however, *Concerto Barocco* is light-years removed from *Serenade*. If anything, *Apollo* is its distant ancestor. The ballet contains some of the most beautiful classical steps ever created, but Balanchine also included a number of the same "distortions" that appear in *Apollo*—in particular, a posture leading with the hip and timing that is practically jazzy in its syncopation. To match the juicy, bouncy quality of the music, Balanchine has invented some unusual steps—during one sequence the *corps* does something resembling the Charleston on pointe. Here are also some of the "daisy-chain" formations that Balanchine became famous for (and which were later spoofed because they were so well known), in which the dancers, often with arms joined, weave under and over the arms and heads of others, forming a maze, in lines that coil and uncoil, sometimes ending up in a tight cluster. The timing throughout—stop-start-stop—again, like *Apollo*, "against" the music, gives a particularly "catchy" rhythmic feeling. This syncopation has been called an "American" quality (once again supporting the assertion that the roots of "American" dance style lie to some extent in the experiments of an expatriate Russian working in pre-Depression Paris—Balanchine creating *Apollo*).

The ballet is in three parts, with three different moods and impulses, corresponding to Bach's score. The first movement, *vivace*, and the third, *allegro*, are both highly energetic. In the *vivace* section, there is a good deal of repetition as well as repartee between the soloists and the small ensemble. Here one will find knees pointing straight front ("turned in") and *arabesques* held an instant longer than the music. The second movement, musically and choreographically, is the emotional center of the work. The melody soars in unbroken arcs (rather than being fragmented and bouncy, divided among several voices, as in the first and last movements). In dance, this is realized as a pulsating *adagio* (man and woman), with the *corps* forming background patterns, adding weight to the stage setting but interacting very little with the two principal figures. The *corps* does not perform any of the same steps as the two soloists, as it does in the first and third movements. Often the *corps* merely walks, with a determined, measured gait. Here, as in *Apollo*, Balanchine created innovative partnering. In one sequence, the man almost throws the ballerina across the stage so that her entire body is close to the ground; from this she swivels and rises onto a single pointe, pulling away at arm's length from her partner in a full-blown *arabesque*. At another moment, he holds her off the floor and she simulates a big leap (never touching the ground) by swinging one leg forward across her body and then backward, opening her body fully to the audience while being supported on her partner's back. Finally, she leaps from side to side (assisted by her partner), in higher and higher arcs, as the music intensifies.

The third movement, like the first, is characterized by a feeling of motor energy, but the rhythmic (and the dance) patterns are more irregular and restless. The ballerinas seem to be engaged in a dialogue with one another, to which the *corps* adds punctuation. Several movements are seen sequentially; that is begun by one or two dancers, followed a beat behind by two more, then two more and two more—like a canon. This section contains many small (and some large) leaps, after which, in a final burst of exuberance, all kneel as the curtain falls.

Concerto Barocco is so precisely constructed to the music and so rigorous in dance terms that there is no room for error. The steps are as clipped as the facets of a diamond. Technically, as

Otto Neubert and Heather Watts in *Concerto Barocco*,
New York City Ballet.

well, the ballet allows little latitude. If dancers do not have beautifully turned-out legs and dartlike feet, they will not be attractive in this ballet no matter what other dance attributes they possess. No excesses are permitted. The slight flutter of a wrist, *rubato*, ritard, incidental flourishes—small liberties that can sometimes heighten the theatrical effect in other ballets—ruin it here. Balanchine measured this ballet to the last ounce.

THE FOUR TEMPERAMENTS

Choreography by George Balanchine, 1946; music by Paul Hindemith; costumes for first production by Kurt Seligmann (since 1950, presented in practice clothes).

Balanchine worked in many veins and styles, but the ballets for which he is best remembered—those most distinctly his and certainly those that have most radically departed from prevailing notions of how ballet "should" look—are his reductive, movement-packed, plotless works done in practice clothes, set to modern music. One of the earliest—in fact, probably the earliest—to embody all of these elements is *The Four Temperaments*. It is safe to say that these Balanchine ballets launched a whole new aesthetic of dance—one that featured movement for its own sake, with little or no emotional associations. There are no characters in these works or reference to any situation outside the dance—each ballet is "about" what happens between the dancers participating on a particular stage at a particular time. Balanchine's dance vocabulary also departed significantly from what had gone before, but not in the sense of breaking away. He started with a classical ballet base, then streamlined and heightened it, sharpened it, turned it upside down and inside out, but never abandoned it. Classical dance—and classical dance training—is always essential in his dancers, no matter how much they turn their legs or convolute their bodies.

The Four Temperaments is perhaps Balanchine's first "avant-garde" creation. Here he unveiled a new world of movement, more distantly related to the classical school than any of his preceding works. His movement syntax has something in common with the contractions through the torso and the "contortions" of the modern dance of the 1940s, and in this ballet, also, Balanchine sometimes tried for a sense of weightedness, which was a quality that Martha Graham also stressed at the time. After an initial elaborate production, with fantastical costumes, the ballet was presented in leotards, which proved much more suitable. It is now performed by companies around the world.

Hindemith's music has a three-part theme which is stated at the beginning and is then followed by four variations. To each variation the composer assigned a "temperament" or mood—Melancholic, Sanguinic, Phlegmatic, and Choleric. These correspond to the four body fluids of medieval physiology, but it is best to forget this while watching the ballet.

The theme is realized by three successive duets. In these *pas de deux*, Balanchine explores some very basic movements—pointing and flexing the foot; bending the body; *arabesque* and its opposite, swinging the leg forward; turning; small darting jumps; and an elemental feature of partnering whereby the woman is manipulated by the man to make new designs, learning to "lean" on him literally and figuratively. The couples are lit by bright lights. Then the stage dims, and there is a greenish cast overall. In the Melancholic variation, a seemingly boneless man droops and lunges. He falls to the ground. A *corps* of women slashes through the air with high kicks. Two female soloists block the man's path. He collapses. His rubber back allows him to bend in an S-curve. Gravity pulls his torso from side to side. With a high kick, he too travels forward, only to lose momentum. In the final backbend, he is almost dragged off stage. The lights brighten.

Sanguinic is a dance for a couple—aggressive and highly virtuosic. The woman, in particular, is speedy, energetic, and unharnessed, with feet like arrows. Her torso is held high, and she is assertive, brilliant, untamed. She kicks the air, she bucks. The man invades space, turning sharply. Their lifts at half-height displace the atmosphere as they travel low across the stage.

A man enters, quizzically, his arm stretched out before him. This is Phlegmatic. He examines the hand at the end of his arm as though it were not a part of his body. His feet also seem dis-

Richard Rapp in "Melancholic," *The Four Temperaments,*
New York City Ballet.

membered. They perform in a rhythm that his body does not know. Four girls accompany the man. He extends a foot between their encircling arms, then pulls back. The women's hands are like cat's paws, snarling, abrupt. The five line up; each protrudes a foot, each withdraws. With taffylike movement, bending deeply over their bodies, and syncopated footsteps, they find their way off the stage.

Choleric is a ferocious woman, who kicks and leaps as though trying to get kinks out of her body. Men throw her to the ground. She writhes. When the three "theme" couples and the Sanguinic couple enter, the dance grows even more ruthless—thrusting and straining. The women are held in splits, almost touching the floor. In the partnering work, their arms and legs seem to be wrested from their torsos. Near the end of the ballet, the three parts of the musical theme come together; the full company of dancers joins to make rich-textured patterns—all the movement particles that Balanchine has used in the ballet unite in a sweeping design.

In this work, Balanchine introduced a pared-down style in which speed and kinetic impact are more important than conventional images of prettiness. Every muscle is exposed and used. Balanchine's movement is very direct, swift, and sure; there is no time for the "politeness" of more gracious eras or more leisurely dance spectacles.

Later he pushed his principles of reductive movement much further and used even more "advanced" music, which sometimes has almost no melody and is "punctuated" by a great deal of silence. His most extreme statements in this vein include *Agon*, *Episodes*, and *Movements for Piano and Orchestra*. To interpret these works, dancers take on the aura of divine machines. Balanchine's stripped aesthetic has gained a wide following, and it does not seem too much to suppose that future cultural historians will see in the lean skeletal structure of his work a reflection of mid-20th-century efficiency, sobriety, and hi-tech beauty.

PAS DE DIX

Choreography by George Balanchine, 1955; music by Alexander Glazounov; costumes by Esteban Francés.

As a master craftsman, Balanchine did not always wait for "inspiration." He often created pieces to fill certain needs in the repertory—whipped them up to order, so to speak. *Pas de Dix* (Dance for Ten) was probably produced in such a manner. It is an attractive, sometimes dazzling bit of entertainment with a pleasingly exotic feeling and several excellent opportunities for dancers of soloist caliber. A number of companies now perform it.

The music, taken from a full-length Russian ballet of the late 19th century (*Raymonda*), is tuneful with a good, strong beat, reminding us of what ballet in those days was about—it was an elaborate diversion, with little thought for art. The general aura of *Pas de Dix* is aristocratic Hungarian, with touches of Eastern mystery, which reflects the story line of the original ballet. There is no attempt at authentic Hungarian steps—just touches of local color. Stamping and clicking heels with arms akimbo give flair to the virtuoso classical vocabulary of which this piece is fashioned. In the age of the Csar, it might have been a sparkling court *divertissement*.

Four couples enter a ballroom. The ladies wear jeweled tiaras, which flash in the light. They circle the stage, followed in a moment by the ballerina and her cavalier. The music, in a minor key, has an Oriental feeling. The ballerina performs a supported *adagio;* her cavalier guides her around in low *arabesque* as she "swims" with her arms. Her glittering *pirouettes* snap to a finish. She raises her leg to the side, balances for an instant without her partner, then falls into his arms in a dynamic lunge. This ballerina role requires a steely flash, yet delicacy.

Now the stage empties. One of the women performs a dance of swift footwork, tiny steps, quick changes of direction, and balances, ending with spins. Another woman does tiny beats forward and back, darting onto pointe in *arabesque*, and finishes with a balance. Next comes a rather boisterous duet for two other women. The music is heavier, and there are slight folk touches. The cavalier's variation is entirely within the classical school,

André Eglevsky and Maria Tallchief in *Pas de Dix*, New York City Ballet.

except that he performs some steps with his knees straight forward, then snaps his heels together, again to give a folk feeling. In general, however, his steps are those commonly associated with male virtuosity—double turns in the air (often landing on one foot), big leaps, beats, and turns. The ballerina enters: She could be a sultry Oriental princess. She darts about the stage on pointe (her feathery little running steps are called *bourrées*) and sinuously undulates her arms, then stretches them forward languidly. Her dance is a seductive mixture of Eastern dreaminess and Russian brilliance. She spins quickly, then stops with breathtaking suddenness, brushing her fingers across her face as if summoning forth a vision. She tosses her head. Her arms ripple. The pace quickens. She moves one leg forward, bending the knee and placing the toe onto the floor (*passé*), then the next leg, then the first and the next, relentlessly, her feet digging into the ground like daggers. After a quick turn, she kicks the back of her head, claps her hands imperiously, and snaps her chin haughtily into the air.

Animated music announces the *coda*, a kind of free-for-all with folk touches, almost gypsy in feeling. The dancers leap around the stage. Suddenly the ballerina enters and all are quiet. Again she spears the ground, one toe after the other, in a diamond-hard display of *passés*. Her cavalier performs more virtuoso male steps—multiple spins and beats, ending with a *grand tour* in second position (a hopping turn with one leg extended to the side, which concludes with spins generated by the momentum of many revolutions). The ballerina, after a series of delicate measures, ''turns on the dazzle'' again in some large leaps with a swivel. All the dancers come together, and, in the final moment of flourish, the ballerina pirouettes many times with her partner, stopping for an instant after each series with gusto.

The sharpness and verve with which the movements of the piece are performed, in addition to the high level of technique required, are characteristic of the style of late 19th-century Russia, what today we call the age of Classicism. This manner of presentation, more than the steps themselves, contrasts profoundly with the gentle, gossamer style of French Romanticism (exemplified by *Giselle* and *La Sylphide*) that flourished a half-century earlier. Ballet had undergone a virtual revolution during those years. Both of these styles, of course, are current today, demonstrating once again that the classical ballet has many and enduring faces.

AGON

Choreography by George Balanchine, 1957; music by Igor Stravinsky.

This rigorous modern ballet won immediate popular approval when it was new, despite the fact that there is very little in it that is conventionally pretty and that the music is often without melody. Now an acknowledged masterpiece, *Agon* seems more a cerebral than an emotional experience. Its construction has the logic of perfectly interlocking parts that fall into place with apparent inevitability. For this reason, some commentators consider it a "perfect" work. Certainly part of the thrill of watching it derives from an intellectual appreciation of its structure.

Balanchine said that he admired Stravinsky's music preeminently for its timing—the clear, ultraprecise rhythm that gives his movement pulse and drive. (Stravinsky, on his side, said that Balanchine's choreography made his music "visible.") *Agon* was the last score Stravinsky composed especially for Balanchine, thus bringing to a close the active phase of one of the most fecund collaborations in the musical theater of the 20th century. (Stravinsky died in 1971.) The music is loosely based on ancient airs and dances from the 17th century, completely transformed by Stravinsky. Balanchine referred to *Agon* as the "IBM ballet"— "more tight and precise than usual, as if it were controlled by an electronic brain." Mechanization is implied throughout. The noted dance critic Edwin Denby contended that the dancers continually "flirted with the edge of risk." *Agon* is all muscle—no embellishment—dry, intense, strong, and razor-sharp, yet with moments of humor and even tenderness. Lincoln Kirstein, General Director of the New York City Ballet, wrote, "There is more concentrated movement in the [20 minutes of] *Agon* than in most 19th-century full-length ballets."

Unrelenting bright lights glare onto the stage from the wings, starkly outlining the dancers' bodies. *Agon* is a spare work, using only 12 dancers in practice clothes who are rarely on stage at the same time. The underlying rhythm, as is often the case with Stravinsky, is like a driving motor in its insistence, and many of the steps are of extreme rhythmic intricacy. The music becomes more dissonant as the ballet progresses. At the same time, Balanchine's vocabulary becomes less classical, and the feats of balance and timing become more exacting. In general, one could say that the ballet does not display brilliant technique. Many of the individual steps are quite small and uncomplicated, but even the mere articulation of the foot, for example, can have tremendous impact when it is echoed elsewhere on the stage. It is the split-second precision of the timing that gives the steps and patterns—often simple in themselves—their extraordinary power and density.

The curtain rises in silence to reveal four men in practice clothes with their backs to the audience. Together, sharply, they turn. To rather strident music with a determined beat, they take small steps, then march forward, then leap together. A trumpet sounds. The first man kicks forward and pirouettes, finishing with arms out; the others follow in canon. The music roars; they march with a "limp." They walk back. Another trumpet; more movement in canon. In quick contrast they walk softly around the stage, swinging their arms and swaying their bodies from side to side in an apparently casual manner. Suddenly they turn—bam!—to face one another, as though in confrontation. Two women enter, then more and more (there are eight in all). The music roars again. The dancers lift their legs at various times. Deployed about the stage, all do deep knee bends and appear to collapse. There are "marching" steps in unison and more raised legs. Now all line up in a double row. As one leaves this formation, he or she is replaced immediately by another. They do more unembellished movements—for example, a single *pirouette*, a pose with one knee bent—but the timing is so exact that the design seems complex. There is a *pirouette* by all in unison, then they seem to be shuffling about. Suddenly they freeze, creating a tableau, each dancer looking front with hand on shoulder. End of section. All exit abruptly

To a flourish of trumpets, two women and a man enter. They dance together briefly, then the man does a slightly quizzical solo, concentrating mainly on the heel and toe. He rocks through his foot onto his heel, digs the ball of his foot into the floor, pauses, takes three or four steps forward, and in conclusion, bows in a courtly manner. The two women return, and to consonant music do some dainty small steps either in unison or one a fraction of a second behind the other. The man rejoins them briefly. All bow.

The same flourish of trumpets is heard, introducing the second *pas de trois* (dance for three), this time for two men and a woman. The movements here are more "dangerous." As the ballerina perches on a single pointe, arms outstretched, the men suddenly let go and switch positions before grabbing her again; then as she is stretched low in *arabesque* (still on a single pointe), they again let her go, turning in place before catching her. She leaves with a slightly self-satisfied air. The two men dance together in a kind of competition, like two young athletes testing each other. They end in a splendid formation reminiscent of Greek statues.

To jaunty music, featuring castanets, the ballerina performs a tiny heel-and-toe variation with little shoulder gyrations—it is all nuance. The men return, with some ferocity. They throw her in the air as she is beating her legs. In the air, lightly supported, she does two splits, legs slashing the air like scissors, landing on the floor in a split. They twist her around with one leg raised. Then at the last second, she leaps into their arms in another split. Finish.

Again the trumpet flourish (Balanchine said the music was so difficult that it had to be heard three times for the audience to make anything of it). The *pas de deux* that follows is the most "dangerous" part of all. It is as though the dancers are teetering on tight ropes. A man and a woman walk slowly forward, holding hands. The music is dissonant. She leans on him, half balancing on her toes, with her knees bent. She slips backward through his legs. During this dance, the woman is completely manipulated by the man. He balances her precariously, at one point supporting her in *arabesque* while he is lying on the ground. Sometimes she folds her body into his. The duet finishes as he kneels and she is partly bent over him.

To percussive and restless music the other dancers enter, moving in counterpoint. Then the women leave the stage. As in the beginning, only the four men remain. They repeat some of the earlier steps, then begin to shuffle and sway in an aimless walk. On the last split-second of music—bam!—they face each other in the pose of confrontation. Curtain.

Peter Martins and Suzanne Farrell in *Agon*, New York City Ballet.

Kirstein wrote: "The innovation of *Agon* lay in its naked strength, bare authority, and self-discipline in constructs of stressed extreme movement." He also considered *Agon* "an existential metaphor for tension and anxiety."

STARS AND STRIPES

Choreography by George Balanchine, 1958; music by John Philip Sousa, adapted and orchestrated by Hershy Kay; costumes by Karinska.

Balanchine, although Russian in upbringing, took to America immediately on his arrival here in 1933. His American numbers met with varying degrees of success—but with *Stars and Stripes*, he hit the jackpot. Whether Balanchine was inspired by a forthcoming State Department tour of his company to the Orient, or whether he found the music of John Philip Sousa irresistible, is not known. But in *Stars and Stripes*, as someone said, "Every day is the Fourth of July."

With marches of Sousa as accompaniment, how could he lose? Everyone in the audience could whistle the music; for everyone, there were nostalgic associations—college songs, school proms, adolescence, parades, small-town America, Norman Rockwell. Even those who had not lived through such things knew of them from legend and folklore. The Sousa marches might just as well have been written by "anonymous"; they are so much a part of our heritage and popular culture.

The ballet was also an important milestone in the history of the New York City Ballet. In those days, the company was not "establishment," as it now is; it was still an underdog. *Stars and Stripes* was the largest and most opulent ballet it had produced up to that time, with the exception of *The Nutcracker* (1954). And in addition, there was a feature in *Stars and Stripes* of major importance to the past and the future of American dance—Balanchine was at last able to give male *corps de ballet* a highly demanding *divertissement* of its own. Balanchine was often criticized for neglecting men in ballet, an objection which is unfounded, since he began creating great roles for men in the 1920s. But there may have been a practical side to the story. It was not until 1958 that he had, in the company he helped to found, sufficient strength in the male ranks to create something really demanding—and exciting—for them to do. All dance companies in the West had suffered in the male contingent because of World War II. In the U.S. the problem was acute for another reason as well—there had never been a tradition of men in "serious" dancing, and male ballet dancers were considered effeminate. This, of course, discouraged many talented boys from taking ballet lessons and resulted in a dearth of accomplished male dancers. So quite naturally, whatever his inclination, Balanchine glorified the woman—at least, in part, because he found more women than men who were excellent dancers. The few outstanding men were almost all European.

Rather than having his dancers merely strut around in dazzling costumes to the toe-tapping music (which might have made a ballet in itself), Balanchine packed *Stars and Stripes* with clever choreography. The curtain opens to the music of "Corcoran Cadets," revealing a miniature corps of drum majorettes in wedge formation. Keeping the wedge shape, they perform various perky steps in unison, then split off to the sides of the stage, while the lead girl does a solo with baton twirling, leg lifting, and splits—a kind of takeoff on a vaudeville variety act (no juggling here, however). On one side of the stage is a group of three, on another a group of four, and on the third side, a group of five. Ingeniously, these three lines interweave in a wheel formation, from which all move forward into a "lineup," backing the soloist as she leaps from one side of the stage to the other. Running back to their wedge, all the girls do enormous high kicks to the side, reminiscent of a Las Vegas nightclub or the Rockettes. But with their years of ballet training, the kicks go a great deal higher, and these girls are apple-pie wholesome. With a salute they march off the stage on pointe, and on comes the "Rifle Regiment," a second group of "cheerleaders," in the same wedge formation.

These girls are much taller, and their movements are larger, looser, and "plushier" than those of the first group. They, too, do high kicks, but this time to the front, hitting their outstretched hands. The soloist of this group plays the bugle, sashaying forward on pointe with hips swaying slightly from side to side. Around her, groups of girls prepare to "shoot." They paw the ground like horses, shoulder rifles, exit with spinning turns in

Robert Barnett and Melissa Hayden in *Stars and Stripes*,
New York City Ballet.

a circle and bouncy, running steps with knees held high, like trotters.

"Thunder and Gladiator" announces the arrival of the men (again in a wedge), and the excitement begins to build. One way or another, the men's variation is filled with every male specialty in the ballet textbook, including split jumps, beats, *grande pirouette à la seconde* (the leading man does multiple turns with his leg held out to the side, while all the others leap around him in a circle). Many of these steps are performed in unison, which adds to their spectacular quality, and many others in sequence (one group, then another, then another), which lends musical and choreographic variety as well as a dash of humor in some cases. As the final "pow," the entire group does a series of double turns in the air together, finishing in a perfect salute. Off they march, as though in military parade.

Even this lighthearted ballet has a Grand Pas de Deux—and it is at least as "grand" as all those that grace the classics as a matter of course. The music is "Liberty Bell" and "El Capitan." Here, Balanchine combines fiendishly difficult steps with amusing characterizations—the man, although good-natured, thinks a lot of himself (his chest precedes the rest of his body by quite a bit when he marches onto the stage), while the woman, although a technical powerhouse, with whiplash legs of steel, is also a dainty, rather sentimental "sweetheart." After some exceptionally demanding steps, she lays her head on her partner's shoulder and bats her eyes at him. The *pas de deux* follows the traditional form—the two dance together, then there is a male variation, a female variation, and an exciting *coda*, which is literally jampacked with eye-boggling steps. These include lifts in which the man throws the woman into the air and supported *pirouettes* in *arabesque* (the man at arm's length looking unconcernedly the other way, only to catch her at the last split second). The lady, in her variation, picks her way on pointe across the stage, moving faster and faster. Later, the man leaps high, but with toes straight out to the side instead of pointed. In a rousing finish, the man rushes off the stage, holding the woman high in the air, saluting. This virtuoso *pas de deux*, with its humor and its dazzle, is often presented as a concert number, without the rest of the ballet.

For the grand finale of the ballet, to the march called "Stars and Stripes," all the regiments together do those enormous high side kicks we saw at the beginning, and a giant American flag appears as a backdrop to all. There's nothing subtle about the spirit of the ballet—it's red, white, and blue patriotism—but the choreography, as always with Balanchine, is anything but empty gesture. It has some very amusing tongue-in-cheek touches, both small and large.

TODD BOLENDER

*T*he choreographer of *The Still Point*, Todd Bolender (b. 1914), had a notable career as a dancer with various ballet companies, including the New York City Ballet and the several groups that preceded it—Ballet Caravan, American Ballet Caravan, and Ballet Society—as well as with the Ballet Russe de Monte Carlo. Since 1980, he has been Artistic Director of the State Ballet of Missouri. In addition to his ballet training, he studied with the important modern dancer Hanya Holm, who was herself a pupil of the German Expressionist dance pioneer Mary Wigman. Bolender's dancing was distinguished by sensitivity and theatrical imagination rather than by virtuosity; he derived a great deal of meaning from gesture, particularly in such roles as the quizzical Phlegmatic in Balanchine's *The Four Temperaments*. He was also very witty. The ballets he has choreographed are characterized by the same traits as his own dancing. By and large, they have stories, slight in themselves, that provide a framework for exploration of an emotional condition. In three of his ballets—*Mother Goose Suite*, *Souvenirs*, and *The Still Point*—he also has shown great insight into the sensibilities of young women.

THE STILL POINT

Choreography by Todd Bolender, 1955 (revised 1956); music by Claude Debussy.

The Still Point is a chamber ballet, a small-scale dramatic work. Originally choreographed for a modern-dance company, its chief impulse, in common with many works of modern dance, is the

166

projection of emotion through movement. There is a bit of a story, but the primary subject is the revelation of a state of mind. *The Still Point* uses a simple but meaningful dance vocabulary. The steps do not draw attention to themselves. What is important is the emotional impact of the movements as a whole. Debussy's music—the first three movements of his only string quartet—is intense and passionate. Its agitated, restless surface is articulated by the frequent use of *pizzicato* (a plucking rather than a bowing of the strings), which produces a pinched, staccato sound that points up the prickly, sharp, defensive feelings of the heroine, a troubled outsider.

The Still Point is about a woman—perhaps still an adolescent—who feels the anguish of rejection by others, but who finally finds comfort in the presence of a strong, quiet man. Two couples enter. Their movements have a youthful flow, and they are obviously intimate; each partner knows the movements of the other. They seem to be playing—the girls run, their partners catch them by the hand. Another girl enters. She is not at ease. She goes up to one girl, then the other. They dance together, but the lone girl is not accepted; although they are all dancing the same movements, she seems to be subtly out of step, to be trying too hard. The three girls hold hands; then the two males touch their partners. The three girls again dance, turning in a line toward the front. The two outer girls join hands; the center girl reaches out to touch them, but they draw quickly away in a sharp movement. The center girl then puts her arms around the other two; together they crouch, then swing out, but the two girls appear to be pulling away. There is a tense standoff. The two girls exit, and the lone girl runs halfway across the stage after them, then gives up, hopeless.

She steps backward, touching her face. She touches her neck with both hands as if seeking solace. She rushes to the other side of the stage. The couples reenter, and they all leap together, holding hands. But the other girls do supported *adagios* with their partners; it is painfully obvious that the lone girl has no partner. This is a dance for two—or four. The couples leave again, and the girl lunges after them. Slowly she straightens up; she is alone. The music is slow, thoughtful, then becomes faster and more agitated. The girl does some of the large, space-covering movements the others did at the beginning. She kneels, throwing her torso forward violently. She leans back; again she reaches for her throat, now pawing it as though suffocating. She touches her body. Is there something repellent about it? She runs forward, still grabbing for parts of her body as though she is covered with leeches, as though she wants to remove her skin. She reaches forward, almost gasping, then seems to grope the space around her, appearing to be enclosed in a cage, a prison. Slowly she lowers her arms, clutching her ears forlornly. She is helpless, lost.

The couples return, but they do not seem to see her, much less to notice her torment. They are in their own world, and she is definitely outside it. It is no use. Almost defiantly she reaches out. She runs around the stage, now frantically clutching, turning, and imploring. Her head is thrown back, with her hands in a prayerful posi'ion. She dances a few measures with the couples, mimicking the previous flowing leaps but now with a jerky compulsiveness. Violently, she is pushed from one man to another. She pitches forward onto her knees. Rising, she twirls faster and faster, arms flailing, like an outcry. She rolls on the floor. The others pull her up and again thrust her forward. She falls in a heap. The four link their hands above her head; she reaches up to contact them; they pull away and disappear.

She is alone again, but this time she is still, only rotating her head slightly, as if trying to release tension. She loosens her arms dejectedly, letting them fall one after the other. She does not see a man walking toward her from the rear. He kneels as she continues her slow-motion movements, gesturing to herself. She walks around in a circle; he imitates her (to give her assurance that he is on her side). He comes closer and they walk forward together. He manages to be in step with her. He touches her on the shoulder, but she freezes and does not look at him. Slowly she reaches up as if to take his hand, but instead flings it away, then runs around the stage. The man merely stands there, calmly, offering his hand. Finally she returns, takes his hand, and faces him at last. He steps forward, and she leans back and away, then allows herself to be supported by him. Together they circle their arms. The man dances a few measures of his own. There is nothing flashy; his movements are slow, large, steady, and full of strength. He bends to reach for her, but she is not yet ready to yield. He tries again, spinning to the ground with both arms extended. They reach to each other; he lifts her; she runs around him, but at every turn his outstretched

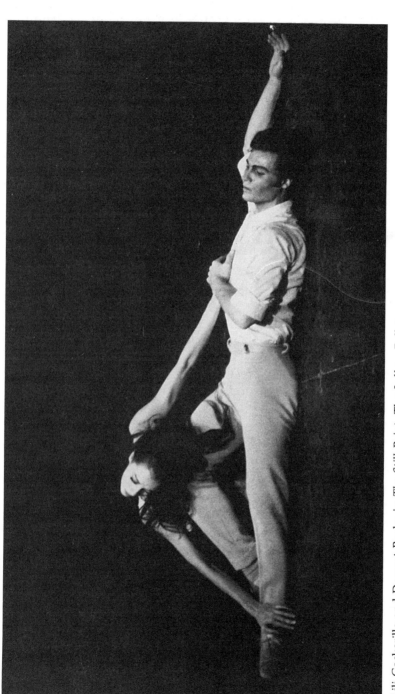

Lili Cockerille and Dermot Burke in *The Still Point*, The Joffrey Ballet.

arms are waiting. She leaps into his arms, now trusting his support. She permits him to touch her around the waist. Then he lifts her so that she is wrapped around his shoulders as he slowly turns. They slide down to their knees; their arms touch, and they lie down together.

The Still Point has been in the repertories of the New York City Ballet, Joffrey, Alvin Ailey, Dennis Wayne, the Norwegian National Ballet, and the ballet companies in Cincinnati and Kansas City. It was created for the Dance Drama Company, a modern-dance troupe headed by Emily Frankel and Mark Ryder.

RUTHANNA BORIS

Ruthanna Boris (b. 1918), who danced as the Wallflower in the original production of *Cakewalk* (although not the premiere), performed with many companies. She was a charter member of Balanchine's first company in America, the American Ballet, and attained the rank of ballerina with the Ballet Russe de Monte Carlo during the 1940s. Boris is one of the few female ballet choreographers who was young enough to dance in the works she created.

CAKEWALK

Choreography by Ruthanna Boris, 1951; music by Louis Moreau Gottschalk and minstrel music, adapted and orchestrated by Hershy Kay; scenery and costumes for first production by Robert Drew.

Cakewalk harks back to an aspect of America's past—the tradition of the minstrel show. It is a series of acts, perhaps on an old showboat, using period costumes (tails for the men, fancy dress for the ladies). At the same time, it is a classical ballet—the dancers are not in blackface, as they customarily were in the minstrels, and the women wear pointe shoes. The cakewalk was a black dance that became exceedingly popular in the 1890s, an exhibition dance that inspired a craze for contests, with prizes awarded to the best cakewalker. Originally, it was a takeoff by plantation slaves on the fancy manners of the white masters—thus, it contains a lot of strutting about with chests puffed forward.

A glance at the presentation of the *Cakewalk* ballet gives a good idea of its flavor: "Part First: *Grand Introductory Walkaround* (following a minstrel show tradition in which couples dance and promenade in a circle); *Wallflower Waltz; Sleight of Feet* (Interlocutor); *Perpendicular Points* (Endmen); *Freebee; Skipaway* (all); Part Second: by Louis the Illusionist, assisted by Moreau and Lesseau, and featuring Venus and her Three Graces, a Wild Pony, and Hortense and her Lover, Harolde; Part Third: *Gala Cakewalk* (in which all are invited to participate)." The music is a medley of authentic minstrel tunes and melodies in minstrel style by Louis Moreau Gottschalk, a composer of the 19th century with an interest in Creole and other American folk themes. Toots of the tuba and plaintive wails of the oboe add humor and underline the foot-tapping beat.

After a rollicking overture, with the catchy syncopation of the cakewalk rhythm, the curtain rises to reveal a forecurtain with a large painted showboat. Across the front come a parade of high-kicking ladies and gentlemen. The curtain goes up, and the assembled company skips off into the ballroom, shaking imaginary tambourines. They sit on gold chairs. The Interlocutor (master of ceremonies), assisted by the Endmen (two sleek ladies in long black tights and top hats, one tall, one short), present the acts. The Wallflower, a demure and dainty vision in pink, tries to join a dance resolutely designed for couples, becoming more and more dejected and limp as she continues to fail. Between each of her attempts to find a partner, a "chorus" of men comes up and looks her over. In mock despair, she grows weak, collapses, and prepares to shoot herself. Just in time the chorus lifts her away.

The Interlocutor, a debonair soul, performs a clicky little solo full of tiny foot movements and jumps. He bounds about, nonstop; the Endmen become worried and follow him around with a chair, which they place in exactly the right spot for him to fall into at the end of a phrase. In *Perpendicular Points,* the Endmen pick their way around on their yard-long legs in geometrical configurations, doing variations of heel and toe and landing in the Interlocutor's lap. The gay leader of the *Freebee* energetically rouses the entire stage to action. After a boisterous "skip around," hand-over-hand in a circle, all collapse on the ground in exhaustion, but then they manage to rise and skip off, ladies swishing their skirts and men collecting all the chairs. The showboat backdrop lowers.

Berissa Wells in ''Venus and Her Three Graces,'' *Cakewalk,*
The Joffrey Ballet.

Part Second begins with three mysterious Magicians (clearly the Interlocutor and the Endmen in the flimsiest of "disguises"), who stalk across the stage. They shake their cloaks and run furtively around. Bells ring. Suddenly Venus and her Three Graces (four scantily clad women) appear from behind the cloaks, frolicking about with a giant balloon. They gambol, they prance, but an unkind gentleman with a pin puts an abrupt end to the act. More mysterious music sounds, and now a horse (a frisky lady) darts forth from behind the cloaks, flicking her tail. The Magicians approach with a lasso, but the Wild Pony eludes them, pawing the ground and leaping away.

"Schmaltzy" violin music announces the arrival of the Wallflower, now reincarnated as Hortense, Queen of the Swamp Lilies, with her ardent swain, Harolde. She flies in on a swing, then descends from her perch for an *adagio* that mocks the poses of French Romanticism. She attempts to appear a thistledown creature. Ducking behind the rustling cloaks of the Magicians, she reappears with giant butterfly wings. Harolde is confused; he doesn't recognize her. After a momentary disappearance, she reemerges with an enormous bunch of flowers. Still he can't find her. What more is left in life? He exits in the swing.

The forecurtain falls, and it is time for the gala concluding cakewalk. The dancers appear, kicking high. They jump from foot to foot, legs thrust out in front, bodies leaning back. They strut. The Interlocutor and the Pony leap on, twisting in the air. The two Endmen lead the Wallflower, picking their way on pointes across the stage. Everyone grabs a partner and high-steps around in a snake formation. Then all promenade across, zipping along, kicking high to the front and shaking their "tambourines." A gay time—and, for the audience, possibly a slightly nostalgic one—has been had by all.

AGNES DE MILLE

*I*n 1942, Agnes de Mille (b. 1909), having struggled unsuccessfully for years to gain major attention as a dance recitalist, was uncertain about the direction her career would take. A late start in ballet training had inhibited her developing a polished classical technique, but it had encouraged her to integrate other elements such as social dance and ethnic forms into her early solos and duets. And her flair for satire was evident in the amusingly wicked danced "morality play" she staged for Ballet Theatre, *Three Virgins and a Devil*.

But her brand of humor was too special and her vehicles too small-scaled to lead to many job offers. The story goes that, one day on her way to ballet class, a friend told her that the Ballet Russe de Monte Carlo was looking for a new work with an American theme. Despite her lack of experience with large ballet troupes, but feeling she had nothing to lose (having no employment in sight), de Mille submitted a story about cowfolk on a ranch out West. The libretto of the ballet that was to become *Rodeo* was accepted. Her tale of an awkward tomboy, rejected by the guys and taunted by the gals, who secretly longs for the heart of the head wrangler and gets her man in the end, would clearly be an audience pleaser.

The difficulties began, however, as soon as the choreographer started rehearsing. Gone were the seemingly weightless jumps, the perfect fifth positions and classically shaped arms the company was accustomed to. Instead, de Mille insisted that her dancer-cowboys learn to squat as if they were saddle sore and jolt their whole bodies as they might when tossed by bucking horses. She urged the dancers to fully use their backs when lassoing the imaginary steer, and demanded that they slap their thighs and use a rolled-in walk in dusty boots. She also insisted that they learn to tap and square dance. Recalling her rather cool reception by the *régisseur*, de Mille admits, "I couldn't compose a classical ballet—my language is American vernacular."

Rodeo became the first hit ballet on an American subject. A year later de Mille choreographed the dances for the musical *Oklahoma!*, and after that she was seldom unemployed on either the Broadway or the ballet stage.

In the mid-1970s, de Mille suffered a near-fatal stroke. Now confined to a wheelchair, she has nevertheless continued to create dances, to write books, and to speak out tirelessly (and eloquently) in support of government funding for the arts.

RODEO

Choreography by Agnes de Mille, 1942; music by Aaron Copland; scenery by Oliver Smith; costumes by Kermit Love.

In *Rodeo*, the curtain rises on the straight, stark lines of a corral fence set against the background of endless plain and sky. Among a half-dozen cowboys lazing around the fence, we see the Cowgirl, awkward and belligerent in baggy brown trousers, heavy boots, and bright red shirt. The cowboys dance to vigorous music, imitating the tricks of the rodeo—they ride bucking horses, lasso the air, and jump and spin energetically. The Cowgirl rushes to join the men, and although she is clearly being ignored, she stays put, her glance lovingly, if discreetly, fixed on the Head Wrangler. The Cowgirl hitches up her pants, scuffles her feet, slouches, and turns abruptly, with the gestures of a determined and vulnerable adolescent.

The mood changes with the arrival of some Eastern girls, friends of the Rancher's Daughter. Frilly, giggly, and flirtatious, they present a strong contrast to the rough and tumble Cowgirl, who is especially jealous of the Head Wrangler's attention to the Rancher's Daughter. Other young women arrive to watch the danced rodeo, until they are suddenly interrupted by the Cowgirl, who enters jolted and tossed by an apparent bucking bronco. She falls off the horse amidst the titters of the other girls. When she shrugs her shoulders and tries to rejoin the boys with a friendly poke in the ribs, they ignore her. The Head Wrangler

Christine Sarry in *Rodeo,* American Ballet Theatre.

jerks his thumb toward the house, and she realizes it is time to leave.

Soon the rodeo ends, and the daytime sounds of clicking horses and tapping boots melt into the softer sounds of evening. The women move slowly across the stage, joined by the cowboys, who slip their arms around the girls and urge them forward. The Cowgirl watches as the Head Wrangler lifts the Rancher's Daughter and carries her off. She remains alone and still, then falls to the ground, clearly hurt and confused as the stage blacks out.

A curtain decorated with galloping horses falls, and four couples do a lively square dance to the sounds of a caller's voice and hand-clapping. They all shout and run in a circle as the pace quickens.

The next scene takes place inside a ranch house, where the Cowgirl sits watching the cowboys dance to warm up for the Saturday night party. Couples stroll in and out and the Champion Roper urges the Cowgirl to dance, but just then the Head Wrangler enters with the Rancher's Daughter and the Cowgirl falls to the floor in tears. The room fills with the local folk, and the men and women line up facing each other for the dance. The Cowgirl resolutely joins the women's line but when everyone chooses a partner, she is left alone. The Champion Roper performs a tap dance solo, and when he is finished, again asks the Cowgirl to dance. But the sight of the Head Wrangler and the Rancher's Daughter together is too much for her, and the Cowgirl disappears. All the couples resume their lively and folksy dance until the sudden reappearance of the Cowgirl—this time wearing a shockingly bright dress. The Champion Roper and Head Wrangler both want to dance with her now, and they playfully toss her back and forth between them, both eager to kiss her. Now, everyone—Cowgirl and all—dances happily, and the ballet ends with the girls stepping into stirrups formed by the men's hands. Holding the girls high in the air, they circle in celebration.

De Mille's *Rodeo* was an instant hit and, despite the misgivings of the management, the dancers learned to perform it with appropriate gusto. The ballet proved to be a turning point in de Mille's career. In *Rodeo*, she used the body in a variety of ways to express dramatically a situation or character. When, one year later, she introduced this idea to musical comedy with her choreography for *Oklahoma!*, she established the role of dance in musical theater as more than merely decorative. Her dances were fully integrated elements of production. Always attractive and energetic, they also added dimension to character and plot development.

While it would be an exaggeration to call *Rodeo* a turning point in the history of ballet, it was, nonetheless, a lively and well-received illustration of a new idea. It showed that the movement of ballet could be extended beyond the classic idiom and enriched by indigenous American styles. The characters could be just plain folk, and gestures, such as dusting one's self off after a fall, hitching up baggy trousers, or jerking with a thumb for someone to "get lost," were now acceptable. Ballet did not have to be a performing art reserved for those with highly refined taste; it could have popular appeal and offer frank entertainment.

Rodeo was the first ballet with American subject matter choreographed for a major company and, with *Billy the Kid*, clearly indicated an important direction in the American ballet—a concern with the domestic manners and particular feeling of the American people.

FALL RIVER LEGEND

Choreography by Agnes de Mille, 1948; music by Morton Gould; scenery by Oliver Smith; costumes by Miles White.

On a sultry August morning during the summer of 1892, in the little town of Fall River, Massachusetts, Mr. Borden and his second wife were hacked to death by an ax murderer. The shocking crime attracted the attention of the nation. Their unmarried daughter, Lizzie Borden, was accused of the crime and, despite rumors of blood on her dress and other circumstantial evidence, Miss Borden was acquitted of the murder of her father and stepmother. Lizzie returned to her father's house, where she lived as a virtual recluse. The murderer was never found (despite the rather eerie and ironic unearthing of a buried ax years later in the Bordens' backyard).

One has only to recall the rhyme "Lizzie Borden took an ax and gave her mother 40 whacks, when she realized what she'd done, she gave her father 41″ to understand how this bizarre and grotesque incident lived on in the national imagination. The very idea that Miss Borden, a respectable, churchgoing woman, might have been capable of such monstrous violence proved haunting. In *Fall River Legend,* Agnes de Mille, too, was intrigued by the psychic history of a New England spinster, whose frustrations and anger could have been unleashed in a sudden and solitary act of murder. Invoking poetic license, de Mille renames Lizzie the Accused and portrays her as guilty and condemned to hang. The ballet opens at the moment she faces the gallows, and we travel back in time to the Accused's childhood, witnessing the painful events that led her to her final fate.

The curtain rises to some alarming and discordant music, and the audience sees the Accused standing in a spotlight on stage right. To the left stand the gallows, stark against a troubled dark sky. A man monotonously intones the murder charge and his recitation reminds the Accused that she committed the crime in the same house where she lived happily as a child with her father and real mother. The drop curtain rises as her memories trigger her imagined return to childhood. The frame of a Victorian house, its façade missing to enable the audience to see the interior, is revealed behind the curtain. A little girl appears, and from the solicitous manner in which the Accused follows and imitates her, we realize this is she as a child. The little girl runs lovingly to her mother and is frightened by a severe, prim-looking woman who enters and scolds her. Her own mother has a fainting spell and the townspeople rush in to help her. The forbidding woman in black, clearly a widow or a spinster, walks away. After a while, the Borden family relaxes, and the Accused sits happily on the steps of her house watching her parents dance. But her mother suffers another attack. She is carried into the house and two neighbors come out and dress the little girl in black. Her mother is dead, and the matronly spinster stands in the doorway of the house; she has now taken control.

The next scene takes place inside the house where the Father and the Stepmother sit in straight-backed chairs, rigidly rocking back and forth. The Accused runs up and down the staircase behind them and then takes flight to the yard where she meets the young Pastor. They dance; he seems to be her only friend. The Accused reenters the domestic scene, this time carrying an ax. The girl is surprised when her Stepmother starts in fear and she runs back out to chop wood. Later, on a street outside the family house, young couples dance. Alone, the Accused dances spasmodically and in her frantic movements almost runs into the ax, which clearly holds some fascination for her.

Just then the Pastor enters and they dance briefly until interrupted by the parents. The Accused at first falls to the ground and kicks her feet as if she were a child. She then regains control and, defying her parents, takes the Pastor's arm and walks off with him. The next scene is a prayer meeting. The people are friendly to the Accused when she arrives, and she dances a long duet with the Pastor while the others continue their folksy, country-revival-type dancing. This time, however, when her Stepmother enters and whispers to the Pastor, he leaves. The Accused flinches as if struck in the stomach and, doubled over, writhes in agony. The others continue their dancing throughout the scene. Later, inside the house, the parents continue their rocking.

The Accused, seemingly in a daze, walking stiffly and determinedly, picks up the ax and enters the house. The action is swift and abrupt—her Father and Stepmother spring to their feet in terror, the Accused covers her face with her hand, and the lights black out. A curtain falls. Painted on it are the family's parlor chairs, now overturned, and a floor stained with blood. In front of the curtain, the Accused enters in a dream. She dances with her real Mother, who at first embraces her but then slaps her when she sees the blood on her dress. In a strange reversal, the girl picks up the Mother and rocks her in her arms as if to comfort her. We return to the opening scene. Part of the framework of the house now forms the gallows we saw in the Prologue. The Accused stands back in the present, before the gallows, with the near-pious anguish of a martyr. Her body twitches violently, her head falls to the side—she has been duly punished.

Fall River Legend, like *Rodeo*, greatly enlarges upon and often even discards the classical ballet idiom. It relies more heavily than *Rodeo* on literal dramatic gesture—the Accused kneels before her Father begging for his attention; the Stepmother blocks the doorway to the house; the Accused clutches her stomach in anguish; she is slapped reproachfully by her real Mother. De Mille makes very effective use of striking visual images—the child standing alone and confused suddenly dressed in black; the young girl

Georgina Parkinson, Victor Barbee, and Cynthia Gregory (kneeling) in
Fall River Legend, American Ballet Theatre.

nervously running up and down the staircase while her parents chat; the tense family drama at the prayer meeting against a background of dancing townsfolk; the murderous daughter who only now is able to give love consoling her dead Mother. There is also effective use of scenery and props—the ominous gallows; the ever-present frame of the house; the forbidding ax; the stiff-backed rockers finally overturned.

The heroines of both *Rodeo* and *Fall River Legend* are outsiders to society, rejected because they are misunderstood. The Cowgirl in *Rodeo*, simple-minded as it may sound, changes her attitude along with her clothes. She "outgrows" adolescent rebelliousness and finds acceptance. The Accused, the victim of a loveless life, is denied any outlet for pent-up emotions and meets a gruesome fate. Both dramas are clearly played against a background of American sensibilities. Both ballets provide a challenging role for a dramatic ballerina.

Video: HOME.

KURT JOOSS

Kurt Jooss (1901–1979) was an experimental choreographer who began his work during the 1920s in the wake of the fertile Expressionistic period in German art. He had an ability to distill the essence of a character or emotion and communicate it directly and meaningfully. In 1920, as a young man, he met Rudolph Laban (1879–1958), the great theorist of human movement, who taught that body language reveals inner emotion. Jooss, who considered himself a "lifelong disciple" of this "master," embraced Laban's principle that manipulation of a movement's speed, weight, direction, and shape would determine its expressive effect. Jooss worked with these variables to compose expressive dance that avoided literal gesture.

After studying with Laban, Jooss directed the dance company at the Essen Opera House and, following a period of exile in England during the war (where he started a school), he was able to return to Germany in 1949, where he directed the Folkwang Ballet in Essen. He was a ballet choreographer much influenced by the Central European modern-dance school, and he was exceptional in his belief that a modern (that is, Labanesque and Expressionist) approach to dance could be enriched by ballet. In fact, Jooss was considered (and considered himself) a ballet rather than a modern-dance choreographer, despite the Expressionistic motivation in his work. However, although he worked with classical dance technique, he deliberately simplified it: his female dancers did not wear pointe shoes, and all the ballet steps were done without embellishment—there were no beats while the dancer was in the air, and multiple *pirouettes* were not really a part of Jooss's vocabulary, although the plain ("simple") *pirouette* certainly existed. His works today, therefore, have a more "modern" than balletic look.

While he is also known for his *Pavane on the Death of an Infanta, A Ball in Old Vienna,* and *The Big City,* it was *The Green Table* that bought him worldwide attention.

THE GREEN TABLE

Choreography by Kurt Jooss, 1932; music by Fritz Cohen; costumes for first production by Hein Heckroth.

The most enduring of Kurt Jooss's ballets, *The Green Table* was presented at the competition held at the International Archives of the Dance of Paris and won first prize. While most ballets rely on themes that are either entertaining and escapist or purely abstract and musical, *The Green Table* is a significant exception. Choreographed in 1932, between this century's two great wars, the ballet was a timely and strangely prophetic indictment of both the horrors of war and the futility of insincere diplomacy. The effect and durability of this masterpiece are due both to the continued topicality of its sobering message and the power of its movement images.

An antiwar satire subtitled *Danse Macabre,* or *Dance of Death,* the ballet combines an Expressionistic approach with the feeling of a medieval morality play. A few broad movement strokes make clear the identity of each of the symbolic characters. Like a medieval play, the action unfolds in a series of loosely connected vignettes. There is an implacable, martial figure of Death (also in the medieval tradition), who claims each of his victims in a manner fitting their individual personality.

The ballet's opening scene reveals ten diplomats, the Gentlemen in Black, all dressed identically in black suits and white gloves with rubber masks for faces. They surround a large green table, tipped at an angle so its broad top is visible. To a mock tango played on two pianos, the gentlemen begin ''conversing.'' They gesticulate circuitously, applaud one another, mime fencing, bow exaggeratedly, and, once or twice, even rise in a handstand on the table to emphasize a particularly empty point. There is an air of shallow friendliness and false dignity in their bearing. At the end of the scene, they line up in a row, bow, and suddenly draw their pistols. They fire a single, resounding shot in the air; the lights black out. This is war.

As the lights are dimly raised, the huge, menacing figure of Death becomes visible, frightening in his massive, black war armor. Death begins his repetitive, lumbering solo, a dance that serves as an ongoing motif throughout the ballet. He hammers the ground with his heavy boots, and flexes and straightens his outstretched arms relentlessly, like a reaper. Death dancing is the background for the recruitment of the proud and vigorous Standard Bearer and the other eager soldiers who march on the scene. Their women follow, bidding them a reluctant farewell. The wily and shrewd Profiteer also makes his appearance. With lunging, acrobatic movements, a small group of soldiers engages in battle. Each time one is killed, Death appears to claim the victim. Next, we see the war's refugees, a band of tattered, displaced people huddled together. When Death suddenly appears to them, all break and flee except for one Old Woman. Bent and slow moving, she finds Death's presence a comfort. He is, this time, touchingly tender as he lifts her gently in his arms and carries her off. The poignancy of this scene is shattered by the strident Guerrilla Woman—a maddened, impassioned creature leaping from side to side, waving a red handkerchief. She shoots an enemy soldier and is in turn shot down by a firing squad. Death appears to take her away, again in an attitude of consolation and pity.

The next scene takes us to a brothel, where the Profiteer presides over the bandying of a Young Girl from soldier to soldier. She moves as if frozen in terror, her arms raised stiffly over her head. The soldiers brush against her lecherously. When she is left alone to dance a macabre waltz with one soldier, Death suddenly appears to take her partner's place. It is he who completes the dance with her, and we understand that she has at last been delivered from her cruel fate.

The scenes of war are followed by The Aftermath. Death reappears heading a macabre procession, a veritable *Totentanz*, or dance of death. All those who have died follow Death in a funereal line. Significantly, it is Death alone who carries a tattered victory flag. Even the Profiteer has been forced at last to join the march. Now Death, left alone, repeats his dance, hammering the air with his fists, pounding the earth under his feet, continuing even as the light fades.

Suddenly, in an ironic change of tone, we are back in the conference room, as if nothing at all has happened. The ballet's

The Green Table, The Joffrey Ballet.

final scene is identical to its opening tableau. War is someone else's nightmare; the Gentlemen in Black are once again gathered around the green table, once again gesticulating, bowing, and applauding one another as the curtain falls.

The personages in *The Green Table*—Death, the Profiteer, the Old Woman, the Standard Bearer, the Guerrilla Woman—are types rather than individuals, and Jooss characterizes each one clearly. Death, the gatherer of souls, stands with his weight firmly planted. He pounds the ground with an even, relentless rhythm. All his movements are energized inward; his clenched fists seem to pull the space around him centripetally. Even his leaps have a downward accent, as if he is claiming rather than releasing energy. The shifty Profiteer moves lightly, sinuously; he skims surfaces and is hard to pin down. In this he resembles the Gentlemen in Black, with their devious way of moving. When the Profiteer focuses on an exploitable object, his approach becomes direct and swift, not unlike the straightforward march and unison shot of the negotiators when they decide to declare war. In contrast to the indecisiveness of the nonfighters are the bounding leaps of the soldiers. The defiant Guerrilla Woman is especially direct, strong, and propulsive, and there is no doubt as to her direction and commitment. The Old Woman and the Girl at the brothel are war's dazed victims. They move as though they have neither the motivation to go forward—or the morale to resist.

Jooss had an individual approach to choreography. His achievement in *The Green Table* is perhaps best summarized by Michel Fokine in his call for a new direction in ballet: "Not to form combinations of ready-made and established dance steps, but in each case to create a new form corresponding to the subject, the most expressive form possible for the representation of the period and the character."

DAVID LICHINE

*D*avid Lichine (1910–1972) choreographed many ballets for major troupes, but *Graduation Ball* is the only one to have survived. As a piece, it is more serviceable than inspired, but as a bit of delightful fluff, artfully constructed for sheer entertainment, it has deservedly become a repertory standard.

Lichine was typical of the stateless gypsies of the 1930s, 1940s, and 1950s, who toured almost endlessly with large ballet companies and had no real homes of their own. Many, like Lichine, had been uprooted from their native countries (he was born in Russia) and grew up in various parts of the world, joining ballet companies when they were virtually still children. The companies were the only home they knew. Without these large troupes, such as the Ballet Russe de Monte Carlo, the Original Ballet Russe, and Ballet Theatre, which traveled all over the United States (and many other parts of the globe), it is doubtful that today's ballet scene would be so lively. Not only did they bring sumptuous, exotic productions to areas that had been completely unexposed to this type of thing, but they also contributed teachers to all sections of the country. Once their dancing days were over, many of the homeless dancers opened studios in the small and large towns of America, which they remembered fondly from one-night stands. They played a major role in spreading the Russian method of ballet technique.

With his wife Tatiana Riabouchinska (b. 1916), one of the three "baby ballerinas"—adolescent dancers discovered by George Balanchine in the 1930s and turned into stars overnight—Lichine settled in Los Angeles after retiring from performing, and taught there for many years.

GRADUATION BALL

Choreography by David Lichine, 1940; music by Johann Strauss, compiled, arranged, and orchestrated by Antal Dorati; scenery and costumes for first production by Alexandre Benois.

A gay, lighthearted piece, *Graduation Ball* is an ideal ballet to end an evening and send the audience home happy. Because the choreography offers a little something for everyone and because the ballet makes few demands on the viewers—it is pure fun—it has been a staple (off and on) for nearly 50 years and has been seen all over the world. At present, it is widely performed by regional companies in the United States.

A potpourri of Strauss music sets the festive mood. The scene is the drawing room of a proper girls school in Vienna, where cadets are about to arrive for a graduation party. The senior girls are dressed in their best; the juniors, in their blue smocks, watch them with a mixture of excitement and envy, primping with mirror and powder puff. The girls are reprimanded by the fluttery Headmistress, who snatches the puff to dust off her own nose. This comic part is usually played by a man, as are a number of female character roles in the international repertory, including the Widow Simone in *La Fille Mal Gardée*, the evil Carabosse in *The Sleeping Beauty*, and Madge, the witch, in *La Sylphide*. It is an old tradition. The juniors have discovered two tutus—fancy short dance skirts—and parade around with them excitedly. They leave for a moment and come back wearing their white party dresses. Lining up in a double row and trying to maintain discipline, they can barely contain their curiosity until a corps of cadets, headed by the Old General, the headmaster, marches on in regiment formation.

The cadets and the girls face each other, as the Old General and the Headmistress offer elaborate salutations. The General is old and creaky but still regal. The cadets bow on cue. One of the junior girls, urged by her friends, approaches the cadet regiment but, embarrassingly, she trips and falls—splat—right in front of them. The boys are good-natured about it, however, and do not tease her. Then a shy young cadet, virtually pushed by his buddies, approaches the girls and bows; one of them

Graduation Ball, American Ballet Theatre.

accepts his offer to dance. They start to waltz, and the others, encouraged, all choose partners. Soon the entire room is waltzing.

It is time for the entertainment to begin. A drummer struts to martial music, beating his drum, twirling his drumsticks. He marches around locking his knees and clicking his heels. His solo is full of flashy tricks. In contrast, a moonlit *pas de deux*, in the Romantic style of the mid-19th century, follows. The woman wears a long gauze skirt and the man is dressed in a kilt, an obvious reference to *La Sylphide*. He lifts her in *arabesque* so that her torso rests on his shoulder; she appears to be floating.

Meanwhile, the Old General and the Headmistress are losing no time in getting better acquainted. One of the youngest girls, who has trouble with her wayward pigtails, does a gay and perky solo, full of skips, turns, and leaps. The students mill around excitedly in anticipation of a contest. Exercise barres are set up, and the two contestants, now dressed in the tutus, do their warm-ups. They kick high, stretch their legs, and for their feet, do a series of *relevés* onto pointe—that is, they rise to pointe from the full foot, descend, and rise again—an exercise that is more than familiar to all female ballet students. The first girl shows off with multiple *fouettés*, inserting double spins in between and ending with a flourish by jumping onto pointe; the second girl turns with one leg extended to the side, then pirouettes backward in *arabesque* and *attitude*. More turns follow, and soon the two are spinning together, causing great excitement among the audience, both on stage and in the theater. Lichine, as a dancer, was adept at *pirouettes* and used many, many of them in this ballet—not the first instance in which a choreographer has favored steps in which he himself excels. (August Bournonville, the most famous choreographer in Danish history, oriented his technique around his strong points as a dancer.) It is a tie! Both girls win, and red prize ribbons are placed around their necks.

All the youngsters depart for supper, leaving the Old General and the Headmistress alone, and they seize the opportunity for a flirtatious *pas de deux*. He bows low, and they do a little *czardas* together. While he kneels and extends his hand, she circles around him. She seems to flee, shyly; he pursues her, and the pace actually becomes quite lively. He even lifts her several times, but she suffers a slight fainting spell. Suddenly all the students return, and there is a gay, helter-skelter finale with a lot of running around. The party is at an end. The boys resume their rectangular regiment formation and march out in unison, headed by their Old General. The girls look after them and wave goodbye. For the audience, too, the fun is over.

EUGENE LORING

*I*n the 1930s, ballet, an old-world art with hundreds of years of tradition, was in the process of digging roots in virgin American soil. For ballet to become an integral part of the American scene, it had to add an American flavor to its European tradition. For the first time, ballets with American themes were clearly in demand. Most of the ballet teachers in the United States were Russian and consequently the technique taught was of Russian origin. But, while building on the inherited academic foundation, the stylistic possibilities of ballet were transformed by its exposure to a radically different cultural climate.

Eugene Loring (1914–1982) was in many ways representative of the spirit America brought to ballet. He was an energetic if unpolished all-around "theater person," who started his formal ballet training late but eventually succeeded in combining his native agility and sense of rhythm with the rudiments of a Russian ballet technique. The story goes that when, in the early 1930s, a youthful Loring journeyed to New York to audition for the ballet master Michel Fokine, the young man could not even complete a double *pirouette*. Nonetheless, even the stern Fokine was so impressed by Loring's gymnastic build, musicality, and intense determination (in many ways the raw material of American ballet), that he encouraged him to continue. Only a few years later, Loring was accepted as a dancer in Ballet Caravan (one of the precursors of the New York City Ballet), a small touring company playing in school gyms and movie houses across the country; he was soon choreographing for that same company.

BILLY THE KID

Choreography by Eugene Loring, 1938; music by Aaron Copland; scenery and costumes by Jared French.

Ballet Caravan's director, Lincoln Kirstein, suggested that Loring compose a ballet based on the well-known legend of Billy the Kid. Kirstein's libretto for the ballet, which unfolds in 12 scenes, paid more attention to fiction than fact, as do most treatments of the famous outlaw. William Bonney was actually a mean-spirited American desperado who went west with his mother just after the Civil War and is believed guilty of some half-dozen murders (not counting Indians and Mexicans) before meeting his own demise at the hands of Pat Garrett at the age of 21. He seems to have been of an unpredictable, possibly psychopathic nature, albeit somewhat of a lady's man. The ballet version emphasizes Billy's savage temper, desperado gunslinging, and romantic appeal, while blaming Billy's murderous instincts on the fictional murder of his mother in the opening scene. Kirstein also invented an Alias figure, a single man who returns in various guises to represent every man that Billy shoots. (Kirstein wrote that the single recurring victim avoided having to clutter up the stage with corpses.) In all, the story of Billy is approached as one step in the necessary establishment of law and order in the West.

Because the ballet's larger theme is the time in which Billy lived, it both opens and closes with pioneer men and women marching westward through a flat and arid prairie. A pioneer figure leads the way for the wagon train; men and women press forward with insistent, strong movements, fall backward, and again press forward with renewed determination. In the next scene, we arrive on the main street of a desert town, where demurely bonneted housewives, brazen dance-hall girls, energetic cowboys, and assorted Mexicans mingle. Billy as a small boy and his Mother enter, Billy shyly clinging to his Mother's skirts. Just then, a fight breaks out and a Mexican's stray bullet strikes and kills Billy's Mother. Blazing with rage, Billy stabs the Mexican in the back so quickly that no one can stop him. This is the first man Billy kills, and the victim will return as Alias in subsequent scenes.

After an interlude in which the dancers rotate in concentric circles, presumably to represent the completion of several year cycles, Billy returns as a grown man. Swaggering defiantly, Billy then practices spinning and aiming his gun, concentrating with animal intensity. Billy hides and then, seemingly for the sheer thrill of it, shoots down a Land Agent passing on horseback. Next, Billy plays cards with Pat Garrett and some others gathered around a campfire. When Billy is accused of cheating, his fearsome temper flares, and the Kid once again hits the trigger and kills a man. Garrett sticks a gun in the young bandit's back and leads him off to jail. As if relieved by Billy's departure, the townsfolk dance, leaving only Billy's Mexican Sweetheart to wander plaintively through the crowd in search of her beloved.

In jail, Billy convinces his guard to play some cards, but the moment the jailer turns his back, lightning-fast Billy grabs his gun and shoots him. Billy then gallops off into the hills, led by an Indian guide to a hiding place where his Sweetheart will join him. Left alone in the desert, Billy falls asleep and dreams of his Sweetheart, an idealized feminine figure veiled in gossamer, who appears to dance a *pas de deux* with him.

Awakening suddenly and instinctively sensing danger, Billy strains to hear distant sounds in the silence. Indeed, his instincts are correct, as his Indian guide has betrayed him and is sneaking up on him with Pat Garrett. Tense to the breaking point, Billy abruptly yells out "*¿Quién es?*"—"Who is it?" in Spanish. Waiting in the menacing stillness, Billy strikes a match to light a cigarette. The moment the outlaw's face is illuminated, Garrett shoots him dead. The stage lights up as Mexican women file by, shrouded in dark shawls, to mourn the slain youth. The Epilogue—a continuation of the Prologue's march westward—immediately ensues. This time the pioneers hesitate even less in the march forward, as if the demise of Billy, symbol of lawlessness, has given them new strength to go forward.

Billy the Kid is more of a danced theater piece than a traditional ballet. Loring's concern was for theatricality and strong characterization rather than for recognizable ballet steps. Indians sneak around stealthily in moccasins, dance-hall girls flaunt their legs, housewives have straight backs and a demure gaze, and

Terry Orr and Marianna Tcherkassky in *Billy the Kid*, American
Ballet Theatre (Courtesy *Dance in America*, WNET).

the townsfolk dance in a down-home, folksy style. The cowboys, moving with bent, parallel legs, provide plenty of jumping, lassoing, and rhythmic horseback riding. Throughout, a constant, underlying theme is established by the "one-two-three-hop" rhythm of the men riding horses. The swaggering, defensive Billy grows from a coltish boy to a stalking, pacing "beast," characterized by abrupt, virile, tense movements. In all, Loring chose his movements "democratically," using what Kirstein described as "a grain of gesture which only someone who has been brought up here could have felt."

Loring turned to the classical idiom twice in the ballet, both times for explicitly expressive purposes. Every time Billy is just about to commit a murder, he whips around in a double turn in the air. Loring explained, "This isn't a technical thing but an emotional one. It seemed to me that before doing such an act, one would be in a state of white heat—an explosion of temper would go through the body—and that's how he expresses it. The leap and aerial turn are an extension in movement of his inner feeling." The Mexican Sweetheart, in contrast to the other women, dances her tender duet on pointe. This is to express her unreal, dreamlike quality. Danced by the same woman who plays Billy's mother in the beginning, she is clearly more of an idealized than specific feminine figure.

Billy the Kid may not be brilliant ballet, but it has proved to be very successful theater. There is a careful sense of pacing and sustained tension throughout. Loring collaborated with Aaron Copland, who provided the evocative score. Composer and choreographer agreed that silence was the most violent of sounds, and every murder, except Billy's, is executed in abrupt silence. The idea of a character suddenly yelling something out is also a novel approach to sound effects in a ballet.

Billy the Kid was not only Ballet Caravan's biggest hit, it is the only work from that company's repertory that is still seen today. When the Ballet Theatre was organized in 1939, Loring joined as dancer and choreographer. His *Billy* has been performed by that company since 1940.

JEROME ROBBINS

Jerome Robbins (b. 1918) has been called the greatest American-born choreographer of classical ballet. He is also known as a brilliant Broadway, Hollywood, and television director and choreographer—as *West Side Story, Fiddler on the Roof, The King and I,* and *Peter Pan,* among others, attest. Robbins seems to have a golden touch in all branches of theater. Since his overnight success as a young man with *Fancy Free,* he has created both serious and commercial works in a steady stream. Years ago he could have retired on the royalties from one of his smash hits, yet he has continued to produce and to dare to do just about anything. A glance at Robbins's career shows that his success is not built on trends or gimmicks, although he seems to have been born with an instinct for theatrical showmanship and for clever tricks and jokes. But, rather than relying exclusively on these inherent talents, he has honed and enlarged them by reaching beyond. Above all, he is a choreographic craftsman, creator of works of substance.

Robbins went through the most exacting kind of apprenticeship—performing in ballet companies and shows, studying all kinds of dancing, researching in libraries. He was and is a constant spectator in the performing arts arena. (Many choreographers rarely venture out of their own theaters; Robbins can be seen at performances all over New York.) He is the product of a thoroughly American type of training. In this country, we have never had the large state-supported dance academies of Europe; in addition, there have been no state-supported, official, or national companies—hence, no single, accepted way to dance. There are also few pensions and no guarantees (as there are in Europe, where dancers are civil-service employees). In America, one must make one's own way from beginning to end.

There is no security in the dance profession; but, on the other side of the coin, there is tremendous freedom because there is no "one way" to succeed. Formulas do not work for long, and dancers cannot rely on official institutions to back them up when they get older or cease to produce. Even in the big companies, a dancer is only useful as long as he or she can dance well; new contracts are negotiated every season. Broadway shows offer even less security, opening and closing with regularity; show dancers, like actors, are always looking for their next job. All this is to say that American dancers must be ready for anything, because the more skills they have, the more opportunities they make for themselves.

Robbins grew up in this atmosphere of training for any contingency. He studied not only ballet, but Oriental, Spanish, and modern dance. He was also a student of acting, piano, and violin. Although he seems now to have settled into choreographing for ballet, for a long time, both as performer and creator, he used many of his other skills as well. He first appeared in Yiddish theater, then danced in summer-stock musicals, before joining Ballet Theatre (now American Ballet Theatre), where he achieved the rank of soloist. There he excelled in humorous character parts, but also danced the dark Petrouchka. As a choreographer, none of his training remained unused. He is known for his extraordinary versatility, and every Robbins work is different from every other. He has created classical ballets, works in which jazz dance predominates, and dances based on all kinds of ethnic material. His work also shows an awareness of modern dance. He has produced comedies, dramas, and plotless works, using concert music, popular music, and no music at all.

In 1944, at the age of 25, Robbins choreographed *Fancy Free*, his first ballet, to music commissioned from Leonard Bernstein; it is still in the active repertory. It formed the basis for the musical *On the Town*, first a Broadway and then a Hollywood production, and Robbins went on to choreograph one ballet and one musical each year, on the average. In 1949, he became associated with the New York City Ballet as dancer and choreographer while continuing his activity in the theater. Seven years later he left to run his own company, Ballets: U.S.A., which toured in this country and in Europe. Then came a period devoted to Broadway and an experimental workshop at the American Theatre

Laboratory (New York). No one knows exactly what went on—the participants were sworn to secrecy. In 1969, he returned to the New York City Ballet, where he remained almost exclusively until 1990. In attaching himself to the preeminent choreographer of our day, Robbins perhaps believed that Balanchine's vision was the only solid bedrock in a field—show business—in which flashy fakery and expediency are common coin. He has also said that he was interested in working alone with dancers rather than in the collaborative atmosphere that musicals require.

On Balanchine's death in 1983, Robbins was named co-Ballet Master in Chief of the New York City Ballet, sharing leadership duties with Peter Martins. In 1988, he took a sabbatical to direct *Jerome Robbins' Broadway*, a retrospective of his dances for the Broadway stage. The award-winning show became one more in his long list of smash hits.

FANCY FREE

Choreography by Jerome Robbins, 1944; music by Leonard Bernstein; scenery by Oliver Smith; costumes by Kermit Love.

At the time of its premiere, *Fancy Free* was as topical as a newspaper headline, and, amazingly, it retains its freshness even now. The ballet concerns three sailors on shore leave for the evening in Manhattan. They come into a bar, have some drinks, try to pick up some girls, and do a lot of dancing. In 1944, World War II was still in progress, and sailors were a common sight in the streets of port cities, but no one had thought of making a ballet about them. Robbins's work revolved around a type as American as the cowboy—this time, however, not a creature of folklore but one that was completely contemporary.

In his scenario, he described the work as a ''jazz ballet, light in mood.'' Although it was created for a ballet company and utilizes the technique of classically trained dancers, it has few recognizable classical ballet steps; rather, it reminds us of show dancing, vaudeville, and hoofing. There are no toe shoes, and the costumes are white summer sailor suits, slinky street clothes, and high heels. The ballet is full of brass and brashness, jazz, jive, boogie-woogie, and blues. Its good humor is pervasive.

Peter Martins, Bart Cook, and Jean-Pierre Frolich in *Fancy Free*,
New York City Ballet.

Some slick movements, such as sliding across the floor in a split, hip wiggling, "over-the-barrel" leaps, and syncopated jumps (with the dancer landing a second after the musical beat) bring to mind Gene Kelly movies of the 1940s (and, indeed, Kelly did star in *On the Town*). Robbins also used acrobatics, ballroom dancing, and a touch of Harlem rhythm.

The scene is an empty bar, with Manhattan skyscrapers visible through the windows. It is a hot summer night. As the Bartender awaits the next customer, with a crash from the orchestra, the three sailors burst in—an ingratiating trio full of high spirits and in search of adventure (that means girls). After downing beer, they split a piece of gum, leave the bar, and look around for action. A girl appears, carrying a red purse, and is immediately surrounded by the three. After a bit of a skirmish, two of them pursue her; the other, giving up, soon finds his own companion when another girl pauses under a lamppost to read the newspaper. They go into a bar. Blackout.

When the lights come up, it is clear that the two have been sitting over their beer for quite a while. They get up to dance a blues *pas de deux*, complete with jitterbug lifts—a dreamy interlude after the fast-paced opening. Robbins described this dance as "somewhat torchy." The two are attracted to each other, alternating lighthearted gestures with movements of some intensity. A sexy undercurrent is not missing. They resume their conversation but are interrupted when the others return. Now there are three sailors for two girls—impossible arithmetic. After more skirmishes, the sailors decide to compete for the girls by presenting solo exhibitions of virtuosity. Their personalities are succinctly revealed by the way they dance. The first sailor, an extrovert, ends by jumping onto the bar, after somersaults, splits, and double turns in the air. The second is more lyrical, almost wistful. His variation has been described as "a danced love song in three parts, with a flavor of jazz," and he is known as the "romantic" sailor. The third dances to Latin rhythms, with snakelike movements of agility and humor. Robbins designed this part for himself. These variations are the choreographic high point of the ballet.

But as they end, the situation on the stage is still unresolved—there are still three and two. A fight breaks out, this time a serious one, and the girls, afraid, make their escape. The sailors fail to notice; they are much too involved with their knock-down, drag-out struggle and wind up in a heap on the floor. When they finally see that the girls are gone, they realize their fighting is pretty silly. They make peace and laugh at their own stupidity. Perhaps it's time for another drink and another three-way piece of gum. A third girl walks past. The sailors look at each other and shrug, then one of them bolts after her, with the others following in hot pursuit.

INTERPLAY

Choreography by Jerome Robbins, 1945; music by Morton Gould (American Concertette); *costumes by Irene Sharaff.*

With *Interplay*, Robbins was instantly recognized as a serious ballet choreographer, more than a one-shot success (after *Fancy Free* in 1944). It was also clear the he had something very American to say.

In those days, the American idiom in classical ballet was still in the process of evolution. Only a day before, so it seems, *Rodeo* (by Agnes de Mille) made a splashy debut—a cowboy saga, destined for long life. About the same time, other aspects of Americana—*Billy the Kid, Yankee Clipper, Frankie and Johnny*—were beginning to gain acceptance as the legitimate province of the ballet, supplanting kings and queens or foreign exotica. And, with *Frontier* (1935) and *Appalachian Spring* (1944), Martha Graham, in modern dance, brought American pioneers to the concert stage. But there had not been many (if any) abstract works in which the characters were recognizably American types. *Interplay* was such a ballet.

Robbins presented a new image of American dancers—sporty, energetic, "loose." The movements were as typical of the era of bebop, boogie woogie, and 1940s jazz as the *West Side Story* street-gang dances would be for the 1960s. In his use of contemporary material, Robbins took his cue from the music and, like the score, incorporated this within a classical framework. *Interplay* uses pure ballet technique, with a few syncopations, hip wiggles, and cartwheels. It is an entirely formal composition with neither story line nor character. Robbins's four pairs of dancers—in crew cuts and ponytails—could only be

Americans—"Dead End Kids right off the sidewalks of New York." They run, skip, and leap for the sheer fun of it and compete with each other in fancy turns and nonstop locomotion. It all gives the impression of unharnessed exuberance and youthful highjinks. In keeping with its image of youth, there is also a romantic interlude—a soulful blues *pas de deux*.

The curtain rises on a single man—an athlete. He swivels around, raises his arms to the ceiling, and bounds across the stage. Another man enters downstage, also with a swivel. They signal to each other, obviously comrades. A third and a fourth man enter. All join arms, facing the back, and do a rhythmic step across the stage. One breaks away, pirouettes, turns in the air. All swivel and dance together, copying each other's movements. Their steps are long and loose. They do more turns, play leapfrog, and challenge each other to turning duels. After many spins, they lie on the floor.

Playfully, the girls enter, one at a time, frolicking among the men. All form a diagonal line to do sequential spins. They clap hands, then leap in a split. The girls fall against the boys on the ground. They are spun around on their behinds. All do a *pirouette* to a split as one man struts along. The others get up and imitate him. They all run around in a circle and down to the edge of the stage, looking into the orchestra pit. They are silhouetted. The music "sends" two of them off into a jitterbug. More spins, more high kicks, more jitterbugging. The dancers circle the stage, "glad-handing" each other. The men flip the girls over their backs, then somersault forward to a cross-legged seated position, as the girls perkily hold their hands high. The second movement is for the most exuberant of the men. He is a kind of a jokester. He does a *pirouette* with his head stuck into his shoulders, takes an *arabesque* fluttering his hands above his head like bird's wings, shuffles about, wiggles his behind, and snaps his fingers. Occasionally, he persuades one of the girls to join him. He bounds all over the stage with flips in the air. After double turns in the air, he peddles as though on a bicycle, then kneels as two girls extend their arms in his direction, as if presenting a vaudeville act.

The lights lower and the music becomes more moody. It is time for romance. A man and a woman sway back and forth together. Their *pas de deux* is a mixture of "showbiz" and ballet. After some syncopated shuffles, she leaps onto his shoulder,

Peter Frame and Lourdes Lopez in *Interplay*, New York City Ballet.

wrapping her arms as though swimming underwater. He lowers her into *arabesque*; she pulls back, and they hold each other at arm's length. She extends her leg forward and swivels around, winding up on his back (as he turns), then slides down to her knee with one leg extended in *arabesque*. She swivels up, and they again sway together to blues music, snapping their fingers. In the background, silhouetted figures sway and snap their fingers, too.

After her tiny steps on pointe in a circle (*bourrées*), he lifts her in a fish dive—probably the first time this famous and grand step has been done to jazzy rather than imperial music. She goes into a *pirouette* and catches him at arm's length, with one leg extended to the side. She turns backward and he lowers her, holding her under the arms as she ''propels'' her feet forward on pointe, while still remaining low, like a wheelbarrow. Entwining while turning, both eventually slide down to an intimate seated position together. In this *pas de deux*, full of original and different steps and partnering combinations, Robbins demonstrates how new material can fit within a traditional framework.

Like a sunburst, the first man bounds out of the wings, urging his companies to join. Soon all are jumping, spinning, lunging, and skipping about. They choose sides; two teams are lined up diagonally. One side performs, beating and kicking. Both groups huddle in circles, as though discussing football strategy, stopping to look at the opposition from time to time. The two sides then shake hands and cartwheel to the edges, and each dancer has a moment of showing off. The men do double turns in the air, the girls spin. Soon all are leaping and skipping across the stage. After a cartwheel, all run to the back. They dash down to the footlights. The girls spread their legs and the boys scoot between them, lying on the stage and smiling out to the audience.

Interplay is a young man's—and a young performer's—ballet.

THE CAGE

Choreography by Jerome Robbins, 1951; music by Igor Stravinsky (Concerto in D for String Orchestra); costumes by Ruth Sobotka.

This ferocious ballet—savage, thrilling, terrifying—has the impact of a knockout punch. Robbins created a glittering, feral world in which a tribe of females destroys any male who penetrates its ranks. He left the precise nature of the protagonists ambiguous; they seem part human, part insect. The working title of the ballet was *The Amazons*; perhaps Robbins imagined some sort of superrace, yet many of the movements recall the insect kingdom. Stravinsky's music, although not composed for this ballet, is uncannily apt in its drama, drive, and suspense, interlaced with strains of tenderness.

The curtain rises, taking with it a tangle of ropes, which become taut as the curtain goes up, suggesting a trap or noose. In the half-light we see a group of women in brief costumes decorated with what appears to be vertebrae and intestines. Their hair is completely frizzled, like Medusa. The tallest of these creatures is the Queen. To pounding chords, the women prance on pointe, slightly sway-backed, holding their stomachs. They turn wildly, finishing with a forward thrust of the hand, palm upward. The *corps* circles the Queen in low, sliding steps; they draw forward a small creature whose head is completely bandaged.

This "chrysalis," called the Novice, cowers, knock-kneed, then takes a few tentative steps. The women come closer and run their fingers all over her body. They slither and slide away. The Novice tries to get her bearings. She takes long, slinky sideways steps, then raises her leg in a turned-in position; her hands twitch like antennae. She begins to stalk, in imitation of her sisters, then runs forward, catching her raised legs with her hands, as if locating it in space. She crumples in a heap, then sits on the floor, extending one leg along the ground, flexing her foot. On her hands and knees, she flexes her back, feeling every vertebra. She scrapes one leg with the other, as though exploring its texture—or removing slime. Upright, her arms puff out, and she seems to be touching the space around her.

The music sounds like a roaring train. A male intruder grabs her. Savagely they roll on the floor; she spears him with her foot as he lies there, then kicks him so that he rolls over. She seems to pull out his intestines. There is a pause—a chord— she takes his neck between her legs and twists. He falls away limply. The Novice has one or two seconds of contemplation. She wipes off the insides of her legs thoughtfully. Another pause. The music collects itself as the Novice marches backward with deliberation, then stalks forward in triumph. Out of the darkness the women return, exulting. They throw back their heads as if in a primi-

The Cage, New York City Ballet.

tive victory cry; the Novice has fulfilled her destiny. The women snake around, then pair off for a brief *adagio* (the Novice dances with the Queen).

All harken to a noise, freeze, then rush off. It is another man. The music becomes lyrical for the first time, and the emotional tone changes from relentless to yielding. The man draws the Novice along the floor. He lifts her and turns her. After an *arabesque* and other extensions of one leg, she falls backward into his arms, giving in, using him for support. All her movements are still insectlike in character, but now the Novice is vulnerable, no longer in command. As the man stands with bent knees, she sits on his knees, extending both legs forward off the ground. Her fingers twitch violently. They dance in unison. He lifts her and again she falls in a lunge, depending on him. After a turn, she finds herself twined around him, as both stand upright. Facing each other, they kneel, leaning against each other's palms. He supports her in a series of small leaps, then lifts her high as her feet peddle. With their arms interlaced, they "feel" each other's fingers. He walks forward alone; she imitates him, then does a *pirouette* and falls against him. In the final pose, she is supported between his legs, reaching upward to frame his shoulders as he reaches downward to frame her face. All we really see, in the still-dim light, are the faces and arms. But there is an ominous, nervous tapping sound.

The Novice is sending a warning to the tribe—or a cry for help. She is not completely under the spell of the man. The women reenter immediately, pull the lovers apart, and attack him savagely. They leap viciously around the stage. They pounce and virtually dismember the man. At the moment of the kill, the Queen gives a signal, and the Novice is allowed to pull out his gorge. Nothing is left but to break his neck, like the last Intruder. This the Novice is also permitted to do. There is a triumphal march. Long, low steps alternate with giant perches on pointe. The women extend their arms up to full height, appearing enormous. The Novice, still in wonder, again rubs her legs. Her chest swells, as though she gains strength from the realization that she has again fulfilled her destiny. She wipes off her arms. The music still "rumbles" suspensefully; then, with a clap—like a thunderclap—the ballet is over. As the curtain descends, the ropes go slack.

AFTERNOON OF A FAUN

Choreography by Jerome Robbins, 1953; music by Claude Debussy; scenery and lighting by Jean Rosenthal.

Like the music, Robbins's ballet is essentially a mood piece. It concerns the encounter of two young dancers—a man and a woman—in a practice studio. Although brief (about eight minutes long), the ballet depicts a complete episode in their lives; it also exudes enormous atmosphere.

The world of dancers is a very special one. Because the body is their instrument of expression, dancers have both a unique attachment to and a special distance from their own bodies. Because of the difficult training and the constant physical effort expended, they are more aware of their bodies than other people; at the same time, they are able to analyze them clinically, almost as though they were objects. They are obsessed with their bodies, because they live through them; but they can view them with immense detachment—as a violinist might view his violin or a pianist a new piano. The ballet takes this passionate yet removed self-absorption as its starting point. The sunlit studio is constructed on three sides of white silk walls that billow mysteriously in the wind; on the imaginary fourth wall—the audience—is the mirror to which all dancers are so narcissistically yet, in truth, impersonally, drawn.

A wavering flute, the principal instrument in the piece, ripples down the scale. A young male dancer, nude to the waist, is asleep on the floor. He awakens and stretches languidly, flexing his foot, lifting his chest. He stares at himself in the mirror, swivels, kneels, and stands. He bends to touch his toes, always in slow motion. He examines his foot, then reaches forward to touch the mirror, but steps back as though mesmerized. He stretches, fascinated by the movement of his muscles, then rolls over, and sleeps again.

A young woman—the Nymph—picks her way into the studio on pointe. Her hair is loose, and she is just tying the sash of her practice tunic. She approaches her image in the mirror. Watching, she kneels, bends back, then forward, brushing her long hair forward off her neck, seemingly to exult in her physicality. She brushes her hair back, arches, and turns slowly from side to side. Just at the moment she catches sight of the man, he wakes up and sees her. Although they see each other only in the mirror, they are almost uncomfortably aware of each other's presence. The atmosphere is electric.

Slowly the woman begins her barre exercises. In the middle of a side leg extension, he wafts her up and away, so that she appears to be floating unaided. As they dance together, he manipulates her as if trying for sculptural designs; both watch the effect in the mirror, always with wonder. They do not look at each other, but make contact through their reflections, and both move slowly, almost as if under water. The man caresses the woman's hair, stroking it to the tips. As he bends to kiss it, she rises suddenly onto pointe, facing him in *attitude.* Very slowly he lowers her (still on pointe); both sit, joining their arms in an arc above their heads. She runs away. From opposite ends of the studio, they approach each other in long sliding steps along the floor. Guiding himself in the mirror, he cups her face in his hands, then reaches through his arms and in a minute he is holding her off the ground in a tense horizontal position. She wilts and goes limp. They face each other kneeling. For the first time he looks at her rather than her reflection, and kisses her cheek. She seems transfixed, barely awakened from her reverie.

Slowly she raises her hand to touch that cheek. It is not at all clear whether he has made a sexual advance or has merely tried another pose for the mirror. The woman walks backward, as if in a daze, then picks her way on pointe out of the studio. The man remains, lies down, stretches again, rolls over, and sleeps. The brief encounter, with all its ambiguities, is over. Nothing, really, has happened.

The music generates a hot, lush atmosphere, as does the constant contact of beautiful, almost nude, bodies and the woman's long hair frequently brushing across the man's face. The dancers' trancelike involvement in this seemingly highly sensual situation gives the work a special fascination.

More than 40 years earlier, in 1912, Vaslav Nijinsky created a work to the same music, originally given under its French title, *L'Après-midi d'un Faune.* Nijinsky's work was a pivotal one in the history of 20th-century ballet. Thus, Robbins's use of the same

Allegra Kent and Peter Martins in *Afternoon of a Faun*,
New York City Ballet.

music to choreograph a completely different ballet with the same title—which could not help calling to mind Nijinsky's notorious and important work—was particularly audacious.

DANCES AT A GATHERING

Choreography by Jerome Robbins, 1969; music by Frédéric Chopin; costumes by Joe Eula.

With *Dances at a Gathering*, a joyous exhibition of dance, Robbins returned to the New York City Ballet. For more than 10 years he had been active elsewhere—directing his own company, Ballets: U.S.A., and choreographing and directing some of the most successful Broadway productions ever, including *Fiddler on the Roof, West Side Story, Oh Dad, Poor Dad, Mother Courage, Bells Are Ringing, Gypsy,* and *Funny Girl.* He had also been involved with two movies, *The King and I* and *West Side Story,* and had choreographed *Les Noces* for American Ballet Theatre. Many fans of the New York City Ballet had almost forgotten that he had been Associate Artistic Director there from 1949 to 1956.

Dances was an auspicious homecoming, and Robbins was given a thundering welcome by press and public alike. By his admission, his inspiration was Chopin's music. The ballet has no programmatic content, no reference to a story or situation, and barely any hint of relationships among the participants. Clearly, they are good friends, but it is hard to say more. The ballet takes place in a large open space with a blue sky and clouds in the background—perhaps it is a sunny meadow at midday. Robbins's original idea was to create a *pas de deux* to Chopin piano music, but the more he listened to Chopin, the more ideas he had. Soon he added four more dancers, then more, finally arriving at a cast of ten. After he had completed several dances, he showed them to George Balanchine, who encouraged him to add more—enough to make a full hour of dancing.

Following the music (a number of short piano pieces), Robbins created a series of *divertissements,* ranging in mood from dramatic to lighthearted, from brooding to flirtatious, from competitive to wistful to exuberant. Indeed, he touched on a wide array of human emotions. The five women wear calf-length chiffon dresses and have ribbons in their hair, the men are in shirts, tights, and boots. They are identified in the program only by the color of their costumes.

The ballet makes immense technical demands on the dancers—steps range from the understated to the openly spectacular. Particularly inventive are the many lifts. A man scoops a woman off her feet into a beautiful arc, another into a dramatic upside-down thrust, a third into an unexpected lunge upward. Robbins tinged the steps with a Slavic feeling (Chopin was Polish, and there are traces of this in his music)— the dancers brush the floor with their feet, stamp the ground, and put their arms akimbo or their hands at the backs of their heads.

As the ballet begins, a boy in brown comes on, his back to the audience. He gazes at the sky, lost in thought. Almost unnoticeably he begins to move, swaying gently to the music. He clicks his heels as in a *mazurka*, then suddenly he is running freely across the stage. A boy in green and a girl in lavender enter. To a lilting waltz, they walk arm in arm, then become more open and expansive in their gestures. He sweeps her up and off.

The girl in pink and boy in mauve dance to another *mazurka*. He lifts her in an angellike position, her arms wide. They look squarely at each other while continuing their dance, with slight hints of *mazurka* steps in their hops. Lifting her upside down, he carries her away. Now others enter. The pace quickens, and the mood becomes more lively. The boy in mauve does double turns in the air, landing in a very deep knee bend (*plié*). Other boys leap. In an amusing section, the assembled company stares straight forward stiffly, as though posing for a Victorian photographer. With a laugh, they break it up and leave.

The stage darkens. To a slow, dirgelike *mazurka*, three couples enter. The atmosphere is elegiac, thoughtful. The girl in lavender is lifted; her foot seems to paw the ground. Many of the steps are based on ballroom dancing. In a playful mood, a couple enters, waltzing around each other. They tap each other's hands, like patty-cake. She perches atop him, her body curled around his shoulders. Then she dives into his arms. Dark clouds seem to gather, and a ruminative mood descends. The girls slowly turn from foot to foot (*chaîné* turns), without apparent motivation. They seem to be going nowhere. There are abrupt

Sean Lavery, Judith Fugate, and Robert Maiorano in *Dances at a Gathering*, New York City Ballet.

mood changes, from dark to light to dark again. This is followed by a spritely contest between two boys. They try to stare each other down; one tries to outdance the other. They sidle up, the smaller boy following the taller like a dog yipping at his master's heels. There is a comradely exit.

A thoughtful solo for a woman is a highlight among many highlights—one of the most original moments in the ballet. The woman seems to be half-dancing. She is ''marking''—that is, indicating—the steps. All the accents are there, but the movements are not executed in full. It is as though she had not danced for many years and is remembering what it was like to dance once, long ago. She curtsies, wistfully. There is no one to see (or applaud) her.

The real fireworks begin with a brilliant waltz for three couples. It contains showy steps, including some very fancy supported leaps. The beat is large, and the dancers dig in with gusto. They waltz, ballroom style; then the girls are swung around, low to the ground, by their partners. The climax comes as each girl is thrown by one man into the waiting arms of another; the last girl daringly flips twice in the air before being caught. Covering space—both the ground and the air—seems to be the motif of this dance, as everyone runs all over the stage.

When the excitement dies down, a lone girl enters. As she dances, a man walks by. He keeps on walking—right off the stage. Another man enters, and the girl dances for him, circling him with leaps. How can he fail to notice her? But he does, continuing on his way. A third man is equally oblivious. Three tries are enough, so with a wistful wave and a shrug, the girl is off. A vigorous jumping dance for a man and a woman, full of dramatic intonation, follows. To whirlwind music, lighter in feeling, the man leaps in large, soft arcs with many changes of direction and *pirouettes* with very pointed accents. The next moments are dramatic, with an almost tragic feeling—by turns dark, brooding, and agitated. The jumps seem almost angry, the whipping turns slice the air—thrusting, troubled. When the stage is almost empty, a couple sits on the ground, each dancer reaching out to touch the other. Others reenter. Then all the dancers hurry off the stage in different directions.

The finale is mellow, reflective, a nocturne. The dancers come on one by one, now calm, now thoughtful. They acknowledge each other's presence. The boy in brown touches the floor. There is a sudden rumble, an ominous portent. The dancers all appear to be watching something in the sky. Invisibly, it crosses the stage, and all follow it with their eyes. Finally, there is a gentle resolution. The boys bow, the girls curtsy. Peace and calm are restored. The dance is over.

When Robbins created this rich, overflowing work, he described it as ''a fairly classical ballet to very old-fashioned and romantic music . . . a revolt against the faddism of today [1969]. . . . I find myself feeling just what's the matter with love, what's the matter with celebrating positive things?'' In this radiant ballet, he did just that.

ANTONY TUDOR

Antony Tudor, like Sir Frederick Ashton, was an integral part of the effort to establish a national ballet in Great Britain in the 1930s. In the same years that Ninette de Valois and Ashton were working to found a British company with a mostly classical repertory, Marie Rambert operated her own Ballet Rambert, which was exclusively interested in fostering new and original choreography. Tudor joined the Ballet Rambert in 1930 and remained with the company for seven years, working as dancer, choreographer, and teacher, as well as often filling the jobs of stagehand, electrician, accompanist, and secretary for the financially crimped organization.

In 1936, Tudor choreographed *Jardin aux Lilas (Lilac Garden)*, considered by many to be Britain's first ballet masterpiece. This helped to earn Tudor's reputation as one of the "founding fathers" of the British ballet. Actually, Tudor's major contribution to ballet was not to be in England, for in 1939 he accepted an invitation to work with Ballet Theatre, a new company then forming in New York. Ballet Theatre (now American Ballet Theatre and ranked among the foremost in the world) saw itself as, in part, a ballet museum, with a repertory that ranged from classical to contemporary to specifically American ballets. From the beginning, Tudor, with his novel approach to creating dances, contributed much to the company's reputation.

Tudor was interested in using ballet to express the workings of his characters' minds. His approach is often called "psychological" because of his interest in projecting internal emotions, in delineating relationships among people, and in sustaining a dramatic mood. He said, "Drama usually deals with the spoken word. Drama in ballet is the same thing but without the voice and without anything that the voice could say rather better than it is said in movement." How could one "say things" more eloquently in movement than in words? Tudor, a sharp observer of the human scene, believed that everything about a person's movement reveals something of his personality. Consequently, he used all elements of carriage and motion as clues to an individual's state of mind. The way someone walks or holds his arms—his very posture—are keys to a character. Subtle juxtapositions of body parts—a pelvis thrust forward counterbalanced by a twisted torso, for example—can indicate conflict in Tudor's choreographic language.

Nonetheless, Tudor's works are essentially balletic in that they fully utilize the resources of the classical dance, albeit in a highly selective and expressive manner. A series of fast *pirouettes* becomes an expression of frenzy, a bounding leap the equivalent of a sudden release of tension, an *arabesque*, with its oppositional stretch between the leg and torso, becomes symbolic of internal discord. Although the classical ballet provides the underlying fabric of Tudor's work, there is a complete avoidance of the "stop-and-start" *divertissement* style. Never is a step performed that does not serve the dramatic progress of the work. The ballets are seamless, flowing, "all of a piece," giving the impression of a stream-of-consciousness outpouring of movement.

Gesture, too, in a near-pantomimic if somewhat stylized sense, is an important tool for Tudor. He uses movement from everyday life—straightening one's clothes, pushing back some stray hair, a handshake. It is the way in which the individual does these familiar things that helps set the psychological tone. The gestures fit unobtrusively within the fabric of movement, suit the music, and seem part of the dance flow while making the dance more "readable." Tudor said, "I would only do dance drama in an obvious way because I want everyone in the audience to understand."

Tudor, although not prolific, choreographed an interesting variety of ballets. Among the most outstanding are *Jardin aux Lilas* (1936), *Dark Elegies* (1937), *Judgment of Paris* (1938), *Pillar of Fire* (1942), *Romeo and Juliet* (1943), and *The Leaves Are Fading* (1975).

LILAC GARDEN
(Jardin aux Lilas)

Choreography by Antony Tudor, 1936; music by Ernest Chausson; scenery and costumes for first production by Hugh Stevenson.

Tudor's first and most enduring masterpiece is a ballet about conflict between the characters' real feelings and the poses they must maintain, between individual passions and the demands of a structured social world. The program of the ballet summarizes the plot: "Caroline is about to enter upon a marriage of convenience, but gives a farewell party before the ceremony. Among the guests is the man she really loves and the woman who, unknown to her, has been her fiancé's mistress. The ballet is a series of meetings and partings and interrupted confidences, until at the end Caroline, without the opportunity to take a final farewell of Her Lover, has to leave on the arm of her fiancé." The ballet portrays the four characters as they struggle to suppress their true feelings. Flashes of genuine emotion break through, only to be checked by a social force they are all sadly resigned to accept.

The action is set in a gracious, fragrant lilac garden through which the four protagonists and their guests pass in a whirl of furtive meetings, interrupted encounters, hasty resumptions of propriety in a frustrating crisscross of desire. It begins with Caroline and the Man She Must Marry standing among the lilac shrubs. Caroline's true lover enters, but she motions him away and takes the arm of her fiancé instead. The fiancé's ex-mistress enters and Caroline greets her, unaware of who she really is. Caroline, left alone, is joined by her real love. They dance together briefly, Caroline constantly glancing around nervously. Just as Her Lover kisses her hand, the fiancé's ex-mistress enters and turns to face them. Caroline quickly retracts her hand. Two men join the scene and exit with the woman. Caroline, left alone, dances a soliloquy, ending with spinning *pirouettes* on the other side of the garden, where Her Lover catches her and lifts her high in the air. Three couples and a single girl now join them, and Her Lover takes the girl for a partner, leaving Caroline alone. The Woman in His Past wanders back on the scene, searching

Fernando Bujones, Natalia Makarova, Gayle Young, and Martine van Hamel in *Lilac Garden*, American Ballet Theatre.

for someone. All the others clear the stage, allowing for a brief meeting of the Woman and Caroline's fiancé. The Woman runs and leaps into his arms and he holds her high over his head. Just as he releases her, the other guests stroll back into the garden. Ironically, Caroline's Lover lifts the ex-mistress just as her fiancé lifts her.

Caroline is again left briefly alone with Her Lover, but this time two of the older women see the couple together. One of the women clasps Caroline's hand in sympathy, but Caroline pulls away to bury her face in her hands. When Her Lover returns, the older women leave them for a moment before the fiancé comes back and the engaged couple walk away together; the Lover walks off alone. Caroline and the Man She Must Marry dance with two other couples in a stilted manner while the Woman tries almost desperately to approach Her Lover. Caroline and the ex-mistress both wander off, and the fiancé, clearly anxious, follows. Caroline now reenters with Her Lover, and they dance together frantically. When the fiancé enters, his ex-mistress leaps into his arms. The other guests enter and just as the music is about to reach a climax, they all freeze in a motionless tableau.

Caroline is the first to move. The four protagonists step forward slowly, hypnotically, in a straight line, with Caroline and Her Lover on opposite ends. The two couples—but not the right ones—dance. Caroline's Lover rushes off and returns with some flowers that he presses into her hand. The fiancé returns with her cloak. Caroline gestures farewell to all her guests, and as she extends her arm to Her Lover, her fiancé draws it back. She takes the arm of the Man She Must Marry.

All of the action—entrances, exits, lovers' duets, soliloquies, promenading guests—is part of an uninterrupted flow of movement. Exceptionally, toward the end, everyone suddenly freezes, in painfully trapped positions. It is as if they have been fossilized by the unyielding ambience, as if they have been frozen by their inner constraints.

We immediately learn something about these people from their exaggeratedly stiff carriage. Their repressive moral code makes their movements stilted and "up tight." With the general tone set, it is worth examining the ballet for details. Every movement is carefully chosen for dramatic impact. When Caroline's Lover first enters, she falls back against him in a momentary lapse of bearing. When they first dance together, a finely tuned harmony between them makes their intimacy immediately apparent. Later, when they dance, Caroline's arms become rigid. Her Lover lifts her now-unyielding body vertically up, and with Caroline stretched out stiffly he catches her in a horizontal fall, inches from the ground. Later, when the fiancé lifts Caroline, her arms reach directly above her head and she, significantly, does not touch him. Caroline pirouettes across the garden and, omitting the traditional graceful finish, is caught by Her Lover in mid-spin. The ex-mistress propels herself desperately into Caroline's fiancé's arms in a *grand jeté* (large leap) that is more an explosion of passion than a virtuosic jump. He holds her above his head in a balletic lift, but her neck is arched tensely as he barely acknowledges her presence.

Tudor's brand of realistic, often seemingly involuntary, gesture makes personalities and relationships clear throughout the ballet. The lovers are constantly glancing about furtively and motioning secretly to one another. Left alone, Caroline holds her hand to her head in a gesture of anxiety. When others enter the garden, she moves her hand to pretend she is only smoothing her hair. The older woman, who understands Caroline, takes her hand in a gesture of sympathy. Caroline lifts her hand to her face as if to weep and abruptly pulls it away. Caroline's Lover approaches her with his hands clasped before him in a position both of entrapment and entreaty. He presents Caroline with some lilacs (a clear memento of things past), but she holds them lifelessly in her hands. At the end, when Caroline resignedly takes her fiancé's arm, he pats her hand placatingly. All these gestures fit smoothly into the rhythm and flow of the dance.

Chausson's score is rich, repetitive, and overpoweringly romantic. Tudor chose the music deliberately for the contrast it provided to the ballet's forced events and stunted feelings. Tudor, who claimed to hate counting to music, choreographed with the music as background rather than designing the movement to emanate from the music. For Tudor, the emotion and situation dictated movement. It is instructive to compare this approach with that of another great choreographer, George Balanchine. Balanchine was primarily inspired by the music he chose. Out of the music come the shapes and designs; they exist, like the music, for their own sake. As to the kind of complex dramatic situations Tudor was wont to portray, Balanchine remarked, ''There are no mothers-in-law in ballet.'' Both men, in greatly divergent ways, bent the classic ballet to their own needs.

Tudor mounted *Jardin aux Lilas* in 1940 for Ballet Theatre and it has remained in that repertory ever since. It is also performed by the Royal Ballet, the National Ballet of Canada, and the Pennsylvania Ballet.

Video: HOME.

PILLAR OF FIRE

Choreography by Anthony Tudor, 1942; music by Arnold Schoenberg; scenery and costumes by Jo Mielziner.

Pillar of Fire, like *Jardin aux Lilas*, is a psychological ballet. Its heroine, Hagar, is old enough to fear spinsterhood, particularly since she is unable to relate comfortably to men. She is a product of the waning Victorian era and, like many Tudor protagonists, is caught in agonizing conflict. Inhibited by feelings of guilt and shame, she nonetheless aches for the release of private passions.

The ballet begins in what appears to be twilight on a residential tree-lined street. Hagar, her spine erect, her fists clenched, sits on the front steps of the house. Young couples, free and relaxed, pass by, followed by a group of prim spinsters. She watches the young people with the interest of an outsider and turns away abruptly from the others. Her own two sisters now emerge from the house. The older one, proper and straightlaced, is a clear example of the unemancipated woman. The younger sister, playful and perhaps a bit spoiled, represents the younger generation. Hagar is obviously the ''middle sister,'' caught between the two alternatives and unable to find her own way. A young man strolls over from across the street. Hagar is too shy to engage his attention, although it seems she wishes she could. He disappears into the house with Hagar's sisters, leaving her alone. While no one is watching, the tormented state

Nora Kaye in *Pillar of Fire*, American Ballet Theatre.

of Hagar's soul is revealed. She gives in to her pent-up anxieties and collapses against the steps. She gets up, twists and distorts her body, rushes in one direction then the next, pirouettes in a frenzy of turns that end with a fall to the floor.

A house stands across the street where shadows of embracing couples are cast against the wall. This bastion of conscience-free abandon magnetizes and repels Hagar; she reaches toward it and hastily retreats. A man walks out of the house and looks her over. Although her body involuntarily stiffens with desire, she is not able to respond. The man goes back into the house across the way just as her young sister emerges with the nice young man, who had originally come to call on Hagar. The girl is flirtatious, perhaps a touch more seductive than innocent. Hagar watches in 'iopeless envy as the pair stroll away. Her body is now contorted as though she is wracked with pain and she turns toward the house across the way as a final hope. The man who eyed her before joins her, and a torrent of sexual energy is released as she flings herself at him. Her body taut with barely suppressed panic, she leaps desperately into his arms and poses in arrested motion. He leads her into the house holding her by the hand.

Hagar emerges from the house, her hysteria only superficially calmed. She is as alone and confused as before, only now she is guilt-ridden as well. A group of couples, Lovers in Experience, emerges from the house across the way and ignores her as they slink by. She is clearly not one of them. Another group, the youthful Lovers in Innocence, also shuns her as they stroll by happily. Her older sister and passing neighbors stare at her with looks of knowing accusation. The nice gentleman caller returns and reaches out to Hagar, but overcome with shame, she cannot respond. She runs from a group of loose women to a group of respectable people and then to the man to whom she gave herself. She is accepted nowhere. The nice man now returns and, although Hagar rushes past him, this time he firmly stops her and insists on dancing with her. Slowly, we see her relax as she learns to trust him, and deliberately, rather than frantically, she gives herself to him. The ballet ends with Hagar and her new-found love walking away slowly arm in arm.

The first things to look for to understand characters of a Tudor ballet are how they carry themselves and the style in which they move. In *Pillar of Fire* we see clear contrasts between the different people. The older sister and townspeople are strained and exaggeratedly prim. The younger sister and the Lovers in Innocence carry themselves naturally and dance with a free-and-easy flow. The Lovers in Experience vamp and slump and swivel their hips and fling themselves around unrestrainedly when they dance.

From the ballet's opening, Hagar is a portrait of frustration, anxiety, and indecision. We meet her sitting up straight and seemingly poised, but her inner tension is clearly manifest in her tightly gripped shoulders and clenched fists. Her gestures—the way she shakes her head, turns away from people, and clutches her solar plexus—are sharp and spasmodic. Her arms, when not hanging lifelessly, are held at a sharp angle to her body. Other parts of her body are also juxtaposed—her pelvis often reaches forward while her torso twists around back. Her solo dance is full of movements illustrative of her "approach-avoidance" conflict. She reaches toward the house across the way with her entire upper body, except for her sharply angled elbows, which pull strongly away. She turns fully away from the house only to drop toward it in a deep back bend. She rushes toward the house with outstretched arms, as if martyrized, each limb pulling in an opposite direction. She frequently turns completely in one direction only to then turn in the opposite direction, a kinetic equivalent to indecision. She often does a classical *arabesque*, but in Tudor's hands the *arabesque*'s inherent oppositional pull is intensified to express conflict. Her legs and arms pull back while her entire torso arches forward. Hagar's striking leap, which seems to freeze in midair, and her *pirouettes* that end on the floor, are additional examples of Tudor's expressive use of the classical vocabulary.

Pillar of Fire is often described as one of Tudor's "pantomime ballets." Although the ballet rests on a foundation of continuous dancing, much of its message is communicated in gestures from everyday life. Their presence in the ballet primes the audience to look for narrative meaning in the "dancier" movements as well, a rewarding search in a Tudor ballet. As we have mentioned, this approach distinguishes Tudor's work from abstract ballet, where movement unfolds for its own sake. Tudor also contributed something new to the *ballet d'action*, or story ballet. Unlike the 19th-century *ballet d'action*, where there is a schism between the mime that furthers the action and the dance that entertains, Tudor wove it all into a unified whole.

Pillar of Fire, composed for Ballet Theatre in 1942, brought Tudor to international attention.

MODERN AND CONTEMPORARY DANCE

Today the distinction between ballet and modern dance is often blurred. Now that it is acceptable for ballet to be danced without toe shoes, to incorporate the floor, or to use the entire body expressively, and, conversely, now that so much of modern dance has acquired the elegance, lightness, and virtuosity of ballet, the difference between the two seems more historical than contemporary. Nevertheless, back in the 1920s and 1930s, when modern-dance pioneers were exploring new movement possibilities, the demarcation was very real and their work bore little resemblance to ballet. They rejected the idea that to be a theatrical dancer necessarily meant subjecting oneself to a preconceived, centuries-old system of movement. They felt that ballet, which they considered bounded by artificial constraints, prescribed attitudes, and limited vocabulary, was incapable of expressing either serious moral or political messages or the deep truths of human emotion. The early moderns sought an original way of moving that could express an individual vision. They then composed dances as expressive vehicles of their movement technique and personal ideas and trained a company of like-minded (and appropriately built) dancers to perform their choreography.

This quest to discover new ways of moving and expression and the rejection of ballet's aesthetics resulted in a strikingly different dance form. Rather than striving to overcome gravity, modern dancers were earthbound; where ballet was fanciful and decorative, modern dance was frank and austere; ballet appeared effortlessly light, while the moderns deliberately emphasized the effort needed to manipulate body weight. While the ballet stressed grace, flow, and curves, the moderns were awkward, angular, and percussive; while the ballet dancer usually held the torso erect and moved the arms and legs, the modern dancers used their entire bodies. The moderns rejected obligatory turnout and pointed feet as well as what they saw as the deification (and dehumanization) of the ballerina. They approached subjects that the ballet, for the most part, never touched—social criticism, political satire, rituals of life and death, and suppressed sexuality.

In our day, however, much as in art, the term "modern" in dance suggests an era and a point of view rather than a work that was created very recently. "Modern dance" has come to be associated with Martha Graham, Doris Humphrey, José Limón, and several other choreographers who were breaking new ground in the late 1920s, the 1930s, and the 1940s. Anna Sokolow, also, has created within this tradition. The other works described in the following section might more properly be called "contemporary dance," or, in the case of Cunningham's *Summerspace*, "avant-garde" or "postmodern." But it is a tricky business to assign labels to current developments in any field. There is a great deal of activity in dance at the moment, and the situation is fluid. Stylistic assessment awaits the historian of the future.

MARTHA GRAHAM

Martha Graham is the foremost and most prolific genius of American modern dance. She is a tenth-generation American, and it has been said that in her penchant for both freedom and discipline, her quest for truth-telling and the exploration of unknown territory, there is much ''Puritan blood'' and ''American bone.'' Born late in the last century, the daughter of strict Presbyterians, she fashioned dances that often depicted the struggle between sexuality and guilt or repression and liberation, and alternated between a castigation and exaltation of the body. Her father, it is often told, warned her as a child that he could discover if she was lying simply from the way she moved. As a grown artist, Graham retained this belief in the revelatory quality of movement, in its capacity to speak of our ''inner landscape.''

Graham was trained at the Denishawn School, which was directed by Ruth St. Denis (1879–1968) and Ted Shawn (1891–1972). There she learned a kind of barefoot, modified ballet, François Delsarte's (1811–1871) movement theories concerning gesture and pantomime, and St. Denis's westernized version of Indian, Oriental, and Near Eastern dance, as well as an approach to dancing to concert music known as ''music visualization.''

Denishawn is credited with being the first company to introduce a serious nonballetic dance to America. Often lavishly costumed and set in ornate surroundings, it emphasized a unique mixture of innovative movement, spirituality, and vaudeville-type entertainment. Graham was doubtlessly influenced by the Denishawn theatricality; in her own works she uses costumes, sets, and props ingeniously. Nonetheless, in 1923 Graham left her mentors to find her own kinetic vocabulary—one that could speak of harsher issues than those concerning Denishawn.

After a two-year stay with the Greenwich Village Follies, Graham taught at the Eastman School of Music in Rochester, New York, where she had the opportunity to experiment with the possibilities of the body in an effort to ''objectify inner truth in physical form.'' She recalls discovering that the body disciplines more than it inhibits movements. Her theory of movement is based on the inhalation and exhalation of the breath and the torso's consequent expansion and contraction. Rather than work with a soft or fluid breath, she emphasized the sharp, initial beat, stressing a percussive accent. The contraction was a sharp spasm—an abrupt, visceral impulse—which, flowing outward in release, initiated movement in other body parts. This was a way of working uniquely suited to the type of ''inner landscape'' that concerned Graham; its terrain ravaged by unresolved greed, lust, deceit, rage, grief, remorse, love, and ecstasy.

The first dances she composed after leaving Rochester illustrate her style. In *Lamentation* (1930), a woman shrouded in a jersey, seated on a bench, twists, stretches, rocks, sways, and leans off-balance in an abstract expression of grief. Typical of Graham, the dance is stripped of any unnecessary ornamentation, the tensions in the body directly express the emotion, the dance is dramatic rather than pretty, the decor is functional rather than decorative, and the costume, against which the woman struggles, amplifies the emotional message.

Primitive Mysteries (1931) is a group work (Graham had formed her own company in 1929) and an acclaimed masterpiece. The dance was inspired by a trip to the Southwest with Louis Horst, her musical director and general consultant, where they saw American Indian rituals. The main figure is a white-clad virgin, a center of religious power who is worshiped, feared, deified, and adored by a group of women. Each of the three sections— *Hymn to the Virgin*, *Crucifixus*, and *Hosannah*—begins with a slow, deliberate procession. With minimal, tense, angular movements, the women, moving in rigid clusters, greet the virgin. In the second section, their hands clasped behind their backs, bent awkwardly forward as if compelled by some unseen force, the women bound around in a circle with large, predatory, gravity-bound leaps. In the final *Hosannah*, the virgin and her attendants remain in the center and the group rolls on the floor with heads bent to the ground in concluding homage. The movement reverberates powerfully because of its tension and restraint, its unpliable rigidity. The piece, with its atmosphere of ecstatic torture, is realized in uncluttered, stark, angular, and percussive movement, qualities closely associated with Graham's work.

Like most prolific artists, Graham has had many phases and interests. Her Americana period, lasting effectively from the mid-1930s to the mid-1940s, produced dances such as *Frontier* (1935), *American Document* (1938), and *Appalachian Spring* (1944). As time went by, Graham's work became more accessible. In *American Document*, she introduced narration and dramatic role-playing in her dance, pointing toward the later "theater of Martha Graham" in its use of narrative, costumes, music, sets, and drama. At this time, her movement style softened somewhat to emphasize not only the contraction but a fuller palette of movement that flowed from its impetus. For the first time men were introduced into the company, heretofore rather fiercely woman-oriented.

From 1944 on, Graham manifested an intense interest in universal, archetypal issues residing in man's collective unconscious as explained by C. G. Jung, illustrated by worldwide mythologies, and personified in the larger-than-life protagonists of Biblical and Greek literature. Turning to diverse mythologies— the imaginative, analytic psychology of an earlier age—Graham particularly investigated the workings of the female psyche. Her Greek and Biblical cycle of dances focuses unorthodoxly on heroines. In *Cave of the Heart* (1946), the central protagonist is Medea, consumed by her own anger, jealousy, and hatred. In a long solo, with a painfully twisted torso, body-wracking contractions, shudders, and spasms, Medea dances her fury. In *Night Journey* (1947), the story of Oedipus is told from the point of view of Jocasta, his mother-wife. In a famous, ambivalent duet, Oedipus and Jocasta shift from positions that suggest the coupling of lovers to poses of a mother cradling a child. *Clytemnestra* (1955), a rare full-evening modern dance work, focuses on Clytemnestra in hell asking why she is damned. The answer explores a woman's struggle with love, power, lust, man-hating, vengeance, and guilt. In Graham's work, it is the expression of the woman's body that indicates her mental state, be it contorted with jealousy, percussive with anger, retreating in fear, undulating with passion, twisted in deceit, or, less commonly, calm and quiet in contentment.

A frequent structural device in Graham's work is her non-linear organization of time. Many of her dances go back and forth in time and others begin at the end and unfold past events in a cinematic-type flashback. *Deaths and Entrances* (1943), inspired by the Brontë sisters, shows three women trapped in the present, whose pasts float in and out with the appearance of various male characters. Graham is fond of catching her characters on the verge of a personal moment of truth, at a time of self-recognition and catharsis that comes only from rigorous retrospection. Clytemnestra in hell examines her past, as do Jocasta (*Night Journey*) and Saint Joan (*Seraphic Dialogue*, 1955), minutes before their deaths.

Another theatrical device often used by Graham is the portrayal of a single character by two or more dancers, each representing a different aspect of the self. In *Letter to the World* (1940), inspired by the life and poetry of Emily Dickinson, the poet is both the One Who Speaks, representing the public, decorous Dickinson, and the One Who Dances, expressing her inner, emotional self. In *Seraphic Dialogue*, we see Saint Joan as the Maid, the Warrior, and the Martyr.

Graham has influenced dance and nondance theater with her symbolic-functional approach to decor and props. Early in her career, through the 1950s, her sets and props were often designed in collaboration with the sculptor Isamu Noguchi. More recently, she employed the late fashion designer Halston to create stage sets and costumes. In her early solo *Frontier* (1935), ropes extending up diagonally from a simple wooden bench reinforce a feeling of limitless space. In *El Penitente* (1940), designed by Arch Lauterer, a cross becomes the pole of a banner; the banner becomes a curtain. In *Dark Meadow* (1944), a somewhat obscure dance referring to a ritualistic and psychoanalytic journey through birth, sexual consciousness, and rebirth, the tone and stage are set with upright poles, suggestive of totems and phalluses. In *Night Journey*, a rope symbolic of the umbilical cord binding mother and child later becomes the noose with which Jocasta hangs herself. In *Errand into the Maze* (1947), Ariadne follows a curved tape on the floor leading to the Creature of Fear.

The tape then forms the structure within which she confines herself; but after defeating her demon, she undoes the tape and is free. In *Clytemnestra*, a huge pink-and-red cloth is a regal welcome carpet for the returning Agamemnon. Stretched across the stage during the murder scene, it becomes both a screen and a river of blood that Clytemnestra wraps around her body. In *Cave of the Heart*, Medea, in her solo, pulls a single long red ribbon out of her bosom, like the uncoiling of a vituperative inner snake.

Audiences and critics have often marveled at Graham's comprehensive intelligence, which synthesizes ideas from so many diverse sources and incarnates them in a physical medium of tremendous power. Graham, long the company's central dancer and foremost interpreter of her own heroines, retired from performing in her mid-70's, but has continued to direct her company and to choreograph. A one-time rebel who has gained wide acceptance, Graham recalls vowing early in her career, ''I will keep it up as long as I have an audience.''

Video: KUL, VAI.

APPALACHIAN SPRING

Choreography by Martha Graham, 1944; music by Aaron Copland; costumes by Edythe Gilfond; scenery by Isamu Noguchi.

Appalachian Spring is the last dance of Graham's Americana phase, composed just before her period of preoccupation with psychoanalysis and mythology. Until the mid-1940s, many of Graham's dances drew on her personal experience and American heritage. *Appalachian Spring* is a dance about a young pioneer couple about to be married, contemplating their future on the American frontier. Interestingly, at the time Graham herself had just gotten married for the first time at the age of 50, and the character of the bride in *Appalachian Spring* may have been a reflection of her own feelings, a role truly created from the inside. The stern revivalist preacher in the piece is probably inspired by her own childhood memories of fire-and-brimstone clergy.

Noguchi's stage set for *Appalachian Spring* consists of a piece of fencerail, which forms a V-shaped entrance to a farmhouse made of a single wall with a rocking chair on the porch. It is the framework of a domestic setting, beyond which the woods and fields of the frontier are assumed. The four main characters— the Bride, the Husband, the Pioneer Woman, and the Preacher— seldom relate directly to one another. The piece is a composite of the private emotions of the characters, each of whom dances an important solo revealing his or her inner landscape, replete with its strengths, fears, and passions.

As the dance opens, the four characters solemnly walk on stage, each one erect, determined, and self-absorbed. The Bride rushes over to her Husband expectantly and then retreats as if she has been too hasty. The Husband touches the wall of the house with a gesture both of possession and of wonder. The Preacher, in broad-brimmed hat and frock coat, is followed by an adoring flock of four female worshipers. They spring up and down in spritely little jumps, their hands vibrating in a little clap, as though emitting sparks from a core of restrained ardor. These bonneted women are symbolic of the strict religionists who founded this country, and they have a typically Grahamesque suggestion of repressed sexuality in their fervor.

Next, the Pioneer Woman dances with broad jumps and steady, generous movements. There is something sure and sustaining about the way she moves, suggesting that she may be symbolic of a solid faith in the future. The Husband now steps forward and adopts a wide stance, planting his legs firmly on the ground. He jumps up and down, slaps an upraised knee, leans on the fence, and looks out meditatively with his characteristic mixture of assertion and doubt. The Preacher and his followers, who have been on the sidelines, are reanimated. The flock jump up and down and around the Preacher in a circle, hands clapping. The Bride then moves downstage, whirling from side to side and running with small steps that seem to bespeak a cautious optimism. She appears to be thinking of the future as she rocks an imaginary child in her arms, bends as if to greet another little child, blows kisses, looks out in the distance, and then stands with her Husband, who actually seems to lean on her a bit. As the music swells, the couple dances a buoyant, jubilant, folksy dance, which, performed to the lilting Shaker hymn ''Tis a Gift to Be Simple,'' is a joyous dance within the larger

Yuriko Kimura in *Appalachian Spring*, Martha Graham Dance Company.

dance. Claiming his space, the Husband bends and scoops the air around him. Then, running toward each other, the pair lock arms and run around in a circle. The Bride springs into the air as her Husband lifts her, and together they proclaim their happiness.

Presumably provoked by the couple's lightheartedness, the Preacher steps forth for his exhortatory wedding sermon. He contorts his body as if struggling with sin and temptation, stamps the ground, and fiercely leaps about. He gestures upward toward the source of his religious authority and directs warnings to the couple. Then, to soften the apprehensive mood created by the Preacher, the Pioneer Woman spreads a blessing over the couple with her warm, sure, and broad gestures, moving in her quiet and knowing manner. The little flock bounce up and down appreciatively.

But, as the others move to the back, their heads bowed and backs to the audience, the Bride comes downstage alone and kneels in self-doubt. She seems to be looking within, wondering if she has the fortitude to bear future responsibilities; she is perhaps praying for the necessary courage. She gets up and runs one way and then another, expressing her ambivalence. She rushes forward and then retreats. Her gestures slowly become larger, and her torso contracts in a solo passage that can be understood as a fear fantasy of childbirth or perhaps of larger dangers that might threaten her family. At the dance's end, her movements seem steady and firm, giving the impression that she has and will continue to grow stronger. As the piece draws to a close, the Preacher and his flock and the Pioneer Woman walk off, leaving the Husband and Bride alone. In an effectively minimal closing scene, the Bride sits rocking on the porch chair. Her Husband stands behind her, and extending his arm over her shoulder, clasps her hand as they both silently and calmly gaze out into the distance.

Graham had wanted to work with the composer Aaron Copland for some time. All along, the composer and the choreographer made suggestions to one another, so that music and dance are the result of a close collaboration. Copland's now-famous score won the Pulitzer Prize in 1945, and his music, which has frequently been given separate concert performances, gained Copland national recognition. The collaboration is of special interest in that it marked a departure from the early modern dance's avoidance of lush, directive scores. Unlike the music used for ballet, the early moderns generally preferred to commission sparse, ascetic scores, to rely on a simple rhythmic accompaniment or, alternatively, to dance in silence. Surely most moderns would have found the rich-textured violins of *Appalachian Spring* too overwhelming. Nonetheless, by 1944, Graham was ready to dance to this music, which contributes so much to the folksy, lyrical feeling of the work.

The trademarks of Graham's vocabulary—tense jumps, angular gestures, small, rapid runs, torso contractions, slow falls to the ground—are evident in this piece, and the whole is constructed with an economy of movement. Nonetheless, unlike some of Graham's earlier dances, it is not pessimistic or grotesque. *Appalachian Spring* is a dance of optimism—the couple confront their fears and, together with the others, affirm life. It is a dance of hope and encouragement, not only for the pioneer couple, but for all people courageous enough to leave the familiar and, in good faith, embark on the unknown.

Video: KUL.

SERAPHIC DIALOGUE

Choreography by Martha Graham, 1955; music by Norman Dello Joio; costumes by Martha Graham; scenery by Isamu Noguchi.

Martha Graham believed that one's past is alive in one's present; the moment exists only because of its antecedents. Personal enlightenment demands introspection and reconsideration of the past. In *Seraphic Dialogue,* Joan of Arc, now Saint Joan, is on the threshold of her ascension to heaven. Death, for her, is a stepping stone toward recognition, sainthood, and rebirth—a religious and moral canonization that comes about through a journey into her former selves. The present Joan, played by one dancer, greets and observes three former Joans—the Maid, the Warrior, and the Martyr—played by three other dancers. The splitting of a single character into several aspects to allow for introspection is a familiar Graham device.

Although there are three other saints present, it is Joan alone who must decide whether to accept her calling, confront the danger, suffer her losses, and win her beatification. A historical and religious heroine, acting independently and defiantly in a world manipulated by men, one who rejects a woman's traditional subservience, had a special appeal for Graham.

The Curtain rises on Noguchi's openwork polished brass set, which resembles gold tracery for a stained-glass window. Saint Michael, Joan's patron saint, stands on the second rung of the metal structure. His palms face out and his hands periodically vibrate. Saint Catharine and Saint Margaret attend him on either side. Joan, seated before the structure, watches as her three selves, all draped in long cloaks, enter and take their places on three seats to the side. The dance proceeds as a kind of dialogue between the present Joan and the others. Joan dances a short solo as if to encourage each aspect of herself to "speak," and afterward reflects briefly on each reminiscence.

The Maid's dance begins with light runs and quick turns performed with straightforward innocence. In the middle of her skips and swirls, she suddenly lifts her hands to her ears, and her torso contracts sharply. She recoils in fear, presumably from the voices, and begins to tremble. Then as her determination grows, she regains her calm and begins to jump energetically. She stops to tie a scarf on her head as Saint Michael reaches out to her from his gold frame. She contracts and falls back sharply to the ground, as if struck by her mission. The scarf becomes a banner that she waves back and forth as she rises into strong, direct leaps; the Maid has clearly accepted her calling. The present Joan rises and dances with agitated jumps as if to reecho and reflect upon that early stage of her life.

The two female saints then walk over to the side and draw the Warrior Joan out from under her cloak. Saint Michael marches forth with a brass sword and jumps up and down repeatedly, with the Warrior following behind him, walking briskly on her knees. She then climbs onto his back as he presses forward with the glistening sword. She falls back, as if struck by lightning, but recovers and accepts the sword. She and the sword become one as she holds it parallel to the length of her body. Saint Michael lifts the sword and her rigid body together—her doubt and fear have strengthened to commitment and resolve. Saint

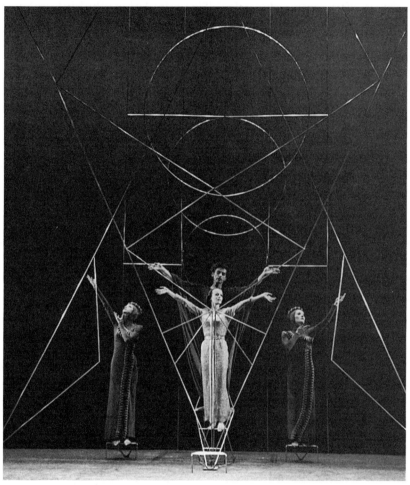

Helen Winter and Bertram Ross (center) in *Seraphic Dialogue,*
Martha Graham Dance Company.

Catharine and Saint Margaret dance briefly, and the present Joan returns to express both pride and sorrow for the zealous phase of her life.

The Warrior retreats under the cloak again as the Martyr comes forth, remaining shrouded in her cloak and dragging herself along the floor with the cross used as a staff. She then leaps into the air holding the cross high. She kneels before Saint Michael and the two women saints cover her again with her cloak. The present Joan now returns attired in a splendid golden gown, and Saint Michael opens the gate of his brass sanctuary. She ascends into her niche beside him as the two attendant saints gently close the gates around the beatific pair. Together, they slowly extend their arms and open their palms, tilting them slightly upward.

Seraphic Dialogue illustrates much of Graham's movement vocabulary—contractions at moments of emotional intensity, backward falls to the floor, brisk walking on the knees, tight, small runs and skips, repeated jumps, iconographic poses, and hand gestures. Joan's evolution from Maid to Warrior is expressed in the change from light skips to forceful leaps. Her approach-avoidance relationship with Saint Michael is dramatized in the duet with the sword, and her total self-sacrifice to her calling is illustrated in the poignant, shrouded crawl of the Martyr with her cross.

Graham's use of costumes and props amplifies the drama inherent in the dance. The large cloaks serve to unite the three Joans as aspects of the same woman and at the same time to isolate each of them as if they are wrapped in separate reverie. Noguchi's set, which he referred to as "the gates of heaven" or "the gates of faith," suggests a wrought-brass church altar or a gold frame for stained glass. When Joan ascends into this structure, we understand that she has entered a sublime realm. *Seraphic Dialogue* was originally a solo for Graham entitled *The Triumph of Saint Joan*, danced to the same Dello Joio score. Noguchi's decor inspired her to rework the dance and to add the three Joans and the saints. It is not at all unusual for Graham to rework her pieces after they have been performed. *Seraphic Dialogue*, still in the repertory of the Graham company, is a successful fusion of decor, music, and movement.

DORIS HUMPHREY

Doris Humphrey (1895-1958) was another student of the Denishawn School who broke away to become a leading figure of American modern dance. Lacking the flamboyance and legendary stature of her colleague, Martha Graham, Humphrey is, nonetheless, considered by many to be equally important. She, too, endeavored on her own to discover new principles of movement. Less preoccupied than Graham with introspection and a release of inner tension, she concerned herself with the nature of movement as a physical and natural phenomenon, basing her technique on principles of physics concerning objects at rest and in motion. She discovered that for movement to be initiated, a body at rest must be "struck" by a movement impulse strong enough to counteract its inertia, and then, for the movement to stop, it must be checked by an equal and opposite force. For example, a deliberate swing of the dancer's head will initiate a turning movement in other body parts as the dancer "gives in" to the weight of the head. Then to stop the turn, the dancer must counterimpose a force of control and balance. Furthermore, Humphrey emphasized that all movement exists in relation to gravity, resisting or giving in to it at varying degrees. Complete resistance to gravity is total control or lack of any movement, one kind of "death"; a total surrender to gravity implies an utter loss of control, another kind of "death." For Humphrey, the drama of movement lay in "the arc between two deaths," in the play between fall and recovery, balance and imbalance, letting go and regaining control.

The excitement of the Humphrey technique lies in the dancer's giving in to the swing of movement and checking the motion at will; the moving through space, rising and falling; leaning far off balance and regaining equilibrium. This approach to dance has psychic as well as physical implications—Humphrey's way of moving was a metaphor for humanity itself caught between its drive for action and the implied danger on the one hand, and its yearning for retreat into inactive repose on the other. Humphrey explained, "Fall and recovery is the constant flux which goes on in every living body . . . all the time." Since the drama lies in the kinetic approach to movement itself, Humphrey's dances rarely rely on obscure symbolism or literary references.

Humphrey was always less militant than Graham, if equally determined. Her dance company used men and women from its early days, and she herself worked closely with her partner, Charles Weidman, in exploring the possibilities for give and take between two dancers. Weidman, a choreographer with an individual, more humorous, bent, often collaborated in composing dances with Humphrey, and the movement approach they developed is known as the Humphrey-Weidman technique. Their style has been described as deliberately unballetic—palms faced forward, fingers were held spread out, toes were left relaxed rather than pointed, the body tilted asymmetrically, and movement was large and pendular.

Early in her career, Humphrey experimented with various kinds of accompaniment—often not music—for her dances. *Water Study* (1929) was danced to silence, and *Life of the Bee* (1929) made use of sounds produced by combs and tissue paper. In *The Shakers* (1931), she arranged her own score of traditional music interrupted by spoken exclamations. In all these works, her organization of rhythm lent drama and structure. At the same time, Humphrey, unlike many other early moderns, was a supremely musical dancer who enjoyed composing to serious music. The first dance she composed after leaving Denishawn, *Air for the G String* (1928), hinted of her future choreographic direction. It was danced to Bach, a favorite composer, whose architectural sense and lyrical flow she mirrored in movement. Like her later major dances to Bach, *Passacaglia* (1938) and her unfinished *Brandenburg Concerto* (1959), the dancers relate to and visualize the music but do not respond to it note for note. Recurring themes such as the progress or ennobling of man can be read into these works, but the works stand on their own as abstract dance compositions.

Passacaglia is an instructive illustration of Humphrey's method of working with music, her approach to composition, and her fusion of form and content. She reflected but did not match the idea of theme and variation found in the score. She selected movement motifs—for example, a walk forward on one foot while widely swinging a free bent leg with arms held at chest level parallel to each other and the floor. She repeated these motifs with variations (much as the musical motifs are recapitulated and varied), but at intervals suggested by the form of the dance rather than the music. She also reflected, but was not tied to, the counterpoint used in the music. She had different groups of dancers do nonidentical movements that were all somehow related, giving an underlying feeling of unity in disunity. She was inspired, too, by the canonical development of the fugue in the music and had dancers pick up themes started by others just before the initiating group completed the movement. The cumulative feeling achieved by the formal structure expressed the dance's implied content—the assemblage of a noble, cooperative society comprised of individual parts.

Humphrey was well known not only as a dancer and choreographer but as an important theorist of dance composition. Many choreographers were trained in her composition classes, where her recurring lesson was that one did not "make up" dances, one composed them. She taught that all movements have a design in space, a rhythm, a type of energy flow or dynamic, and a reason for being or motivation. She urged her students to consider their motivation and then purposefully manipulate their use of dynamics, rhythm, and design.

Some of Humphrey's idealistic themes date her dances in sentiment, but they survive as examples of classic modern dance composition. Her trilogy, *Theatre Piece* (1936), *With My Red Fires* (1936), and *New Dance* (1935), was considered at its premiere "the crowning achievement of the American dance thus far." Its concern with a harmonious society today seems perhaps a bit naive, but her manipulation of design—specifically, her spatial arrangements of different groups of dancers to express the theme of the individual versus society—remains valid.

After her retirement as a dancer in 1944, Humphrey became the artistic director of a company formed by José Limón, her leading male dancer, a position she held until her death in 1958. In this later phase of her career, she created many enduring works, including *Lament for Ignacio Sanchez Mejias* (1946), *Day on Earth* (1947), and *Night Spell* (1951). Several of these works survive in the repertories of the Limón Dance Company. A relatively large portion of Humphrey's works has been recorded in Labanotation scores, and they are often revived by advanced modern-dance students in colleges and studios worldwide.

Video: DHV.

THE SHAKERS

Choreography by Doris Humphrey, 1931; traditional music, arranged for percussion, accordion, and soprano voice.

The Shakers, founded in the late 19th century, were an ultra-austere sect of the Quakers. They believed in extreme simplicity and rigid celibacy, and although they lived communally, they did not procreate. Their name derives from a feature of their worship in their pewless meeting houses where the men and women actually shook their sins away in a segregated dance. The dance would grow from small quiverings into wholesale twisting of the body. A physical means of achieving catharsis, it is reasonable to assume that their ritual dance was also a means of sexual release.

Doris Humphrey had a sustained interest in the Shakers and was particularly drawn to the tension in their lives between austerity and religious frenzy. In 1931, Humphrey composed her first acclaimed masterpiece, called *Dance of the Chosen*, later known as *The Shakers*. Its choreography was based on authentic steps and formations she had observed in the Shaker dance. Its theme was the play of religious passion and repressed sexuality.

The dance begins with a dozen men and women on their knees, their hands clasped, their gazes upward. They are dressed in drab Shaker garb, the women modest in bonnets, high necks and long skirts, the men somber in dark frock coats and broad-brimmed hats. Arranged in two lines facing each other, the sexes clearly segregated, they begin to rock from side to side. They sink back onto their heels and rise onto their knees. They rise and continue the forward and backward motion standing on one leg and lunging with the other leg and upper body to the front and back.

The Shakers, The Limón Dance Company.

The men and the women face front and, one pair at a time, they walk stiffly toward the center, their arms held in rigid paralysis at their sides. When each pair reaches the center, the men and women abruptly turn, face each other, and continue stiffly walking sideways toward the back of the stage, their upper bodies now rocking from side to side. Then the groups of men and women each form a separate, rotating wheel, holding hands at the center and radiating out. As the segregated wheels turn and the outermost members of each one pass each other, they lean out toward each other but do not touch. Now facing front, the celebrants begin to hop from one foot to the other, opening and closing their arms. The small, frenetic jumps are suddenly arrested as one member shouts out a spoken declaration of faith. They resume jumping with their rigid arms periodically jutting out, until their female leader stands on a chair placed at the back of the stage. They all kneel as she claps for order and then exhorts them to continue their ecstatic worship. As if exhausted by her revelatory message, her upper body falls over. Recovering, she leads them in accelerating jumps and the shaking of stiffened hands insistently toward the floor.

Facing each other with this chugging jump in which their hands and feet drive downward, the men and women hop toward the center, then abruptly face front and continue the hand shaking while walking sideways. They return to the falling forward and backward movement, adding turns as the excitement mounts and the drumbeats grow faster. The men and women lean slightly toward each other, then drop their weight onto their back legs. They are interrupted by the leader, who is transported in a series of ecstatic whirling turns, her arms held high, her head tossed back. Those assembled fall to their feet and rise again to jump with increasing frenzy into the air, arms and legs spasmodically stabbing into space. In clusters, they subside and fall to the floor. They then return to the opening position, hands clasped, gazing upward, bodies circling.

As is usual in Humphrey's work, the drama in the dance lies in the movement itself—in the sense of constrained energy beneath the bound, restrained movements and in the juxtaposition of tight, rigid movements with sudden ecstatic outbursts. The sexual tension is made clear but never overstated in the cautious but energetic approach of the men and women, in their subtle leaning toward each other and abrupt turning away. The brief dance (approximately eight minutes long) is actually constructed with very few movements—falling forward and back, swaying, jumping in place, shaking of the hands, and stiff walking steps. The constant sense of falling and recovering, swaying off balance and returning to center are signatures of Humphrey's style. These movement motifs are repeated throughout with some variations, giving the whole a sense of thematic unity. Formally, the dance is a neat A-B-A; it ends, after its build-up, just as it began. The brevity, crispness, and restraint are illustrative not only of the Shaker outlook but of Humphrey's choreographic credo as well.

The score, a combination of accordion, sung hymns, drum, and spoken word, was arranged by Humphrey. The spoken recitations were her first attempt at using words in a dance, an idea she would develop more fully later. In the first performances of *The Shakers*, Humphrey distinguished herself in the role of the leader, and there were more men than women. In contemporary performances, the number of men and women is equal. *The Shakers* is often reconstructed by modern-dance companies, students, and even ballet troupes from the Labanotation score.

JOSÉ LIMÓN

Modern dance is a personality-oriented field, and almost all modern-dance companies are named for their founders. It is most unusual that a company survive the death or departure of its originator, but the Limón Dance Company is a noteworthy exception. Since Limón's death in 1972 (he was born in 1908), the company has continued to perform. Early in his career, Limón had already departed from the familiar "life-cycle" patterns of modern dancers. Most "second-generation" modern dancers either rebelled and left their mentors or remained eclipsed in their creative shadows. Limón, who danced with the Humphrey-Weidman company for 12 years, formed his own company in 1945 with Doris Humphrey as artistic director.

Limón's approach to movement is deeply rooted in his work with Doris Humphrey. The Limón technique, too, emphasizes fall and recovery, balance and imbalance. With an exhalation of breath the dancer lets go, with an inhalation he regains equilibrium. The weight of one body part pulls the others into action. Limón's personal style emphasized agile, elaborate footwork, while the arms and upper body executed large, often pendular, movements. Like Humphrey, Limón was very concerned with composing rather than merely choreographing. His dances show a careful concern for formal structure—themes are stated, varied, and restated. As in his teacher's work, dramatic content is expressed through formal structure. A good example of meaning emerging through form is Limón's *There Is a Time* (1956). Based on the Biblical text "to everything there is a season, and a time to every purpose under heaven," the dance begins, often returns to, and ends with a group circle. The circle lends structural unity to the dance and dramatically expresses its theme of continuity, repetition, and cyclic self-renewal.

Although in the beginning, Limón's large frame and inelastic build seemed to hold little promise for his future as a dancer, he eventually gained an extraordinary reputation for his strikingly handsome appearance and majestic bearing. While still a dancer, Limón began choreographing and often drew his themes from his own Mexican heritage. His career also reflects his great concern with the status of the male dancer. In a field largely dominated by women, he stressed the importance of strong, virile dance that a man could perform proudly. He rejected the decorative and, to him, effete role of men in ballet and spoke admiringly of the examples of dancing priests and warriors in ancient times. He wrote of his determination to show that "a man could, with dignity and a towering majesty, dance." He added, "I saw the dance as a vision of ineffable power." Many of Limón's dances, such as *The Emperor Jones* (1956) and *The Traitor* (1954), are about the anguish of heroic men and were created in the mid-1950s when Limón was working with an all-male company.

Limón's own words—"dignity," "majesty," "power"—describe the feeling and point of view of his works. His themes were grandiose, his characters larger than life; they often struggled with baser instincts or disaster and somehow emerged ennobled. *Missa Brevis* (1958) is a dance about coming together and rebuilding after wide-scale devastation. In *The Exiles* (1950), Adam and Eve try to find comfort and dignity after their expulsion from paradise. His thrust was toward a kind of enlightenment through anguish. He wrote: "I try to compose works that are involved with man's basic tragedy and the grandeur of his spirit. I want to . . . probe the human entity for the powerful, often crude beauty of the gesture that speaks of man's humanity."

THE MOOR'S PAVANE

Choreography by José Limón, 1949; music by Henry Purcell; costumes by Pauline Lawrence.

José Limón did not often work with the subtleties of human nature. He preferred to present characters with full-blown qualities, with corruption, villainy, heroism, or innocence clearly evident. In *The Moor's Pavane,* his danced version of Shakespeare's

Othello, he uses only the four main characters: Othello, the Moor; his wife, Desdemona; Iago; and Iago's wife, Emilia. The protagonists are presented as four opposing poles of human nature—Iago's sinister treachery is pitted against Othello's majestic dignity; Desdemona's unstained innocence is counterbalanced by Emilia's complicity in the plot.

The Moor's Pavane, Limón's undisputed masterpiece (and considered by many the finest modern dance ever composed), is in no sense a mimed version of the play. The drama emerges fully in dance terms with no resort to mute gesture. Its formal elements embody and express the tensions in the story as the four characters move in and out of the *pavane,* a stately Renaissance court dance. The restrained and elegant *pavane,* emblematic of proper social form and a cool exterior, is periodically interrupted by passionate encounters between the couples and between the two men and two women. The alternation between the courtly formality of the *pavane* and the underlying private dramas is a compositional device that is a key to the tragedy as seen by Limón.

The dance begins with the two couples joined in a circle. They are dressed in formal Renaissance costumes; Desdemona's wide-skirted dress is pure white. To Purcell's elegiac music, they begin a *pavane,* widening and narrowing their circle. Still in the circle, the two men face each other and rise on one leg as the two women bow low. A new tableau is formed as they leave the circle. Othello presents Desdemona with a handkerchief, Shakespeare's well-known symbol of their mutual devotion, while Iago slithers around menacingly in the background. They return quickly to the *pavane,* now dancing in diagonal lines with the two couples facing and crossing through each other. True to Renaissance style, the torsos are very erect and there is a slightly decorative touch in the curved arms and hands.

The *pavane* is again abandoned and the two men come into the foreground as the two women freeze. Iago, a slight, wily man, grabs onto the Moor's shoulders and shifts his head from side to side, as if whispering in each of the larger man's ears. Othello, his eyes clouded with displeasure, flings Iago off with a whip of his head. As Othello then dances with the accused Desdemona, Iago slithers in between them. Next, Iago and Emilia come alive as Othello and Desdemona are still. Iago bends Emilia in

Sallie Wilson, Toni Lander, Bruce Marks, and Royes Fernandez in *The Moor's Pavane*, American Ballet Theatre.

a series of asymmetrical poses, manipulating her balance in off-center positions. Emilia then quickly walks over to Desdemona and snatches the handkerchief out of her friend's bodice just before the four return to another variation of the *pavane*.

Next, the two men are alone. Othello has one arm raised as if to defend himself against Iago's slander. Iago, standing behind, again holds onto Othello's shoulders. The two alternate in counterpointed, pogolike jumps. As one goes up, the other comes down, as if they are engaged in a curt exchange of "yes," "no," "yes," "no." They then pull each other into weighty lunges, forward and back. Finally, as the struggle increases in ferocity, a looming Othello forces Iago to his knees. The villain crawls back up and attaches himself to Othello's shoulders. Like a leech, he rides on Othello's back as the Moor strides across the stage. Othello again shakes him off and Iago retreats, crawling backward along the floor.

Then, the two women and Othello, standing in a diagonal line with one arm raised, sink into a *plié* and rise onto one leg in unison. The focus next switches to Emilia, who spins and skips with the handkerchief, tossing it contentedly into the air. In the background, Desdemona, her arms held out, tries to get Othello to look at her, but he is distracted and lunges away.

The four now return to the *pavane*, danced in a wheel formation. Iago beckons Othello away and suddenly produces the handkerchief. He flings it at Othello, who whips away from the evidence in horror. Tensions mounting, the four return once more to the wheel of the *pavane* and then spin away in opposite directions. A broken-hearted Othello and thoroughly bewildered Desdemona emerge into the foreground. He clasps her face in his hands, fixing an intense, loving gaze on her. She collapses backward in his arms, as if in pleading surrender. He, deeply sorrowing, cradles and rocks her, his adoring gaze never leaving her terrified face. The other couple steps in front, and as Emilia slowly lifts her leg her skirt functions as a screen hiding the inevitable tragedy. When they step away, a lifeless Desdemona lies on the ground, her disconsolate murderer bent over her, grieving. Emilia, suddenly aware of the horrible consequences of her deed, produces the handkerchief. Othello realizes with bottomless despair that he has been deceived. A looming, tragic figure, he pulls Iago and Emilia toward him in fury. Knowing it is, of course, too late, he falls over the dead body, embracing it in a futile, impassioned plea for forgiveness as the others turn away.

Although the dance embodies contrast—between tragic heroism and unmitigated villainy, between the rigidity of the *pavane* and the eruption of passion—it is characterized by a feeling of fluidity. The transitions between formal postures and private encounters are rapid and unobtrusive. The drama is intensified by the stylistic contrast between the held posture of the Renaissance dance and the constant push and pull, give and take, of the interludes. Limón "speaks" through this manipulation of weight—the heavy lunges of Othello and Iago, Desdemona's surrender to the arms of Othello, the terrible heaving of Othello's shattered strength at the end.

Although there has been much cross-influence between ballet and modern dance, performances of the *The Moor's Pavane* can illustrate some of the basic differences between the two. While *The Moor's Pavane* is in the repertory of several major ballet companies, it has often been remarked that ballet-trained dancers are not able to emphasize and shift their weight in the requisite way (instead, they are trained to "pull up" and appear weightless). Furthermore, protest has been engendered by such modifications as the insertion of multiple *pirouettes* in the role of Othello. Virtuosic display and arbitrary additions of steps are inappropriate in a modern dance composed with a tight, dramatic structure. *The Moor's Pavane* exemplifies the modern-dance credo of emotion contained in the movement, rendering ineffectual the classical dancer's occasional tendency to emote from the neck up. Nonetheless, the acquisition of *The Moor's Pavane* by ballet companies is a noteworthy tribute to Limón and an interesting challenge to the dancers.

ANNA SOKOLOW

Anna Sokolow (b. 1912) is a major dance choreographer. She grew up with the modern dancers of the 1930s and danced in Martha Graham's company until 1939, when she began establishing an important, independent career. Drawing her themes from Mexico, her own Jewish roots, social issues, and musical scores, she has created enduring works such as *Lyric Suite* (1954), *Session for Six* (1958), and *Dreams* (1961). She has worked as a choreographer and teacher in Japan, Israel, and Mexico as well as at the Juilliard School of Music, New York. While her musical tastes are varied, she has been especially drawn to serious jazz with an edgy, disturbing dimension, a sound she considers "the music of our time."

Sokolow does not have a lighthearted or frivolous attitude toward life or art. Her dances often depict melancholia and suffering, painting the kind of isolation and despair she evokes so unflinchingly in *Rooms*. Yet she never lapses into excess or melodrama.

ROOMS

Choreography by Anna Sokolow, 1955; music by Kenyon Hopkins.

Discussing the inspiration for *Rooms*, Anna Sokolow recalled, of all things, riding the elevated trains in New York City. The tracks were often built very close to the tenements, and as she sped by, she could look right into people's windows. The source of *Rooms*, a study of man's isolation in an urban jungle, was in these fleeting glimpses of figures sitting alone in dilapidated

Rooms, Contemporary Dance System.

dwellings. *Rooms* is a searing yet muted study of extreme alien-
ation and maladjustment among a city's forgotten souls. The jazz
score by Kenyon Hopkins reinforces its statement about a loss
of humanity in an accelerated, explosive age.

Like many works that are deeply moving, the power of *Rooms*
lies in its utter simplicity, in its expression of profound feeling
projected through minimal uncluttered images. The dance begins
with four men and four women simply sitting immobile on
chairs, staring into space. The separate chairs are symbolic of
separate rooms where people are entirely cut off from each other,
even though they are physically quite close. In the understate-
ment of dancers simply sitting, one fully senses the tension and
desperation. They rise slowly and tentatively from their chairs,
then sink back aga in. They then fall far to the side and, still sitting on their chairs, slump toward the floor. Standing, each one
clutching his own chair, they look around frantically. Although
they all occupy the same physical space, it is clear they do not
see each other. Each one is trapped in his or her own ''room,''
doomed to a psychic as well as physical estrangement from the
others.

After a blackout, a single man is left alone. He falls off his
chair and rolls across the stage. He then sits up and draws his
legs toward his chest in a fetal position. He stretches upward
and even dares to cartwheel before feeling impelled to move backward. As if the chair and the hopelessness it stands for exercise
a magnetic pull on him, he crawls toward it on his stomach. He
gets up, tries to run only to fall and, resigned, goes back to sit
in the chair. The name of this section is *Dream*—clearly, one that
is hardly realized.

Next we see a woman sitting in her chair alone. She holds
her arms out as if half-expecting someone or something. She rolls
her head around and then languorously swings her arms and
head from side to side. Getting up, she runs around in a small
circle, her arms again raised expectantly, her head tossed back,
a dreamy half-smile on her face. Then, holding onto her chair,
she slowly raises her leg sideways and lets it fall. She then begins
to tremble in place, her vibrating hand and arms circling her body
as if ushering in an unseen presence. Sinking back into her chair,
she plays sensually with her own long hair, caressing it as one
might a lover. Growing more agitated, she stands up and spins
around in a circle. Then, in a final attempt to alleviate her obvi-

ous loneliness, she sets an empty chair opposite her own. After greeting her imaginary companion, she lays her head tenderly on her own chair and drapes her legs sensually over the other, as if to unite two figures. Then disgusted, her attempts to *Escape* (as this section is called) draw to a futile close as she kicks over both chairs in disgust and continues spinning around aimlessly.

Next is *Going*, which is actually an ironic study of going nowhere. A man sitting on the floor pulses his body energetically, snaps his fingers nervously, and crosses and uncrosses his legs. The music accelerates, and his chest pumps in and out furiously, but he does not move forward. He crouches predatorily, leaps into the air, and lands on the same spot. He then tries to walk forward but his legs are stuck, as if tied together. He continues running, and leaping in place, and boxing hyperactively with an imaginary foe as the light fades.

Next, three men and three women can be seen sitting and clinging to the sides of the chairs. They push one leg forward and then the other, pawing the ground while leaning back. Slipping off their chairs, they lie on the floor in a group, rolling from side to side, as if experiencing a dull, unarticulated agony. Individually they contract into a sit-up and sink back down. They all lift one leg and curve it backward, almost interlocking with a neighbor, but never quite touching one another. At the end of this section (called *Desire*), they return to stand on their chairs. Arms held rigidly to their sides, they have clearly lost all hope of reaching out to one another.

The following section is entitled *Panic*. A bare-chested man runs forward and backward like an animal in a cage. He rushes back to his chair, which is placed among three other men and a woman who sit in their own chairs totally ignoring his desperation. Taking his seat, the single man stretches his arms out, waves his legs around, and hops up and down instinctively, all to no avail. He then covers his face with his hands and sways disconsolately from side to side. The others walk away. Left alone, he crouches on the ground and beats his head violently up and down, only inches away from the floor.

Next we see three women in the throes of a lighthearted *Daydream* (the only relief Sokolow provides in the entire work). Holding onto the backs of their chairs, they rise and fall, waving one arm around. They sink to the floor and contentedly roll over. Next, kneeling, they bounce up and down and then lean their heads on their chairs. Rising to their feet, they stop and stare into space, walk around their chairs listlessly, and sit down.

In the final section, *The End*, the eight men and women walk past each other. One woman places her chair in the center and stretches her arms, vibrates her hands, and throws her head from side to side. She gets up and runs around frenetically before collapsing forward, her hands still trembling. She collapses and rises several times, almost compulsively, before standing on her chair and waving her arms around. Now the others enter and resume their original sitting positions. Some of them do brief sections of their preceding solos and then return to simply sit in their chairs and stare.

As *Rooms* superbly illustrates, Sokolow accomplishes her goals with spare, striking means using a series of hard-hitting, clearly drawn visual images—the woman conjuring an imaginary lover in an empty chair and, in disgust, kicking it over; a man pulsing madly but going nowhere; people rolling on the floor in aching loneliness but never touching each other; a man desperately "beating" his head against the floor. These are examples of her simple but unforgettable movement style. While her choreography does not emphasize technical virtuosity, it demands extreme control and great dramatic intensity.

Like most traditional modern-dance choreographers, Sokolow's works succeed through a careful manipulation of compositional structure. The motif of the chairs appears throughout. (Sokolow confessed to having difficulty deciding how to show eight separate rooms at once until she saw a stage filled with empty chairs. She recalled, "It occurred to me that if each person sat in a chair it could be a room. . . . I could show the amplification of one room eight times before going into each room.") Certain movement themes—outstretched arms, running and falling, rolling the body, waving arms and legs—also recur with variations throughout. The end section returns to the beginning, giving the work a clear A-B-A form.

Although few would deny the stature of *Rooms*, its brutal, unrelenting look at the dark side of life has kept it from attaining widespread popularity. (A few companies have even been forced by public reaction to drop it from their repertories.) It is, nonetheless, periodically revived by modern-dance and ballet companies.

MERCE CUNNINGHAM

$\mathbf{M}$erce Cunningham (b. 1919) continues to inspire controversy. He has been "assaulting" audiences for over 40 years, and he must be one of the most difficult of 20th-century choreographers to "penetrate," yet the suspicion that there is much to glean from his works keeps people coming back. And, of course, he has ardent admirers, including most professional dance watchers (critics, commentators, historians), among many others. So dance sophisticates find much that is bracing—even brilliant—about a Cunningham work. Others may find the going difficult. Some dismiss it completely.

Cunningham's works—or his concept of dance—have been so radical that most of us still have not caught up with him. His fundamental innovations are two: First, he divorced dance from music (or, more accurately, from sound); in Cunningham works, the dance and the accompaniment occur at the same time but are otherwise unconnected. Composer and choreographer do not work together. Cunningham merely tells the composer how long the score should be, and the dancers do not hear it until the first public performance. He uses a great deal of live electronic music, which he likes because he feels the range of sound is greater than that possible on conventional instruments and because it is not bound by the metric beat we are accustomed to hearing in "regular" music. Cunningham scores are often played excruciatingly loudly, and they are often not what we would call "music" at all, but rather collections of noise. His most important musical collaborator has been John Cage.

Second, Cunningham introduced the principle of simultaneity—a number of things happen on stage at the same time, often without apparent relationship to each other, and thus there is no single focus for the attention. Since there are many focal points, it follows that the stage is not oriented toward the center; each dancer creates his own center, and much of the action occurs at the side of the stage. The spectator has a choice of where to look.

Structurally, many of Cunningham's works have no fixed beginning, middle, or end. They just begin, and they just end. In fact, he has described most of his pieces as open-ended. Moreover, it sometimes happens that his pieces begin and end differently at different performances, and that they have different middles, too. This is *not* due to improvisation—each dance is strictly composed—but because Cunningham uses random or chance methods of composition. That is, he creates what he calls "gamuts of movement" (a series of movements, or a movement unit) and then determines the sequence of these movements by a chance procedure such as rolling dice or dealing cards. Sometimes the dancers are given leeway in the ordering of their steps, but the movements themselves are always set. (In fact, without metrical accompaniment, the timing and precision of the steps are even more strict than usual.) In 1964, Cunningham went even further in breaking down accepted notions of structure when he started presenting "Events"—dances made up of movement sequences extracted from various works, strung together without pause, to a score of one sort or another.

Cunningham believes, with Balanchine, that dance need have no reference to anything outside itself (such as a story or a philosophy); good dance is enough. And, unlike some contemporary choreographers, he requires a very high level of technical polish and control from his dancers. A former member of the Graham troupe, Cunningham was superbly trained himself. His dancers are very strong in the torso and able to isolate various parts of the body. They are extraordinarily nimble, capable of quick changes of direction or of scurrying across the stage, seemingly without weight. The technique does not seem to concentrate on big jumps or on low movements (the heavy kind, near the floor, that occur in a number of modern-dance techniques, including Graham's), although, of course, both of these types of movement are used. (In common with other "avant-garde" choreographers, Cunningham has also employed gestures from everyday life.) The Cunningham dancer is characterized by a special alertness, a sensitivity to the smallest nuance of sound or motion.

The dancers rehearse without music. Cunningham times their movement sequences with a stopwatch; once they have the "feel" of how long things take, they take their cues from the other dancers' movements or perhaps a sound, such as a stamp.

Cunningham has made his greatest—perhaps his sole—concession to the sensuous side of theatrical presentation with his decor and costumes. He has worked with two of the foremost contemporary artists of our time—Jasper Johns and Robert Rauschenberg—and obviously has an excellent eye for color and shape himself. Some of his decors are almost lush, in contrast to the frequent rigor of his dance phrases and unyielding electronic accompaniment, neither of which—in their most extreme forms—offer much sensual "balm" for eye or ear, despite their undeniable intellectual and visceral appeal. (It should be noted, however, that Cunningham has also composed many steps and sequences of a classical order and beauty.)

Some observers have pointed out that Cunningham's dances, although devoid of plot or character, make a statement of sorts about modern life, which bombards us all with its rush of events occurring pell-mell, without apparent order, all at the same time.

Video: CDF, KUL.

SUMMERSPACE

Choreography by Merce Cunningham, 1958; music by Morton Feldman (Ixion); *costumes and decor by Robert Rauschenberg.*

Summerspace, with its hot-pink decor and costumes, splashed with blue and green, may have something to do with summer, and there is no denying that it has a great deal to do with space. The dance was created for four women and two men, and chance methods were used in composition. The music, which provides a trickle of sound, can be varied; each player is at liberty to play notes of his choice, so long as he plays the number given for the amount of time specified.

Cunningham wrote of *Summerspace*: ''The notion of space was always present. . . . The principal momentum was a concern for steps that carry one through space, and not only into it, like the passage of birds, stopping for moments on the ground and then going on, or automobiles more relentlessly throbbing along turnpikes and under and over cloverleaves. . . . As much as possible I worked with a single dancer all the way through his actions except where a movement came directly in contact with another dancer. Perhaps this is what gives the dance its sense of beings in isolation . . . along with the sense of continuous appearing and vanishing.''

The dancers in *Summerspace* seem to have little relationship to one another, and yet there are movement fragments that are repeated throughout (sometimes in varied form). Some of the basic steps are running, turning, leaping, walking, and a kind of hitched skip. To these are added crouching, prancing, coiling, and a particular traveling movement in which the dancers appear to be rocking from side to side swinging their arms, as though windblown. Cunningham also uses many recognizable steps from the dance vocabulary, including, for example, his version of the *arabesque*. When the dancers run, often zig-zagging across the stage, they seem to skim the ground, and their leaps are small and light. At times they stare at each other with great concentration or mirror each other's movements, but more often they seem unaware of the rest of the activity, performing in isolation. Much of the action occurs in corners. The dance seems to be about patterns, albeit jagged, arbitrary ones. It is also about the contrast between weight and lightness, jumping and remaining near the ground, sustained and nimble movement, changes of direction, changes of intent, following the leader, and taking cues from other dancers. The dancers' off-centered weight makes the audience very conscious of the pull of gravity.

The costumes, in the same pointillist pattern as the backdrop, render the dancers almost invisible when they are still. In movement, they emerge from the background, then fade into it again—from 2-D to 3-D and back, like shifting fragments of color.

Summerspace, which Cunningham staged for the New York City Ballet, Birgit Cullberg's dance company in Sweden, the Boston Ballet, and the Théâtre du Silence in France, is one of the few Cunningham company works to be performed by a group

Viola Farber and Carolyn Brown in *Summerspace,*
Merce Cunningham Dance Company.

other than his own. Generally speaking, he is not interested in disseminating his works; he creates, performs, and then moves on to something else, discarding or ignoring what is already there, as if reflecting the ephemeral nature of dance itself, as it exists only at the moment of performance. Moreover, in common with many contemporary choreographers, Cunningham seems more intrigued by the process of creating a dance than by the final product—hence, he is always involved in working through new material, which leads to ever more new dances.

ALVIN AILEY

In 1958, Alvin Ailey (1931-1989), a Texas-born black dancer, formed his own dance company with the intention of expressing something of his heritage and experience. Most of his dances on black themes are vivid and dramatic—*Blues Suite* (1958) shows a "slice of life" in a series of scenes from a backwater brothel, where black men and women find release from a down-and-out existence in nocturnal revels; *The Mooche* (1975), with its flashy extravagance, depicts four black female singing stars against a background of the Harlem nightclub world in the 1920s and 1930s; and *Cry* (1971), choreographed, in Ailey's words, "for black women everywhere, especially our mothers," is a solo for his then-leading dancer Judith Jamison, now the Artistic Director of his company. The dance shows the black woman's journey from a proud racial past through degradation in America and back to dignity and self-esteem. Many of the company's dances are set to spiritual or gospel music, as well as jazz, blues, and rock by contemporary composers.

In the 1930s and 1940s, Katherine Dunham and Pearl Primus, two black choreographers, created theater dances influenced by their research into indigenous black dance forms. Primus's focus was Africa; Dunham had worked mainly in the Caribbean. They choreographed dances for Broadway and the concert hall derived from ethnic forms, as well as presenting dances based on Negro spirituals. After their companies disbanded, their dancers and students brought some of their style— the loose fluidity, Afro-Caribbean rhythms, and sensual jazzy accents—into the mainstream of theater dance. Still, in the 1950's, there existed no company whose primary concern was black themes, and performing opportunities for black dancers were still relatively limited—or, at best, stereotyped. When founding his primarily black company in 1958, Ailey explained, ''I feel an obligation to use black dancers because there must be more opportunities for them, not because I'm a black choreographer talking to black people.''

Indeed, in the past 30 years, the Alvin Ailey American Dance Theater has proven that it speaks not only to black people. The company, which has been called ''one of America's great cultural ambassadors,'' has toured extensively and has probably been seen and applauded by more people in the world than any other single company. While still resting on a black cultural and musical foundation, the company is fully integrated, and its repertory has grown to include abstract and lyrical dances without racial references. The company's goals have also expanded and now encompass the preservation of important modern-dance works by choreographers other than Ailey, as well as providing a showcase for young choreographers.

Alvin Ailey moved from Texas to the West Coast as a young man and left college after two years to dance with the California-based Lester Horton (1906–1953). Horton directed the first integrated modern-dance company and was interested in Afro-Caribbean as well as other ethnic forms. After Horton's death in 1953, Ailey directed the company for a few years. Coming East, he studied with a number of well-known teachers, including Jack Cole (1913–1974), Anna Sokolow, Martha Graham, and Doris Humphrey.

If the Ailey style shows some roots in the technique of Lester Horton in its athleticism and the use of a flat, strong torso and long arms and legs, it also reveals the variegated strains of Ailey's own background. It combines a Grahamesque use of the torso with the sensual exuberance of jazz dance, and the pulse of Afro-Caribbean rhythms with the elegance and long line of ballet. It incorporates the body language and street gestures of the urban black and makes use, choreographically, of the strong sense of community and group dance among rural churchgoing blacks. The resulting style is hybrid, theatrical, and flashy. Heads are held high and tossed about freely; dancers sashay and strut; pelvises are rotated and often pushed forward; leg extensions are dramatically high; steps are large, open, and unambiguous. His performers are technically proficient in jazz, modern dance, and ballet. The dances are energy packed, often sensuous and emotionally provocative, and direct in their appeal.

Video: KUL, HOME.

REVELATIONS

Choreography by Alvin Ailey, 1960; traditional music (Negro spirituals); costumes by Lawrence Maldonado.

Even those who consider Ailey too "showbiz" agree that *Revelations* is something of a masterpiece. The company's signature piece, *Revelations* is about a communal journey through baptismal purification from despair to joyous salvation, achieving a danced testimony to faith and spiritual optimism. It is danced to a suite of Negro spirituals sung by soloists and a choir about which Ailey has said, "These are the songs I feel very personally about—they are intimately connected with my memories of the Baptist church when I was a child."

Revelations' opening section to "I've Been 'Buked" shows a pyramidal cluster of dancers, their upper torsos arched over their legs, which are sunk in a low, wide *plié.* Costumed in drab and shapeless sackcloth, they use their outspread, curved arms like the wings of a huge bird trying to take off outward and upward. In the following section, the choir sings out "Didn't My Lord Deliver Daniel" as a woman writhes on the floor, her contractions allusive to birth pangs, while, simultaneously, a couple dances with hands clasped as if bound over their heads. The suppliant, tender "Fix Me, Jesus" duet for a man and woman follows. The woman swoons and leans on the man's arm in the manner of a congregant turning to her preacher for guidance and support. They seem to be yearning toward something together as they lean on one another in sculptural poses that often stretch upward. At the end, the woman, braced on her partner's thigh with one bent leg, reaches with the other leg in an expansive high *arabesque.* The man, arched on the floor, holds her hand and leans backward. A solo to "I Want to Be Ready" follows

Revelations, Alvin Ailey American Dance Theater.

and is danced almost entirely on the floor. A man rises and falls in a series of contractions and releases. He never sits up fully and never finds symmetrical equilibrium; rather, he balances in various off-center positions. Rising to his feet at the solo's end, his strong taut torso provides a steady center for the wide circling and reaching of his arms and legs.

For the "Processional" and "Wading in the Water" sequences, blue and white gauzy cloth is stretched across the stage and rippled at either end, creating the illusion of the flowing waters of a baptismal river. Girls in flouncy white dresses step gingerly through the waves, undulating their own torsos as fluidly as the water in a backward and forward walk. Pelvises pushed forward, heads thrown ecstatically back, arms flung out, their walk bursts briefly into skips. The movement and mood is joyous as they feel reborn through immersion in the baptismal stream. One girl, holding a big white parasol, is carried off in the end. The following section, "Sinner Man," originally a solo but danced as a trio since 1962, shows three men in desperate flight. To the familiar refrain, "Oh sinner man, where you gonna run to?" the three men race around, turning in every direction, their heads rolling. Standing on one leg, they reach out, far off center, and fall, catching themselves with their hands. The flight is futile; there is no place for the sinners to hide.

Revelations now moves toward its climax. To "The Day Is Past and Gone," women dressed in bright yellow dresses and big floppy hats appear on stage with a perky sashay walk, flicking their big palm-leaf fans in the imaginary heat and greeting each other. They turn their backs to the audience and slowly lower themselves onto stools with a kind of mock delicacy. As the ladies gossip and fan themselves, relaxing on the stools, men in bright shirts walk on and begin dancing to "You May Run On." The ladies, to join the dance repartee, stand on their stools and shimmy in response to the men. Onstage and off, all are swept up in the revivalist fervor of the climactic "Rocka My Soul" that follows. The dancers strut around pumping their elbows in and out, swivel their hips, toss back their heads, kick their legs, and clap their hands in an ecstatic outpouring of good spirits. The contagious energy of the finale always has the audience clapping along, half out of their seats, screaming for more.

When the Ailey dancers respond to the audience's shrieks of approval with an encore of "Rocka My Soul," some may feel that the dignity of the usual modern dance concert has been violated. Ailey, however, has little in common with the serious, stark classic image of modern-dance in either tone or intent. His dances, without apology, are designed to be accessible, hard-hitting, and entertaining. If they are at times superficial or commercial, they nonetheless communicate a great deal of kinetic excitement and, as in the case of *Revelations*, sincere sentiment. Acknowledging his tendency toward Broadway-type crowd-pleasing, Ailey said, "First get them in the theater, then show them anything you want."

The original *Revelations* was 45 minutes long and used only eight dancers. Now some 25 minutes long with over 20 dancers, it has a faster, fuller impact. More than any other of Ailey pieces, *Revelations* has been danced to universal acclaim.

Video: KUL.

PAUL TAYLOR

Early in his choreographic career, Paul Taylor (b. 1930) was looked on as a cryptic avant-gardist in the dance world. One critic, Louis Horst, was so incensed (or baffled) by Taylor's *Epic* (1957) that he reviewed it with a column of blank space, which contained only the name of the work and the reviewer's initials. As time passed, however, Taylor, while retaining his stylistic originality and independence, has come to be considered more and more accessible, less and less "far out"—and, indeed, not so difficult or obscure after all.

There are two sides to the Taylor coin—the light, breezy, and exuberant on the one hand, and the dark, cynical, and critical on the other. To project both, he has developed a most unusual movement vocabulary; it could be called modern, in that it avoids ballet's pointe work, turnout, stretched knees in jumps, rounded arms, and so forth. However, it is not like anyone else's modern-dance technique. For example, Taylor seems much more interested in a balletic lightness in the air than in the modern dancer's traditional concern with the ground and the weighti-ness of movement. Taylor studied both ballet and modern dance; he performed with the Martha Graham and Merce Cunningham companies, among others, but the influence of his past experiences is not too pronounced in the dancers he has developed.

Taylor dancers are characterized by an extreme nimbleness and fleetness, an ability to change direction and trip lightly all over the stage at any instant. They also leap for joy at the drop of a hat—either into the arms of a waiting partner or on their own. The preparation for these leaps is often a great loping run, heels first, from a distance far across the stage. Arms are flung out, hair flies. It appears that Taylor tries to make his dances look casual—not studied or consciously refined—although it is obvious that his dancers have superior technical training. A critic once wrote that Taylor's compositions seem to be full of run-on sentences—they just keep bubbling along at breakneck speed.

Like many modern dancers, Taylor has choreographed a number of works with major roles for himself. Unlike many, however, he has been, if anything, more inspired in his choreography since he retired from performing in 1974; often choreographers dry up when they can no longer work out the steps on their own bodies. Today the Paul Taylor Dance Company is considered one of the finest.

Video: HOME.

AUREOLE

Choreography by Paul Taylor, 1962; music by George Frederick Handel.

Aureole, Taylor's most widely performed work, is also one of his most balletic. But even when performed by ballet dancers (as it often is), it does not have the look of a ballet, either traditional or modern. In addition to the dancers' unpointed feet, turned-in legs and flying arms, Taylor's atmosphere of throwaway abandon is all his own and differs sharply from the "finished" look with which ballet movements are naturally endowed, no matter how they are used in a particular dance. Handel's music is a joyous affair (even in slow sections), with a strong, "dancey" beat. Unlike many modern dance choreographers, Taylor does not stick to ultramodern music or specially composed scores, although he has used both. (One of his "juiciest," happiest works, *Esplanade,* is set to Bach).

Aureole is in five short sections for three female and two male dancers dressed in white. It is a sunny work with a meditative side. If any emotional coloring can be ascribed to the dance, it is surely the sheer joy of being alive. The curtain rises to reveal dancers in silhouette. Two women prance about, doing a kind of skipping step with one hip thrust out. A man cradles a woman in his arms, rocking her. The dancers crisscross the stage in runs,

Sharon Kinney, Dan Wagoner, and Elizabeth Walton in *Aureole,*
Paul Taylor Dance Company.

then take little "bunny hops." They do lunging steps in a circle. These lunges are repeated throughout the work and can be considered one of the choreographic motifs. There are more little jumps and hops. The dancers move gracefully, with feet parallel.

There is an *adagio* for a man. It is full of long, large movements, including lunges of great amplitude. The man raises his outstretched arms like a giant bird's wings, thus extending his line. Taylor himself is a tall and bulky man, and this choreography was undoubtedly designed to exploit his physical appearance. The next section is full of light leaping steps, swings and sways, with the dancers moving their hips from side to side. They throw their arms in the air to music that is stately yet gay. Tiny scurrying steps alternate with large leaps. After another *adagio*, the concluding movement is one of gusto. There is a variation on the *arabesque*. Over and over, with their arms outstretched in a V to the ceiling, with one bent leg lifted and their heels resolutely in the lead, the dancers look for all the world like farmers at a hoedown, having a wonderful time. They leap in a carefree manner, roll on the floor, and spin with bent knees. *Aureole* is Paul Taylor at his most exhilarating.

TWYLA THARP

Twyla Tharp (b. 1942) is a true original. Although specialists may trace some of her slinky, slithery, "throw-away" movements to experiments of the avant-garde dance circle in the 1960s, to today's popular concert audience her movement style seems to have come from nowhere. To music ranging from pop to rock to jazz to country to classical (and sometimes silence), and with ballet training as a starting point, Tharp combines popular dance, social dance, vaudeville, soft shoe, jazz, hip wiggles, bumps and grinds, and much more. Her dancers might almost be the teenagers next door, so goofy and informal are they, so young and "groovy," so unknowing, yet so streetwise. Somewhat akin to the Paul Taylor company (with which she once performed), Tharp dancers have none of the grandeur of the originators of modern dance (such as Martha Graham), nor the highly stylized, polished look of the ballet. If anything, they resemble a bunch of energetic, slightly nutty kids.

Tharp's work, for all its apparent casualness and funkiness, depends for much of its effect on a wry, tongue-in-cheek relationship to the musical beat—just that perfect touch of syncopation that makes everything feel slightly cockeyed. She has taken pop music and movement and has made a sophisticated (and witty) gloss on both. Although some of Tharp's early works had moments of improvisation (dancers warming up and talking to bystanders, who were sometimes the audience), many of the recent ones do not; despite their often random feeling, they could probably be plotted with a computer: They are *that* exact.

Tharp studied ballet, modern, tap, and baton twirling as a child. It is possible that elements of each are still visible in her work. After two years with Paul Taylor, she began choreographing for her own small group. Often she had only women to work with, but after choreographing *Deuce Coupe* in 1973 jointly for the Joffrey Ballet and her own company, Tharp was "in," and could afford a larger and more permanent group. She has done choreography for the stage, for the movies (*Hair*), and for experimental television.

At the invitation of American Ballet Theatre's then-director Mikhail Baryshnikov in the early 1980s, Tharp began an active association with that company (bringing some of her dancers) and eventually disbanded her own troupe. As an Associate Director of ABT, she choreographed several works, further integrating her style into a ballet setting. With Baryshnikov's abrupt departure in 1989, Tharp's future with the company is uncertain. Recently, she has worked with Chicago's Hubbard Street Dance Company to revive some of her earlier works. She has also choreographed for the Paris Opéra Ballet and the New York City Ballet.

Video: HBO, KUL, PI-A.

PUSH COMES TO SHOVE

Choreography by Twyla Tharp, 1976; music by Joseph Lamb (Bohemia Rag) *and Franz Joseph Haydn* (Symphony No. 82 in C Major); *costumes by Santo Loquasto.*

Push was without question *the* dance hit of 1976. Rarely, if ever, has a serious dance work received such instant acclaim. Press coverage and publicity were fantastic. For one thing, Tharp used the newly arrived Russian sensation Mikhail Baryshnikov, known for his dramatic ability and purest classical technique, in a completely new (and zany) way; for another, her work was unlike any ever staged before for a full-sized major ballet company. What on earth were all those people doing up there?

The choice of music was a typical Tharp non sequitur—a Haydn symphony preceded by ragtime. The opening movement is a kind of *pas de trios* with a grace note—the participants are three dancers and a hat. The man (originally Baryshnikov), in shiny casuals, alternates between mad spins and jumps—falling off balance, stumbling, stopping on a dime, and changing

Richard Schaeffer, Martine van Hamel, and Clark Tippet in
Push Comes to Shove, American Ballet Theatre.

direction—and complete indifference, slouching around and running his fingers through his hair. One lady makes her entrance enticingly—first her leg and foot are seen, then the rest of her. For reasons unknown, she wears a brow band. The three pass the hat from one to another surreptitiously, swaying and slinking around, in a loose-jointed manner.

As the Haydn music begins, the man continues his headlong, "wrong-headed" movement; the girls breeze about. The trio exits, and we see two ensembles of eight women each. Their dance, carefully crafted, establishes geometric patterns—they move in fours, twos, sixes, and so forth—so that when things begin to go subtly wrong, the result is amusing indeed. All at once, 30 dancers are on the stage, twisting, wriggling, and milling about. The ensemble has been joined by two soloists (a man and a woman), four men, and four ladies dressed ridiculously in long, straight jersey skirts and turbans. There is a great deal of disorder; the feeling of feverish activity is increased by many entrances and exits. For the finale, all come together—including the hat—and there is more roaming about. The dancers seem to be preparing for a final pose; then they prepare again and again. A final dash to the finish line spells the end, but not before two derbies are tossed in the air.

Tharp's movement spasms, shimmies, and smirks, her breathless dazzle, her quirky, off-center movement, her cheekiness, her deftness are all a part of her energetic approach to choreography. Her movements virtually explode. What it all "means" is anybody's guess; and the title of this piece is as much of a mystery as everything else about it.

Video: KUL, PI-A.

GLOSSARY

Despite the existence of a standard vocabulary, the terminology used to describe the various dance steps varies widely due to the number of different schools. This glossary was compiled using several different dance reference works.

ADAGIO   A slow, sustained duet. The first part of the traditional four-part *pas de deux*. Also, there is *adagio* (slow) dancing as opposed to *allegro* (fast) dancing.

ALLEGRO   Dancing that is lively and fast; jumps and turns in the air are forms of *allegro*.

ARABESQUE   A pose in which the dancer stands on one leg with the other leg raised behind and extended fully. The *arabesque* lends itself to many variations—for example, in the *arabesque relevé*, the dancer rises from the full foot onto pointe and back down again.

ATTITUDE   A pose closely related to the *arabesque* in which one leg is raised behind the body, but is bent rather than straight.

BALLABILE   A lively dance for the *corps de ballet*.

BALLERINA   The top female dancer in the company, now more often referred to as the principal dancer, although the term ballerina is still in use.

BALLET BLANC   The "white ballet" of the 19th-century Romantic era. The *white* refers to the long white gossamer costumes that the women wear in ballets such as *Giselle*.

BARRE   The horizontal wooden railing at which dancers begin their practice sessions.

BATTERIE   The beating of the legs in the air in jumps. *Grande batterie* and *petite batterie* are distinguished by the elevation of the jump and the number of beats executed before landing.

BOURRÉE   A quick, tiny step from pointe to pointe.

BRISÉ   A step belonging to the *petite batterie* in which the legs are beaten in the air to the front or to the back of the body before landing on both feet. In the spectacular *brisés volés*, *brisés* are executed alternately to the front and back without a pause.

CABRIOLE   A movement of *grande batterie* in which the dancer swings one leg up to an angle of 90 degrees, brings the other leg to meet it, then lands on the same leg.

CHARACTER DANCING   Theatricalized folk dance performed by classically trained dancers.

CODA   Most commonly, the ending and climax of the traditional *pas de deux*; also, the concluding movement of other dance sequences.

CONTRACTION-RELEASE   A sequence of movements made famous by Martha Graham. The terms refer to the movement of complete inhalation with contraction through the torso and complete exhalation (release).

CORPS DE BALLET   Literally, the body of the ballet. The *corps* performs steps in unison or provides patterns against which (or within which) the stellar dancers perform.

CZARDAS   Also spelled *csardas*, which is indicative of its Hungarian origins. There are no fixed steps in this dance, but there are two distinct parts: a slow first part and a rapid second part filled with leaps and turns. There is a *czardas* in *Swan Lake* and in the first act of *Coppélia*.

DANSE D'ÉCOLE   Literally, dance of the school. The academic technique based on the five positions and the turnout, combined with the elegance in bearing that reveals the courtly origins of the classical ballet. Over the centuries, the term has come to designate a prescribed vocabulary of steps and movements executed in a particular style.

DEMI-POINTE   The ball of the foot.

DIVERTISSEMENT A dance inserted for sheer enjoyment or technical display; a kind of "dance number" only tenuously related to the story line.

EN TRAVESTIE A man performing in women's clothing or vice versa.

ENTRECHAT A beating step in which the dancer jumps from *plié* into the air with legs straight and crosses the feet a number of times.

ÉPAULEMENT The relationship of the head and shoulders to the torso, arms, and legs.

FOUETTÉ A turning step in which the female dancer rises on the toe of one foot while propelling herself around with a whiplike motion of the other leg.

GRAND BATTEMENT A high kick.

GRAND PAS DE DEUX A special duet in classical ballets for the ballerina and her cavalier. This duet for the two leading dancers concludes or climaxes the act or evening.

GRANDE PIROUETTE À LA SECONDE A virtuoso step for a male dancer, in which he hops on one foot while turning with the other foot extended to the side, and ends in a series of *pirouettes*.

JETÉ A leap or jump. It is interesting that the word derives from *jeter*, to throw, and not *sauter*, to jump. In *jeté*, the dancer throws one leg into the air while leaping—and the weight of the body is thrown from one foot to the other.

PAS D'ACTION A danced interlude amplifying the story of the ballet.

PAS DE DEUX A dance for a man and a woman, usually composed of an adagio section, two variations, and concluding fireworks, or coda. Such a duet often emphasizes virtuosity.

PAS DE TROIS Dance for three.

PASSÉ One of the many transitional movements from one position into the next.

PETIT BATTEMENT A fluttering movement of one foot against the ankle of the supporting leg.

PIQUÉ   A step directly onto one pointe from *plié*. *Piqué* turns are traveling series of turns on one foot.

PIROUETTE   A turn on one foot.

PLIÉ   A bend at the knee, often a preparation for jumps and turns.

PORT DE BRAS   Formal arm movements.

PREMIER DANSEUR   The top male dancer of the company, now more often referred to as the principal dancer.

PREMIER DANSEUR NOBLE   The top male dancer of the company, if he has a particularly classical style.

RELEVÉ   The rising onto pointe or demi-pointe from the flat foot.

RÉGISSEUR   An imprecise term usually designating the rehearsal director.

ROND DE JAMBE   A part of the classic *danse d'école* vocabulary, this step is a rotary movement of the leg in which the dancer describes circles in the air or on the floor with the pointed toe.

SOUBRETTE   The female lead in comedy ballet, a young, gay ingenue dancer.

SUR LES POINTES   On the toes.

TARANTELLA   An energetic Italian folk dance.

TURNOUT   The outward rotation of the legs from the hips at a 90-degree angle. The turnout enables the dancer to move to either side as well as forward and back with equal grace, giving him or her a command over a full circle of movement. This is an integral part of the *danse d'école*.

INDEX

Note: Dates for key figures are given at the first significant mention in the text. Ballet terms are italicized and indexed when they are defined in the text: no other mentions are noted. Dance names are italicized and indexed separately from choreographers: dances beginning with "The" are indexed by the second word.

ABOUT THE AUTHORS

Nancy Reynolds, who began her career as a dancer with the New York City Ballet under George Balanchine, is the prize-winning author of *Repertory in Review,* the history of that company which appeared in 1977. She has written numerous books and articles on many aspects of dance. With Susan Reimer-Torn, she is cofounder of *Pictura Dance,* publishers of audiovisual educational materials in dance history. She is currently completing a comprehensive history of theatrical dance in the 20th century, to be published by Viking Press.

Susan Reimer-Torn is a native New Yorker who has been working as a Paris-based freelance writer and editor for the last 10 years. She has been a contributor to the *International Herald Tribune,* the *New York Times, Vogue,* and *Child* magazine. She is founder and editor of *Kids Extra! The International Family's Guide to Paris,* and is presently at work on another book.